THIRD
AND
LONG

A NOVEL

BOB KATZ

This is a work of fiction. Characters, places, events, and incidents are either the product of the author's imagination or are used fictionally.

Third and Long
ISBN # 978-0-9777915-2-1

designed by *the*BookDesigners
cover photo by Chris Dellamea

6 5 4 3 2 1

CHAPTER 1

....

On the day Nick arrived, a thick fog curled down the river valley, blanketing everything, even our thoughts, in a gauzy dreamlike haze. The air was smoky gray, as though clouded from leaf fires, and the visibility, not that we made a habit of measuring such things, was less than the length of a football field. It was, in hindsight, the ideal way for a certain type of stranger to slip into a town like ours – just after dawn, unknown and unannounced, stepping gently into a rolling green landscape nestled in a peaceful fog.

The way some tell it, those with a need to embellish, when the fog finally did lift, he was suddenly standing there as though materialized from nothing as part of some magic act, presto! In truth, his entrance was not nearly so dramatic. He'd simply been delivered by the eastbound Amtrak. The conductor that morning was James Sawyer. As the train made its final southeasterly slant into Longview, Sawyer had dragged himself from his nighttime dozing spot in the dining car and had begun to make his rounds. There really wasn't all that much for him to do. The head count he'd been handed the night before when he came on duty at Chicago's Canal Street station was less than fifty. Not many folks traveled across the breadth of the country by train any more, at least not midweek

1

in September, 1997, after the school year had started, after the long summer had quickened into fall.

Taking his obligatory walk-through, Sawyer found the aisle blocked by the dangling foot of a slumbering passenger. A man in an awkward fetal position lay across both seats. The sheet of newspaper he'd been using to shield his face had slipped and lay fluttering across his mouth with each heavy breath. His bedraggled appearance – matted silver hair in need of washing, several days of facial stubble, a creased sport coat suited to a colder season – led Sawyer to guess the man would be going the distance, all the way to Penn Station. New York City was always a standard end point for uprooted men of a certain stage in life.

But the ticket stub clasped to the headrest told a different story. The California Zephyr had comprised the first leg of his journey and Longview, Ohio, a stop on the Cardinal route, was where he was headed. That is if he didn't slumber right through and miss it.

Sawyer nudged the man's extended leg just hard enough to awaken him. "Your stop, mister."

Drowsily, the man pawed the newspaper off his face like an irritated boxer deflecting a sparring partner's jab. He looked to be in his late 40's, with allowances for what life may have done to him. He had a firm jaw, high cheekbones, thoughtful eyes set deep. His name was Nick Remke, although Sawyer wouldn't know this, or anything, about him until the news accounts that came later.

A gruff announcement coughed across the PA system. "In approximately four minutes the train will arrive in Longview. Longview will be next. Doors open on the right."

The brakes tensed and whined. The man gave a shake of his head as though invigorated by a splash of cold water. He squinted hard out the window, crinkling his eyes as though correcting an astigmatism. The stately limestone bluffs and plateau of rich farmland beyond the river are normally a breathtaking sight, but in the fog and dim light the landscape was but an undifferentiated swath of gray, a vast chalkboard on which nothing was written. Still, Nick kept staring.

Yawning, he lifted wearily from his seat. His full size took Sawyer by surprise. It was as if the fellow had undergone a shapeshift from the inert lump of a few minutes before. He was larger, sturdier, more imposing.

The erratic sway of the train forced him to recalibrate his balance. Once stabilized, he reached into the luggage compartment and effortlessly hauled down an overstuffed canvas duffel. The train eased to a halt, its brakes shuddering with a muted cornet whine. The sliding silver doors, caked in prairie dust, zipped open. Nick shuffled uneasily toward the exit. Sawyer offered to help but he was briskly shaken off.

There was a labored hitch to his gait as he edged down the steps and made his away gingerly along the platform. Each stride was a minor lurch, as though he was jerking a dead weight. A wounded war veteran is what Sawyer thought to himself. Just a guess.

Nick stood for a moment on the long depot platform, getting his bearings. He'd traveled for nearly three days and he looked it, unkempt, unshaven, and suspiciously pale. We already had our share of middle-aged fellows with husky builds from whom we'd long ago stopped expecting very much and it's doubtful much attention would have been paid had anyone even been at the depot to encounter him. Nick resembled a lot of local guys who hung around year after year without any good reason. In that sense, he fit right in.

The Longview railway station served Amtrak as well as assorted regional and cross-country freight lines that tie into the Ohio River port traffic. It was a solid brick construction from the 1920's, nothing fancy, about the shape and size of one of those modular classrooms they employ in school districts bursting at the seams, which is not a problem we've had. The depot office was located mid-way down the waiting platform. An idle transport dolly leaned against the lone lamppost to assist anyone hauling more than he could handle. Wally Pfaff, the stationmaster, was finishing up some paper work pertaining to a shipment of Styrofoam packing materials. Wally functioned as our ticket clerk, shipping clerk, freight handler, and custodial crew. He was the first person in Longview to speak with Nick, and nearly the last.

"Looking for Made Right," Nick said flatly. His face was pressed so close to the window that he nearly filled the frame.

Wally, sixty-nine years old at the time, was in some ways a child of the Great Depression. Glancing at Nick, he was reminded of an image – he couldn't tell if it sprang from his own childhood in a Youngstown Hooverville or a PBS documentary he'd seen – of idle men with long gray faces in bread lines stretching down a city block and around the corner.

"Don't think they're hiring these days," Wally answered, trying to be helpful. "Had a half a dozen more layoffs just last month."

Nick did not flinch. "Just tell me how to get there."

Wally leaned his head out the ticket window, and pointed: across the tracks, up the bluff, across the cast iron bridge, over there. "See that big red brick building? Kind of like a castle? Way up there?"

In the fog, all that was visible was the shapeless mustard-gray outline of the row houses directly across the tracks.

"That's Made Right, up top the bluff," Wally said, jabbing his finger toward a phantom shape in the distance. "But I tell you, they're not hiring."

Nick broke into a smile so bright and hopeful that it struck Wally, under the circumstances, as almost daft.

"Everyone, mister, needs the right man. Don't always know it," he added jauntily, hoisting his bag, "'till he arrives."

Wally watched Nick hobble up the embankment and across the iron bridge. Then he phoned Lou Zanay, a buddy from the legion hall, simply to say that a stranger had arrived on the morning eastbound who looked suspiciously like the local news anchor on Channel 4. This was a running joke between Wally and Lou. Whenever they watched the newscast together over a few beers – okay, more than a few – they eventually fell into speculating who in town most closely resembled the news anchor or some other broadcast personality. This parlor game was most enjoyable when the TV personality in question was a saucy young female.

We were not yet a cell phone town. Nor was the worldwide web then a feature in our lives except as a distant technology pumping the stock market into a bullish frenzy, or so we'd heard. The Internet Age, Web 1.0, the Digital Divide, all that would arrive on our shore eventually, though the changes for us would be distinctly less than were occurring elsewhere. At the time Nick came here, Longview's favored communication network was the tried-and-true phone tree. Wally would phone up Lou who called Rusty who phoned Maddy who called Gina who rang up . . . that sort of thing, on and on. The phone tree was what knit us together, joining the disparate pieces of our community of nearly 12,000. It was an emergency broadcast channel, an oral history archive, and, yes, a rumor mill. It was, in retrospect, a precursor to online chat rooms. Phone trees were how we disseminated information as well as allegations. They were how, after the dust had settled, we gathered together, figuratively speaking, to process events and settle on the version of the story we'd tell ourselves and anybody else who might be interested.

The way it worked was simple. No instructional manual necessary. The sole requirement for formal membership in the network was to have a sheet of paper scotch-taped on the wall nearest the most commonly used household phone, generally in the kitchen. On this list was a sequence of names and phone numbers. If you received a call from the name above yours it was your duty to call the next name down, and if nobody answered, the name below that. When anything of consequence occurred, news was transmitted with jaw-dropping speed. From the inaugural call ("each one, call one" was the byword), regardless of time of day or night, weekday or weekend, the entire network could achieve saturation communication within an hour. Give us credit: you can't say that about New York City or LA.

Some of us had separate call sheets serving distinct phone trees. PTA for school emergencies. Made Right workers for communications that needed to avoid the watchful eye of management. Sports parents for rain-outs and re-schedulings. Chamber of Commerce members for windfall tips that rarely materialized. Etc., etc. In theory, these overlapping networks could all coordinate with each other ("link" in contemporary technospeak), but the need for that had thus far never arisen.

Transcripts of these various communications would, if they existed, reveal all that any outsider would need to know about us: our concern for family; our penchant for gossip; our inordinate fondness for sports; our appetite for and susceptibility to hero worship in all its manifestations; our lip service to organized religion; our economic myopia and distrust of financial success; our detachment from national politics; our affection for tradition and preference for mainstream aesthetics; our love of a good joke and our ongoing vulnerability to same. The phone tree, in sum, was our collective voice, our chorus, the one responsible for this account.

CHAPTER 2

·····························

Had he been the sort to decorate his duffel with gaudy stick-on travel decals, it might have been clear at first glance that Nick had been around, that he possessed what amounted to a long distance trucker's familiarity with the American landscape. On this foggy September morning, however, Longview was entirely new to him, as Sacramento had once been, and Nashville and Chicago and Mobile before that. He had journeyed to those locations as he came now to us. Each locale had once been a pushpin on the map of his next best chance.

"Anything can happen" had been his operative outlook upon arrival in all those spots, yet when all was said and done, when the job had run its course and nothing else could keep him there, it was his departure that proved to be the signature feature of his stay. "Move on" is what he'd always told himself when things hadn't turned out. Move on and try your luck anew. Move on, be clear, stay strong. Anything can happen. Like the catchy refrain of a lilting jukebox tune, such phrases had become the background music of his days, propping him up, at times moving him to song. He was in the habit of muttering pep talks to himself, a closet motivational speaker with a private audience of one.

Crossing the railroad overpass, Nick was soon in the center of our business district, gazing down Bluff Street towards High. It was a scene framed like a postcard, although not precisely the postcard that the Chamber of Commerce in their zeal to portray us as a thriving hub of enterprise might print up and distribute. The scruffy tan dog with protruding rib cage sniffing the gutter, no owner in sight, as if Longview was some forlorn Mexican pueblo. The solid stone Cheshire Building on High Street with its windows dust-smudged, even on the ground floor. The retail storefronts with hand-lettered placards advertising "Angela's Classic Cuts" and "Checks Cashed Here." The Riverview Tavern, smelling of varnished wood and last night's bourbon, open for business at 10 a.m. every day except Sunday.

Coming to Longview, Nick was entering a world tethered as much to the intractable past as to the jet stream of the future. Of course, he would not have immediately recognized this, and why should he? Few enough of us did, and we had an excuse: we lived here and had no better perspective on our fragile circumstance than a polar bear on a melting ice flow. What Nick saw – and this said more about the depth of his floundering than it did our actual resources – was nothing less than a land of opportunity. He had no choice.

There were, admittedly, some features about Longview that encouraged romanticizing. The view, particularly from the depot, was reminiscent of those meticulous model train setups with their cute compact houses along sloping hills carefully arranged to depict the countryside at its innocent and bucolic best. Our setting was one that a diligent Lionel hobbyist might have assembled: the depot, with "Longview" inscribed in gold lettering on a board bolted to the lamp post; the ticket office with its window half-open and the shape of a man inside; the sturdy iron bridge with "Class of 94" crudely painted on a buttress; the hillside dotted with miniature frame homes half hidden by the arching branches of tall shamrock-green trees; the length of track vanishing in the distance as it rounds the bend.

Situated on a thumb-shaped protrusion of fertile high ground overlooking the Ohio River, we were in a sense isolated by the river and protected by it. We were nearer to Pittsburgh than Cincinnati, but pretty far from any place you'd call cosmopolitan. We were not incontestably rural like the Dakotas, or antiquated and quaint like New England hamlets, or obstinately rugged like western logging towns. At the periphery of several minor media markets, we enjoyed divided loyalties when it came to pro sports teams, having no preordained affiliation. We could be, as viewers and consumers and fans, whoever we wanted to be. Or we could abstain entirely.

We certainly felt ourselves to be fully contemporary. Cable TV in most homes with a full complement of channels, strip mall out County 12 with a Wendy's and Pizza Hut, a local Savings Bank taken over and renamed by Wachovia, kids taking drugs named for chemical compounds the police had never heard of, a shortage of qualified nurses at the Oak Cliff senior care facility. Yet with the exception of enhanced home entertainment opportunities and a few technological conveniences like ATM cards, we were largely unchanged, or so we liked to tell ourselves.

The Ohio Hotel was Nick's first stop. He'd made a reservation before departing California, although there probably hadn't been more than a day or two in the past twenty years when a reservation was necessary. His appointment at Made Right was not until 1 p.m. He had a few hours to rest up, even to prepare.

The hotel's frosted glass double doors were open to the street. Like much of Longview, the Ohio had seen better days. The original hotel, built in 1889, had featured 46 rooms with a carved walnut staircase ascending from the airy, high-ceilinged lobby. It had been renowned throughout the region as a showplace for the radiance of the gaslight era. Swing bands from Cleveland and Louisville had performed on weekends. In the 1940's, the central staircase had been eliminated and the dining room with its colorful William Morris wallpaper patterns was now mainly a place to watch TV. In recent decades, the Ohio's clientele has been mostly a day-today bunch, salesmen and the not-yet-destitute. Guests who weren't at the Riverview Tavern drinking to excess often congregated here late at night to glumly watch the Jay Leno show. We preferred the affable Leno, wringing his hands like a befuddled buddy, to his more caustic and urbane rival, David Letterman.

Nick plopped his duffel on the beige industrial carpeting. The lobby was silent except for the incessant rasping chatter from the tiny Panasonic that Gus Hoover kept behind the reservation desk. Gus rarely turned the TV off. He was watching *Good Morning, America*. President Clinton was concerned about the Balkans.

"How much for a room?"

Gus waited for the TV correspondent to conclude his summary of the President's dilemma, which had no easy way out. "By yourself?" he asked.

Nick tried a little joke. "Damn," he cursed, swiveling around in exaggerated surprise. "Where the heck did that woman disappear to now?"

Gus was not amused. "How many nights?"

"With a little luck, who knows?"

Gus plunked down a registration form on the Formica countertop. "Sure, mister. With a little luck you could be here forever. Like me."

Gus watched as Nick filled out the form.

"Don't get many Californians," Gus commented.

Nick smiled. "Can't imagine why."

Gus handed over the room key, affixed to a clunky plastic disk the size of a bar coaster. "Any, ah, help with your luggage?"

Nick gave a yank on the duffel strap and flipped it cavalierly atop his shoulder. Then he walked briskly, as briskly as he could, across the worn lobby carpeting and up the carpeted stairs.

CHAPTER 3

························

H e barely napped. Shower, shave, dress. That was all the prep
he seemed to need. That, and a dose of self-administered pep
talk: look smart, stay focused, seize the moment, own the
moment. His penchant for motivational psychology would
later be a curiosity for us. Those self-help books and audio tapes
that were best-sellers throughout much of the rest of the country
were not particularly popular items in Longview, although our need
was as acute as anyone's.

With explicit directions from Gus ("Head straight through
town center till you can't go no further, then look up"), Nick set out
for the short walk to Made Right's main gate.

Our downtown is an orderly intersection of the three primary
streets that laterally span our plateau, perpendicularly crossed by
Bluff and Ohio Streets running northwest from the river. Town Hall
square, with its granite courthouse and stately elms and oaks, appears
much as it did a century before. Office and commercial buildings,
some as high as four stories, were constructed of sandstone, limestone, red brick and concrete blocks, and are as tightly bunched as
if it were lower Manhattan circa 1875. Many of the edifices still bear
the original inscriptions, carved into stone facades, of the original
owners: Rugen Bank and Trust, Valley Furniture, Western Union.

In 1994, the Chamber of Commerce, groping for ways to maximize our assets, commissioned a commemorative etching of downtown Longview as it might have appeared back in the 1890's. The etching depicted wide dirt streets, clean brick buildings, an oxcart piled with sacks of grain, a saddled horse tethered to a hitching post, a barber's pole of intertwining red and white stripes, men in derby hats standing in the shade of a lime green canvas awning, amicably discussing important affairs of the day. The idea was to turn the artwork into a postcard and promotional poster. For budgetary reasons, it never did happen.

Along High Street, Nick passed storefront windows advertising a range of local businesses – Zelk's Footwear, Benson's Department Store, Ramsay's Market, Tina's Travel – as well as several vacant retail spaces pocked with uncollected refuse that advertised something else. As he strolled past in his cream-colored suit, white shirt, and wide magenta tie, Nick resembled a city slicker, one from another, more prosperous era. A few of us lurking in doorways took note.

Longview has no skyline to speak of, which is why directions for locating Made Right are so simple: once in the vicinity, just look up and there she is. The factory looms atop the highest bluff above the river. It is a brick structure, soot-colored with faint red highlights, and nearly a hundred feet tall. There is something foreboding and dour about the building. It projects authority with an implied haughtiness, a hint of judgment verging on displeasure, like a respected yet feared grandfather. A concrete retaining wall, the type you find in old European cemeteries, surrounds the grounds ("campus" was the term preferred by the Ziglar family, who owned the company, though it never caught on). The building gives off a powerful suggestion of confinement, of being designed to keep nature out and people in.

Nick entered through the Arrowhead Street gate, an imposing iron structure with gargoyles carved into the railings. A cluster of workers were enjoying a break outdoors, smoking cigarettes, soaking in the sun, squeezing in a fast game of hearts at one of the wooden picnic tables the company provided. Nick did his best to minimize his limp and to conceal the grimace it sometimes caused. But we took note.

Ricky Figueroa, a floor mechanic, called out in a tone that was not exactly mockery, but not far from it. "Hey fella, that a Made Right suit you're wearing?"

Nick to his credit did not flinch. He shot Ricky a beaming sales-man's smile, the type we don't encounter much in Longview. "Good point, pal," Nick saluted. "I like that. Fact you're looking out for the team . . . I like that. Keep it up."

We scratched our scalps and wondered what the heck that was about, then watched him disappear into the plant.

The Made Right factory had the cavernous interior of an ancient stone cathedral. The central space was larger than a gymnasium, with exposed brick walls nearly three stories high, tall windows opaque with dust, and a roughed-up maple floor. Unlike a church, there was no solemnity or stillness here, not for a moment, certainly not during working hours. Instead there was the shrill hissing of the presses, the frenetic clatter of stitching machines, the whirr and snap of the Eastman cutters, the jangle of dollies on steel wheels stacked with bundles of bound fabric whipping down narrow aisles, the low whine of churning metallic parts, the snip and clip of doz-ens of hands simultaneously doing their job. Above all else, this was a domain where things got made, the hard way.

A mezzanine overlooked the factory floor. Here were the admin-istrative offices, payroll and accounting, a showroom, a conference room mostly used by sales reps, and the executive suite. A wind-ing steel staircase led from the mezzanine to the shop floor. Marie Zanay, Jeremy Ziglar Jr.'s administrative assistant, was skipping hurriedly down the stairs as Nick approached.

Marie was around forty years old (an estimate rounded off for public consumption; of course we knew her exact age, year of high school graduation, and personal biography all the way back to her parents' courtship). She wore a neatly ironed blouse and a dark skirt that was tighter at the pelvis than was customary at Made Right. But that was Marie. She did more or less as she liked. Or so we believed.

Nick was not alone in stealing a glance. Her face was heart-shaped and she had a delicate dimple in the center of her chin. Her rich auburn hair was cut to shoulder length and flared at the wings with an easy zest. There were delicate puffs beneath her eyes, a few fine crease lines around her mouth. There was a style about her – her outfit, her figure, her dancer's carriage and the self-assurance it implied. Nick the newcomer must have wondered what she was doing in a place like this.

Marie deftly dodged an onrushing rack of Prussian blue blazers heading toward the loading dock, and found herself directly in front of Nick. She held a clipboard to her chest, as a schoolgirl might. A giant rotating fan used to keep the air circulating kept blowing her hair across her eyes and she kept sweeping it away.

"I'm looking for Mr. Ziglar," he said. Several others were nearby, so it caught our attention that he chose her to ask.

Marie gave him a shrewd once-over. That's about all she gave anyone. "Which one, junior or senior?" Sensing Nick's befuddlement, she softened. "The plant manager position?"

He nodded.

"I thought that . . . " She checked herself. "Oh, well," she trilled. "Follow me. Office is upstairs."

She climbed perhaps more quickly than normal, wishing to put a bit of distance between her hind side and the smartly dressed stranger. Halfway up, she glanced back and saw just how far he'd lagged behind. She waited as Nick caught up.

"You okay?"

"I'm fine. Just an old injury."

"We have a freight elevator if . . . "

"I can manage."

"Tell him it's from football," she chuckled.

"Why's that?"

Marie resumed climbing. "This town's nuts about football. The Ziglars especially."

"And you?"

"Me?" They were directly above the row of Reece button-hole machines and the rising clatter forced her to lift her voice. "Other things interest me more."

At the mezzanine, Nick followed Marie. They passed the long glass case with its chronological display of Made Right styles, starting with World War I doughboy uniforms, on which the Made Right reputation was first solidified, and continuing on to the nifty flight attendant jackets, red trim on Navy blue, produced for Valley Air, the start-up regional airline that fed into US Airways routes. The mezzanine walkway dead-ended at a bank of glassed-in offices that peered down at the factory floor like sky boxes in a pro sports arena. A grayish tint to the interior-facing glass windows made it hard to see in. Marie swung open the door, and held it for Nick.

"Second office down. Remember," she said, "tell them it's a football injury."

CHAPTER 4

····························

The door to Jeremy's office was open. Nick tapped gently on
the mahogany veneer, and waited to be acknowledged. From
the threshold he could see out the tall windows and what
struck him was what struck every new visitor to the Made
Right executive suite, the sweeping panoramic view across the
river valley, both east and west, for miles each way on a clear day.
At this elevation, the landscape below appeared more than ever
like the idealized layout of a model train hobbyist. Down there
were cargo boats and church steeples and tiny autos silently gliding along rolling hills.

Jeremy Jr. was seated at his large walnut desk thumbing through
a manila file folder, seemingly too absorbed to immediately look up.
His mannerisms were well known and most of us long ago had got-
ten over being annoyed by them. Junior was not naturally cheer-
ful. A perpetual tension churned in him, even though by rights he
enjoyed more comfort and suffered far less insecurity than any of
us. Happiness, when it did befall him, played quirky tricks with his
face. His mouth widened but never opened, and the smile always
came out crooked. It might have been mistaken for a phony smile,
but it was the only one in his repertoire and we'd come to accept it
for what it was, the best he could do.

The consensus was that Jeremy Jr. was basically a decent guy under a lot of pressure that he was possibly not equipped to handle. Unlike his elderly father, who was far less decent and superbly equipped to handle just about anything. Junior, the name everyone referred to him by, had too easily achieved the dimensions of power and responsibility he held. As a consequence, he was wary of people who might, in a true meritocracy, be more deserving. That syndrome, which Junior tried his best to disguise, possibly explained his assortment of irksome quirks, like always arriving late and always keeping you waiting.

Nick tapped again on the door. Jeremy, trim, balding, dressed in a starched white shirt and smart saffron necktie, nonchalantly summoned him closer with a flick of his index finger.

"You must be . . . " Junior grabbed another folder off his desk, not the one he'd been perusing. His shirtsleeves rolled up, he had a health club devotee's pride in displaying his sinewy forearms. "Yes, Nick Remke. How was your flight?"

"Fine."

Junior waved Nick to an armchair at the corner of his desk.

"Get a chance yet to see the town?"

"A bit. Very nice." Nick took his seat.

"Not exactly California, is it?"

"Like I told you when we spoke on the phone. I'm ready for a new challenge."

Jeremy tilted back as he gave the resume folder another swift peruse. While he did so, Nick was able to steal a quick survey of the surrounding shelves and wall hangings. It wasn't difficult to identify the recurring theme: a navy and gold Notre Dame pennant; a framed aerial photograph of the South Bend football stadium packed with 80,000 fans; a dramatic LeRoy Nieman oil depicting a handsome quarterback with grease-blackened cheekbones poised to launch a desperation pass; a bronze football mounted on a stained walnut stand; a hard plastic football helmet, polished to a gleam with a black stripe down the midline. Nick could have been forgiven for thinking he'd stumbled into the alumni association headquarters. The Ziglars' infatuation with Notre Dame football was well known to us, in no small part because they so frequently referenced it when proclaiming that Made Right, within the realm of clothing manufacturing, represented a comparable tradition of excellence and integrity. It was a fetish we were willing to humor.

"Remind me. How'd you hear about this opening?"

"Production managers association."

"So tell me, Nick, why come way out here?"

Nick sat taller. "You mean, why would I give up all that sunshine and easy living for hard labor in a tiny burg deep in the rust belt? Is that the question you're asking?"

Jeremy nodded.

"Well, that's not how I see it, Mr. Ziglar. I see this as a great opportunity. For me, and for your company."

"Nicely put." Jeremy flipped to page two of Nick's resume. "Says here, you worked at Hart, Schaffner in Chicago. Reason for leaving?"

"Greener pastures. I was young."

"Let's see. Ransome Industries in Nashville. Assistant plant manager. Reason for leaving?"

"U.S. Navy. It should say that."

"Five years? Kind of a long hitch." Junior had a passing familiarity with military jargon, which came in handy in dealing with procurement officers from the armed services. "And a, shall we say, unusual career move."

"It went by quickly."

"Hobbies? Says you like fishing, music, reading. Quiet stuff, huh?"

"Work hard, then relax. That suits me."

Jeremy put down the resume. "I'll be perfectly frank. You're one of three candidates. One young man, I can tell you, comes highly recommended. Made Right's at a crucial juncture. Pressure's on from off shore. The Koreans. Chinese. Guatemalans. You name it.

Labor costs, shipping, tariffs, inflation. Styles changing faster than you can blink. None of it's making life easier. Or more profitable. The fact that you've moved around so often, well that suggests . . . "

"A refusal to settle for second best. Mr. Ziglar, those other shops weren't Made Right."

"You can say that, but still . . . " Jeremy lost interest in his argument, and returned to the resume. "Sacramento. St. Louis. Don't stay put, do you?"

Nick was a man for whom the vocational world had been an upstream struggle. Clothing manufacturing had been, from an employment standpoint, his default position. In that regard, he was not alone.

"I'm not a rookie any more, Mr. Ziglar. I've spent twenty years, on and off, in this industry. You'll be getting a seasoned veteran with plenty to offer."

"And your references. The Greek fellow . . . "

"Gil Stamos?"

"Deceased."

Nick gulped.

"News to you?"

Nick held it in. "Gruff old goat, but a good man."

"Sorry."

"Me too." Nick took a moment to collect himself, then plunged into his pitch: he was the right man for the job, he knew how to do it, knew it cold and would be willing to prove it, even on a short-term trial basis. He vowed to work long hours, to be responsive to all directives, to do in essence whatever it takes. "Give me the chance. That's all I'm asking. Give me a shot. You won't regret it."

Such a naked plea from a grown man discomforted Jeremy. His upbringing had been privileged, certainly compared to nearly everyone else in Longview. He'd attended private schools in Connecticut, which we took to be somewhere near Europe. He'd excelled at lacrosse, according to his father. All that was required of him in order to successfully inherit the family business was to be an obedient son. Nick's urgency made him squirm. It came as a relief to be interrupted by a loud buzzing from his phone console intercom.

Junior picked up the receiver, listened a moment while looking out the window, nodded. He plunked the receiver down, and pushed back like a diner at a four-star restaurant who'd had his fill.

Probably Nick could tell something was up. For all his studied self-confidence he must have been privately on-guard for the unforeseen setback, the fly in the ointment.

"That, Nick, was our top candidate . . . he's accepted our offer. I tried phoning you yesterday to say maybe you should wait, but this phone number" – he tapped Nick's resume – "was disconnected. I should've mentioned it, that we'd extended an offer. I'm very sorry. You make a good case. I'm sure you'll find something. We'll keep you on file. I certainly hope you haven't come all this way . . . "

As he rose to escort Nick to the exit, there was a knock on his door. Marie, his personal assistant, breezed in carrying a tray of sugared donuts and a pot of coffee.

Jeremy frowned. "Leave it," he commanded, pointing to the Bristol blue glass coffee table.

Marie's instinct was always to liven up a moribund gathering, even when she had no business doing so. It came from being an only child with querulous parents. "How's the injury?" she asked with the perkiness of a truck stop waitress. When she got no reply, she added, "We've got a great sports doc in town. Athletes swear by him."

Gingerly, Marie set down the coffee tray. With that, she departed.

With only the slimmest apparent interest, Junior asked Nick, "Sports injury?"

Later, when he had ample cause to reflect on the nuances in this conversation, Jeremy would see that his question was but an innocent scrap of conciliatory small talk meant to soften Nick's obvious disappointment. He liked the guy. Or at least he had no reason not to. Jeremy was not so self-absorbed as to be blind to how badly this must have stung Nick. To have come so far, and then to be rebuffed so cavalierly must have filled him with the urge to smash something valuable, to leave broken shards behind as he stormed away. There would have been no surprise if Nick had done so.

"Football," Nick replied glumly, hauling the dead weight of his body up from the armchair. In his mind, he was already shuffling down the long trek back to the depot for the next train departing, east or west, it hardly mattered.

"What level?" Jeremy's harmless follow-up was but a continuation of his diversionary banter meant to defuse any mounting anger the man might harbor. So far, Nick had remained perfectly calm. Jeremy wanted to make certain it stayed that way until he was safely out the Arrowhead gate. Executives and senior management throughout all industries were on warning these days, what with so many going postal. Two years before, in Ashtabula, a guy had shot up a custom auto parts shop, killing three and wounding six, just because the raise he'd been promised had been postponed indefinitely. "I mean," Jeremy added, "just out of curiosity."

"College."

"Really?" Again, Jeremy employed this conversational mode only to move things calmly, peacefully, uneventfully, out the door, out the building, and off the premises. If he sounded a trifle bored, with the hint of a stifled yawn, that was the reason.

The iconic blue and gold pennant behind Jeremy's desk and the framed photo of the legendary stadium stared Nick smack in the face, taunting him, shouting at him. His reply was like an involuntary twitch. "Notre Dame," he conceded.

Jeremy swung his arm backward, indicating the wall behind his desk. "Guess you can tell we're fans."

"I never graduated, so I didn't put it down."

"What year?"

"Mid-seventies. Red-shirted one season."

"Position?"

"Mostly tailback. A little flanker." Nick patted his belly, a stock self-deprecating gesture. "A few pounds ago."

Nick was in no mood to play along as though he had nothing better to do than idly shoot the breeze. He'd come too far and had fallen too hard. Once again, it was time to drag his ass out and move on. He started out the door.

Jeremy blocked his path. "Don't go just yet." With his hand extended as if holding Nick at bay, he shouted down the hallway after his assistant. "Marie, could you get my father in here? Right now."

When she failed to respond, Jeremy rushed out to fetch the old man. Left alone, Nick circled Junior's desk, studying the meticulously arranged photos, each in its own ornamental frame. It was like taking a capsule tour of Junior's life, and a good life it seemed: posed with arms around his wife and two daughters, sun-tanned and smiling ferociously against a backdrop of snow-capped mountains; in a tuxedo with a wooden smile receiving a plaque from a woman in a wheelchair; standing with an elderly man – his father? – on a football field taking a mock hand-off from a player with golden hair who Nick halfway recognized from a deodorant commercial.

Jeremy Jr. entered with his father. Jeremy Sr. was no longer the towering lion who'd served with the OSS during the war, had engineered bold business transactions throughout Europe and South America, and had been admired not just in Longview but at the statehouse in Columbus. Physically, he was now a shadow of himself, stooped, hawk-nosed, with bulging spectacles spanning the width of his thin face. His skin was an unhealthy olive color and he had difficulty walking, even when propped by his son.

"Dad, Mr. Remke here played for Notre Dame."

The old man re-balanced the eye glasses which had slipped down his nose. "That so?"

Nick nodded.

"The Parseghian teams," Jeremy Jr. added. "You might have seen him play, Dad."

"Parseghian," the old man mused. "He was some coach."

Nick must have sensed the slimmest of openings, a tiny glint of daylight. With a touch of pique, he allowed, "Coach gave everyone a fair shot. If that's what you mean."

Jeremy Jr. led his dad to the sofa by the window. He handed him the resume folder.

The old man studied it closely, his nose just inches from the page. "But nothing about football."

"Some wear it on their sleeve," Nick explained. "Some move on."

"Remke?" The old man was still inspecting the resume. "Don't recall any Remke. You ever get any playing time?"

"A bit."

"Those years, we went to nearly every home game. Plus Columbus and Ann Arbor for away games. My son here nearly memorized the programs, right?"

"Right, Dad."

"So how come . . ."

"A long story."

"Go on. We're listening."

"When my dad left, we switched to my mom's maiden name."

"So, what name?"

Nick gazed across the big desk and the expansive view of the sunlit valley. In the river below, a rust-colored barge as long as a city block was being towed by a white tug. On the shaded slope of the far bank, he could make out the miniature shapes of two men who appeared to be fishing. A large bird swooped up from the water. The scene was like some eighteenth-century oil painting depicting the Promised Land, dappled and serene with benevolent light streaming through a break in the dark sweep of clouds.

"Nocero," Nick replied.

Jeremy Jr. eyed his father.

The old man cupped his hand to his ear. "Did he say . . .?"

"Yes, Dad. Nick Nocero."

"And he knows the clothing business?"

"Yes. He definitely does."

The old man stared – he still had a fearsome, withering stare – in disbelief at his son's obtuseness. "So what the hell we waiting for?"

································

L ongview's only phone-tree free zone was the Riverview
Tavern. It was a dimly lit establishment where patrons,
mostly men, went to avoid the outside world. There was a
black metal pay phone with a white rotary dial back by the
dartboard, but the Captain never answered it. "Could be a wife,"
was the pat explanation he gave when questioned about this practice. We all knew what he meant.

On mild days the Captain liked to keep the door open. Nick's
entrance that autumn afternoon was not even noticed until he
plunked onto a stool directly facing the bar, and the long mirror
behind it. He still wore his cream suit, and to say he was over-
dressed was a serious understatement. Only a few of us were present at the time, all guys except for Blanche Thompson, a bleached
blonde substitute teacher who often arrived around 4 p.m. and
downed a few stiff drinks before merrily heading home to grade
papers. If there was grade inflation in her classes, we thought we
knew the reason.

The Captain was a big bear with an Amish-style beard, neatly
trimmed at the jawline with shaved upper lip. There were several
Amish settlements in the hills to the east, but their impact was
minimal. The only time you'd hear about them was when someone

struggling with mortgage payments or stressed out in other ways wished aloud that he could be Amish and have a whole community to fall back on.

Nick scanned the liquor shelf. For such a modest joint, there was a lot to choose from.

The Captain (why'd we call him by that nickname? nobody knew) set a cork coaster down. "Take your time," he said affably. "Celebration or sorrow?"

Nick seemed to appreciate that formulation of his options. "How about Old Grand Dad? What does that tell you?"

"Tells me," the Captain crowed, "we've got us a winner."

It had only been an hour or two since Nick's Made Right interview. News of his hiring had begun to spread but it was a long ways from penetrating the Riverview. All we knew of him was the visual evidence. A pharma salesman capping off a road trip? An attorney fresh from a closing? A small business owner who'd been down the block begging for a bank loan? Those were our best guesses.

The Captain located the Old Grand Dad with its burnt orange label and gold lettering and poured Nick a tall glass. For a man so large, fully 6'3" and at least one hundred pounds overweight, the Captain had an incongruously high-pitched, phlegmy voice. "A good day?" he asked. Nick took a long swallow. "Great day."

The Riverview, it is true, provided nothing close to a view or even a peek of the majestic Ohio River. Its one tiny window directly faced Ramsay's Market across the street. Even if you stood in the doorway having a smoke, the only sensation you'd get of the river would be a whiff of the mud flats carried up by a prevailing breeze. What the Riverview did legitimately offer was several beers on tap (Strohs, Rolling Rock, Miller, Bud), a vintage jukebox (no tunes more recent than the late 70's), and a pock-riddled 18" dartboard back by the unisex men's room. In the darkest recesses were four varnished wood booths suitable for a variety of illicit transactions. We'd heard the tall tales from the time we were grade-schoolers. The hombres from Bogota who'd held court here for a solid week in the 80's and now purportedly owned a bank down in Pompano Beach. The Miss Ohio semifinalist who'd flagrantly made out with another woman and didn't care who was watching. Rear booth stories were legend, and probably no less exaggerated than the Riverview's name.

The clientele was a melting pot. On any given night, or afternoon, or weekday morning, you might bump into Made Right workers after their shift, bank tellers on break, truckers between loads, an architect reviewing blueprints spread across the bar, gals in high heels pumped from an Amway rally, even old man Ziglar, at least until he became too deaf to handle the ambient noise. The place was a level playing field, as level as they came. Anyone who could tell a fresh joke, crack a deft quip, or raise a halfway earnest toast to another's alleged success was instantly accepted. If you could do those things you were in like Flynn. No other score mattered.

The Captain had been staring at Nick, cocking one eye like an artist appraising his model. Finally, he blurted, "You look kinda familiar."

Nick scoffed, "Don't even try. Never been here before. Never set foot in town till today."

The Captain did not give up easily. "Give me a minute. I'll get it. You'll see. I'm good at faces. If they had quiz shows for faces stead of that pansy-ass trivia shit . . . Who played the dog on Star Trek? Who led the league in doubles in 1968? Who the hell cares? It's faces that count."

"You're the man," cheered Blanche, sliding two stools closer to Nick, and sliding her wine glass with her. Blanche wasn't one to stand on ceremony. New guy in town. Sharp dresser. Might be gone by morning. Might have a bankroll. Heck, why not give it a whirl? She'd lived in Longview less than two years, having come up from Kentucky where she'd been reputedly married to a Derby trainer who left her for a young sexpot (giving rise to many a shopworn filly joke). Bars like the Riverview may be the most hospitable of all places for lonely middle-aged women who like to socialize and drink, but that doesn't mean they're long on empathy. Early on, Blanche had made the mistake of getting tipsy and coming on to Phil Leahy of Phil's Auto Body, touching his knee whenever he talked. If that sort of behavior didn't get a newcomer branded in a hurry, nothing would. So we thought of Blanche as a pathetic lush and it hardly mattered that the Captain had warned us more than once that we were all dead wrong.

"First time here," she informed Nick, "Captain did the same to me. I'd just moved here after my husband passed away. Captain claimed he knew me from somewhere. Took him a while, but you know what he came up with?"

Nick studied her baby blue blouse and yellow straw hair. He knew better than to offer a guess.

"Barbara Walters. You have to understand that I wore my hair diferently then. It was an honest mistake. No telling," she mused, "who he thinks you are."

"I'm nobody."

"The Captain will never accept that. Nobody's nobody. See that guy over there?"

Blanche wagged her finger in the direction of Jimbo Kluge. He was wearing a "Myrtle Beach Is For Lovers" t-shirt and baggy camouflage pants. "Captain insists he's Bryant Gumbel."

"Gumbel's black."

"Not saying the Captain's right all the time. Point is, he tries."

Longview was not a community that prided itself on teeming with lovable eccentrics, like some wacky British sitcom village. To distance ourselves from Blanche's folly, Jimbo and the rest of us moved to the rear for a game of darts.

But we kept our ears tuned. And we could still get a good look. Blanche did not, from what we could tell, slip a hand onto his knee. But their conversation certainly appeared to grow intimate. The Captain too stayed within earshot, loading the dishwasher and carefully stacking the newly rinsed pint glasses.

Blanche asked Nick how long he was in town. A while, he answered. She cautioned him to be careful, and he asked why. She said people here were not as congenial as they might appear. So

what, he replied, he'd learn to make adjustments. She warned that
adjustments were all well and fine, but too many of them and a person might forget what his dreams had been. Well that gave Nick
pause (and us too). Before he could reply, Blanche apologized. She
said she wasn't typically so gloomy and harsh. He said he wasn't
either, except when life got to be too much. They clinked glasses on
that pearl and ordered another round.

Soon you would have thought they were long-lost cousins.
Barbara Walters herself couldn't have done a better job of engaging
Nick in conversation. At one point their voices grew loud and she
insisted, "Tell me." And so he did, his head bowed as if in prayer, his
hands folded around his glass. We wondered what the heck kind of
spell old Blanche had cast over him.

The story Nick told was about a teenage boy he'd been friendly
with back in Iowa where he'd been raised. It was one of those
accounts, intense and cathartic and disturbingly detailed, that you
knew, you just knew, wasn't really about someone else. By the dartboard, the guys piped down to better overhear. Every few minutes
one of us would return to the bar for a book of matches or a refill,
any pretense to eavesdrop.

This teenage boy – we never did catch the name Nick ascribed to
him, and maybe he never did state a name – had been out fishing with
his dad one spring afternoon on a tributary to the Mississippi, just
above Dubuque. The boy and his dad were not close, mainly because
the boy knew a secret. He knew what his dad was really like. The dad
was a well-respected pillar of the community, successful tri-state rep
for Amana refrigerators, summertime stand-out for the men's softball
squad, lay preacher at the local Methodist church. Only the boy, the
boy and his mom that is, knew the truth. Which was that the dad was
a nasty-tempered, sadistic, silver-tongued huckster who could charm
anyone into anything, even persuade good honest folk of his own dubious virtue so long as they didn't spend too much time in his presence.

When the boy finally returned from the fishing expedition,
an entire day later, the anguished account he gave was that he'd

been abandoned. His dad, he said, had steered their outboard to a small island in the river where they'd been planning to put in for lunch. The dad told the boy to wait there while he boated upriver to a nearby town to fetch cokes and chips to go with the sandwiches he'd prepared. The boy waited on the island until it grew dark. The boy was a strong swimmer and could have made it to shore. But he waited through the night, assuming his dad was off on one of those crazed drunken benders only his family knew him capable of. In the morning, chilled and frightened, the boy plunged in and eventually made his way home.

Nobody ever saw the dad again, or heard from him. Townsfolk were dumbfounded. They could not believe that this man they so admired would do something so dastardly as abandon a wife, a son, a daughter in the fifth grade.

"That's awful," Blanche commiserated. She did not need to ask, nor did we, why Nick was telling this tale about someone we did not know and never would. Like many barroom stories, there'd been no ostensible prompt beyond the teller's evident compulsion to get it out and receive affirmation. Even from – or especially from – a perfect stranger.

"It gets weirder," Nick hurriedly added. The boy's fishing story was in reality a cover story, at least in part. The dad had not really gone upriver to fetch cokes and chips. The dad had not gone any-where. The dad had accidentally fallen – he'd not been pushed, Nick emphasized – into the river's swift spring current while trying to free a sinker snagged on a submerged log. He'd lost his balance. The dad was not such a great swimmer. A tobacco habit had weak-ened his lungs. He'd yelled for the boy to help. Yelling was a regu-lar habit of the dad, only this time the boy recognized a dramatic reversal in the balance of power. Many times the boy had called out for his dad's help, for problems large and small, and his dad always answered the same way: do it yourself or you'll never amount to nothing. Sink or swim, the dad was fond of saying. As though that said it all. Well maybe it did.

The dad shouted again, or tried to. But the boy's thoughts were roaring too loudly to hear, roaring with memories of his mom cowering helplessly in the kitchen by the blood-spattered refrigerator, their brand new Amana.

In the river, the dad was in trouble. Reluctantly, the boy saw what he must do, saw the awful obligation he could not avoid. He'd have to save the sonofabitch. By then, however, the dad had gone under once more. The boy cranked the throttle and began madly zigzagging downstream, searching, searching, frantically searching.

To no avail. The boy spent the night alone on the island shivering and thinking dark thoughts. There were sins of commission and omission. He did not believe he had committed either. Aware that others might disagree, he told no one.

By now, you could hear a pin drop in the Riverview. We weren't even pretending to toss darts. Who was this guy? Why was he even telling this to people he could not trust to understand or empathize or leap to uncharitable conclusions. Unless he thought he could trust us. Unless, for reasons we would probably never know, he had arrived at a point where he had no choice but to trust us.

Nick glanced up from his bourbon. He seemed surprised to find that Blanche was not the only one paying attention. Feigning a sheepish smile, he added, "The kid up and moved to California with his mom and sister. Things worked out."

"A happy ending?" suggested Blanche, wanting it to be so.

"Happy enough."

"End of story?"

"Far as I know. We lost touch. Me and the kid."

The mood in the bar had taken a perilous downward turn. The Captain, always looking out for us, moved in. "Hey, I got it!" he jubilantly informed Nick. "The weather. CNN. Weekday mornings. I don't mean the red head with the knockers. The other one, the guy who draws happy faces on the sun. Tell me, am I right?"

Blanche tilted back on her stool, as if to study Nick from an improved perspective. "Captain, I do believe you've hit the bull's-eye."

Nick, to our great relief, was able to switch gears and play along like a sport. That told us something, that he could sound so miserable one moment yet rebound so swiftly. Adopting an artificially suave broadcaster's baritone, he stridently announced, "Precipitation moving down from the Great Lakes off to the south. Followed by a warming trend."

"Love those warming trends," Blanche enthused.

His ebullience restored, Nick was now on a roll. "Looking ahead to the rest of the week, clear and unseasonably mild for . . . hell, forever after."

We drank to that.

CHAPTER 6

It didn't take long for word to spread about the new hire. Eyebrows were raised, but no more than eyebrows. When it came to the management of the plant, the Ziglars generally enjoyed our trust. The decisions they made were of course self-serving, but our lives and livelihoods were so intricately intertwined with the interests of the company that we assumed good faith in all their efforts regarding the welfare of the plant. Even the layoffs, that most difficult of all developments to swallow, were accepted precisely on the terms in which they were presented, a bitter pill that was nonetheless critical to our long term viability and health. Regarding the new plant manager (his predecessor, Vern Collings, turned 65 in August and had already worked a month past retirement), we had every reason to trust the Ziglars' wisdom in recruiting him and to hope that this was the best choice. Or rather, the best that was available.

Longview's economic history had not been an entirely upward trajectory. Unless you count survival as a noteworthy goal. The town's original name, once we were substantial enough to merit one, was Langton's Landing. During these early frontier years, inhabitants were mostly the roughneck and hearty risk-takers willing to undertake the difficult journey over the Alleghenies getting here. By the mid-1800's, with the riverfront a churning hub of commerce, we flourished as a regional center where local farmers could bank their savings, where hardware and dry goods could be purchased, where professional services like medicine and law were dispensed, where disputes could be settled in a civilized way at the new county courthouse. Soon we had ourselves a middle class and by the early twentieth century most of the town, if a poll were taken, would have declared themselves to be just that, middle class. If history were a movie, we might want to throw it into slow motion right around here, the early 1900's. We could grow or get or manufacture what we needed and the world beyond the Ohio was neither our burden nor our worry.

The Great Depression was a setback, as it was for most of the nation. But Made Right, with its uniform-making capability, withstood the worst of the downturn. We had jobs and at least the trickle of an economy. By V-E Day, 1945, Made Right was not only the dominant employer in town but one of the largest in the entire county, at one time putting out upwards of 300 dozen garments per day. Most of us either had an immediate member of the family working here or knew someone who did. Political leaders, school leaders, Scout leaders, 4-H leaders, even religious leaders were employed at the factory. Wages were steady and decent, probably higher than they actually needed to be to attract labor amidst the widespread unemployment. The general consensus, with allowances for the usual allegations of unfairness, was that the plant was a decent and fortunate place to work. If a worker was strapped for cash or had pressing financial needs, if the family car required a costly transmission overhaul or the hot water heater was shot or medical care soared beyond what insurance covered, the company would offer no-interest loans to be repaid through weekly payroll deductions. It paid, somewhat begrudgingly, half the costs of the annual union picnic. A family-owned business, Made Right had something akin to a familial relationship to the rest of us: intense, argumentative, co-dependent, draining, replenishing, supportive, demanding, taxing, fortifying, inescapable. The company was the parents we would never leave. Without Made Right, Longview was an orphan.

Made Right had experienced up cycles and down cycles and the occasional phase when it appeared to be smooth sailing as far ahead as one cared to project. We'd dealt with shortages and rejoiced at abundance, endured periods of apprehension as well as episodes of relative security. But the current situation was different. Economic experts tossed around the term "globalization" as though, like a science formula, that should explain something. What it explained was the mode of our impending demise. Who wants to hear that? It brought little solace knowing that the dilemma facing Made Right, Inc. was shared by just about every domestic manufacturing operation in North America in the late twentieth century. The driving force behind both the cutbacks and the outsourcing was the increasingly fierce competition from LDC – Less Developed Countries. You did not need to be a World Bank economist to detect what was going on. The ground, quite simply, was shifting under our feet. Anyone could see it.

So what did we think about having a has-been former football player recruited to run operations at Made Right? Let's just say we were a lot less skeptical than another community might be. Sports analogies have their limitations but sometimes they apply. We were like veteran ball players who'd diligently practiced an assortment of skills, only to have the rules switched on us. For years we'd labored to achieve a modicum of productivity (and profitability, so we were told), and now we found ourselves unceremoniously challenged from the blind side by upstarts who weren't even in the league just a few years ago. We were like utility infielders, valued for our workaday skills but eminently replaceable. We had to trust that the Ziglars knew what they were doing.

Entering the tall iron gates of Made Right that first time, Nick came as a pilgrim seeking safe harbor. His second time through, he entered as a man who belonged, a man with a challenge.

His first day on the job, Nick got a guided tour from Jeremy

Jr. Pleased to show him around and show him off, Jeremy squired Nick through the sequence of tasks that led to the completion of a Made Right coat. There was design, marking, cutting, bundling, sewing, backs, fronts, pockets, sleeves, linings, shoulders, collars, lapels, buttons, pressing, inspecting. A rough evolutionary logic pertained to the layout of the factory floor, beginning nearest the main entrance by the huge spreading machines that roll out the fabric for marking and cutting, and proceeding rearward to where the neatly pressed garments were finally draped on hangers, sheathed in plastic, arranged by lots according to size, and hauled near the loading dock at the far end of the plant.

Jeremy Jr. used this tour mostly to fill Nick in on what he viewed as the game plan. Unlike his father, a stern adherent to an old school, command-and-control style, Jeremy Jr. tried to acquaint all employees, whenever possible, with Made Right's "mission." That basic survival was currently the mission that overwhelmed all others seemed not to undercut his conviction that management needed to frame the company's objectives in terms that were, if possible, inspiring.

Jeremy Jr. was a firm believer that motivation was the key to business success. His penchant for inspirational speeches, and his belief in their merits, was a bit like religion. For those who had the faith and the need, the benefits were indisputable. For agnostics, it could seem pretty pointless. Junior's shelves were stocked with books by acclaimed experts in the field, mostly sports figures like Mike Ditka, Pat Riley, Rick Pitino, Lou Holtz, the great Lombardi. All were passionate advocates that motivation could save the day when not everything was going your way. Did we buy into that? We did when we needed to.

"Women's jackets, Air Force." Jeremy pointed to a stack of bluish gray fabric twined in compact packets. "The military, thank God, don't get their clothes made in Asia. At least not yet."

Nick pulled a small loose-leaf notepad from his shirt pocket and quickly jotted a note.

"Something catch your eye?"

"General observations."

"About?"

"Just details. Anything adds up, you'll be the first to know."

Jeremy accepted this with a theatrical roll of his eyes to indicate that the acceptance was provisional. They continued past the fabric spreaders and cutting machines. Nick nodded a pleasant hello to several of us but said little. He was like a presiding physician making the rounds of a hospital ward. He'd offer congenial bits of commentary, about the fabric, the machines, the noise, less an invite to converse than a gesture of vague solidarity. We played it close to the vest, revealing no more than mannequins. All we really knew about him was his presumed organizational affiliation, and that was management. At this juncture, it was best to keep our eyes glued to the task, hunched toward our machines, fingers and hands moving efficiently, no small talk, no distractions.

Nick wouldn't have to be a genius to guess what was percolating. Made Right, quite simply, needed to get more productivity out of fewer people. The Catch-22 of apparel manufacturing, from the management perspective, was that the soft, floppy, varied nature of the fabric itself precluded the kind of full automation that would have solved so many overhead problems. There was no way around it. You needed sentient human beings to maneuver the material at the required angles, to adjust the lumps and dips and creases that had to be set just right before a cutting machine or a sewing machine could perform its function. Millions in research funds had been spent and were being spent to develop robotic capabilities that could emulate the nuanced dexterity of human fingers. Someday it might happen. But Jeremy Jr. was not holding his breath.

In the meantime, Made Right, like so many plants, was experimenting with new methods of structuring tasks, or at least in the talking stage of beginning to do so. Modular manufacturing was being touted as the coming alternative to the traditional bundle system. The idea was to have each worker perform many of the assembly line tasks, to essentially be responsible for assembling a complete garment from start to finish, rather than one specialized function. There was probably merit to this idea. But it took time to reengineer and it required the union to buy into the concept. That was hard to achieve when the pressure was on, with everyone so skittish about an uncertain future.

Jeremy kept talking, Nick at his elbow. "It's crunch time. We've structured the operation like a well-oiled football squad. The whole is larger than the sum of the parts."

"Makes sense."

They arrived at a poorly lit region tucked beneath the far mezzanine overhang. Large steam presses, the size and shape of crypts, hissed like dragons, belching vapor. The operators manning these beasts – they were all men – were drenched in sweat. "This," said Jeremy, "is our . . . "

"Pay dirt offense?"

"You got it. Last step before we rack 'em up and ship."

Nick shut his notepad.

"You'll probably hear rumors."

"About?"

"Management decisions, threats from offshore – that sort of thing. I can assure you, Nick, nobody knows anything."

"Except you."

"Me, and my father. That's right."

Jeremy waved to catch the attention of a man bustling at a good clip along the far aisle.

Isaac Ashong was our union rep. He'd come up the hard way, factory floor to elected leader, and had held the position for nearly eight years. A dark-skinned man with a glistening shaved skull and a cherub's smile, he wore the type of loose-hanging, lemon-colored rayon sport shirt that is popular with tourists in tropical resorts. With wide shoulders and a thin waist, Ashong looked like a Calypso star. But looks were deceiving; he had none of that languid cool-mon tranquility, and he did not aspire to it.

Jeremy Jr. made the introductions. "Isaac Ashong, our union rep. Meet our new manager, Nick Nocero."

"I prefer Remke," Nick stated. He didn't want to make an issue, nor, it was clear, did he want to let it slide.

Jeremy bristled. "Nocero's already entered in our system."

"What I mean . . . "

Jeremy cut him off with a scolding stare, letting it be known this was not a matter to be argued. Certainly not in front the union rep, and not with several of us eavesdropping.

Introductions concluded, Jeremy dismissed Ashong with a curt, "Why don't we talk later?"

Ashong obliged. "Pleasure," he told Nick, and stopped just short of stumbling on the surname.

Whatever. We had a new plant manager and he'd have the benefit of our best efforts as long as he seemed worthy, and possibly longer.

The tour of the plant floor completed, Jeremy guided Nick back toward the mezzanine staircase. "This is a fine town, Nick. If you're not busy tonight, you might stop by Riverside Park. It's our annual football homecoming bonfire. It'll give you a better feel for who we are."

"Football," Nick said with emphasis, "is behind me."

Jeremy lifted his eyes with theatrical exaggeration, humoring Nick. "Whatever you say. Try to stop by anyway."

T he annual football homecoming bonfire was a tradition going back at least fifty years, and some said longer. Mayor Ernie Luppert's father, Franklin, who played offensive and defensive tackle for the Bobcats, claimed to have met his wife at the homecoming bonfire when she was part of an a capella chorus performing a medley of patriotic tunes – "Grand Old Flag", "America the Beautiful", "Somewhere Over the Rainbow." That Ernie's mother vehemently denied this – she insisted she was always too shy to do anything more demonstrative than sneeze in public – said more, according to Mayor Luppert, about the nature of his parents' marriage, and his father's veracity, than it did about the historical dating of the event.

Riverside Park had always been the setting for the bonfire. The park featured nearly all a person could want in the way of civilized outdoor recreation except for golf. There were hiking trails and bridle paths that crossed streams and cut through wooded glens and brought you to unexpected clearings teeming with grasshoppers. There were picnic pavilions perfect for sprawling family get-togethers and a outdoor amphitheater scooped from the hillside with rows of terraced seating. There were concrete tennis and basketball courts surrounded by shade trees, and open fields suitable for football, soccer, softball, kite flying, and vigorous dog runs. There was an in-ground swimming pool that was open from Memorial Day to Labor Day. The park even had its own mythology, which made it a place of mystery and fascination, especially after dark, especially for teenage couples. Long ago on a September evening, as darkness was descending, a young woman in love was said to have argued with her boyfriend while strolling through the park. She bolted away, across Richard's Creek and behind Phantom Rock, never to be seen again. The boyfriend, so the story went, returned every day for the rest of his life, just before sunset, and waited for her to reemerge. Sometimes he'd wait an hour, sometimes all night. He was finally found dead, still waiting, at the age of seventy-four.

Nick arrived just after sunset. Making his way amongst the sauntering couples and cavorting children, he was swept like an ember on a cushion of air. He passed beneath the stately American elms so admired for the geometrical precision of the archway formed by their overhanging branches, and came onto the dirt path that slopes deeper into the park. Drawn by the sound of music, and laughter, and the static-riddled croak of a male voice making announcements over a shoddy PA system, he walked on.

In an open grassy field surrounded by maples, birches, alder, and oak, the bonfire was already piled to pyre proportions. A mini-explosion from the pit shot sparks into the air. Children shrieked. A fire truck was parked nearby, just in case. A Good Humor van, its siding lavishly illustrated with alluring pictures of fudge bars, creamsickles, rainbow-colored rocket ships, had pulled up behind the fire truck. Nick considered getting something cold and sweet; the line wasn't long. But cheering erupted from across the clearing and he moved in that direction. He was like a child, navigating by curiosity.

A dozen folk were watching a horseshoe contest. Vintage cast iron-shoes were being flung at stakes situated a dozen yards apart. Curt Vranek, co-owner of Freck's Department Store, was tossing. A

CHAPTER SEVEN

large fellow with a hefty gut, his throw arched masterfully, a perfect parabola, and landed two feet from the pole, where it flipped.
Not a ringer but a touch. The crowd cheered again. We were fans of
any contest where the outcome was in the balance.

That might be what most defined us, being fans. Someone once
wrote, "Perhaps long ago we were a pioneer people, but now we are
a nation of sports fans." That statement was probably intended to be
a sarcastic comment on Americans' dubious progress from fearless
explorers of the dangerous frontier to passive consumers of televised entertainment. We didn't necessarily see it that way. Sure, we
watched our fair share of ESPN broadcasts involving brand name
teams and marquee players. But our true passion had always been
reserved for our local squads, for the sons and daughters (well,
mostly sons) of townsfolk and neighbors. Of course, if the satisfaction that comes from winning was our primary objective, we would
have been far better off, percentage-wise, following the New York
Yankees or Duke basketball. But if winning was all we cared about,
we'd have been smarter to just pick up and leave.

A few fireflies left over from the summer skittered aimlessly as
Nick sauntered into the clearing where preparations for the main
event were under way. Larry Delp, the high school music instructor, was busily stringing wire from an auxiliary generator to a pair
of garage band amps. Ms. Averson, the drama instructor, stood on
a footstool adjusting the imported stage lights attached to a low-
hanging tree branch. A temporary stage had been constructed of
reinforced plywood propped on cement blocks. It had that makeshift
look of a public hanging apparatus from the cowboy movies. Always
a solemn moment. Storm clouds gathering. Grim-faced townsfolk.
A woman in black weeping. God have mercy on his soul.

When the amps were finally connected, a bouncy country
swing number blasted out, electric guitar and amped-up fiddles
accompanied by a twangy female voice oozing with heartache.
Couples emerged from out of nowhere, from the woods, from the
horseshoe pit, hand in hand, high-stepping and twirling, the men

41

in jeans and T-shirts, the women in billowing skirts and blouses. Younger kids and grown-ups inched forward, waiting to be coaxed. Nick simply watched, nostrils filling with the burnt sugar fragrance of autumn leaves.

He felt a tap on the shoulder, and there was Marie from Made Right. His hand jerked to shake hers. "Hey, I owe you big-time." Nick's voice was louder than necessary, perhaps out of nervousness. "They were set to offer it to someone else."

"Someone less worthy?"

"Don't know about that."

"Certainly someone less famous." Marie kept her sparkling eyes fixed on his. She wore a lime wraparound skirt snug at her hips. She always looked more put together than other women at Made Right. In cooler weather, for example, she'd taken to wearing a black woolen cape that she twirled around herself with needless panache. It probably pleased her to be noticed by someone who didn't immediately speculate who the heck she thought she was, dressed so fancy and smart. "My father couldn't believe I'd never heard of you."

Nick winced.

"A good move for the company," Marie elaborated. "That's what everyone's saying."

"Thought the company was doing okay."

"Maybe. But we're about the last clothing plant still standing in a region that gets snow."

"No snow tonight," Nick said.

"No," Marie agreed. "Tonight is lovely."

The mournful Hank Williams classic, "So Lonesome I Could Cry" was next over the speaker system, the languid whine of a steel guitar, the nasal croon of a man out of luck.

Marie asked, "Would you like to dance?" Soon as she said it, she realized her faux pas. Acknowledging his bad hip with a downward glance, she apologized. "That was stupid. I'm sorry."

Nick offered his hand. "The answer is yes. I'd like to dance."

This version of the song featured an extended instrumental

interlude with guitar and bass. Nick and Marie drew closer, dancing slowly, unpretentiously.

"If you're not a football fan," Nick asked, referencing a remark she'd made on the way up the stairs. "Why're you here?"

"My son Brian. He's on the team."

Abruptly, the music stopped. Two men clambered atop the stage. Phil Forrester, owner of Forrester's Shoes and a volunteer fire fighter, was the first to reach the stand-up microphone. But Phil couldn't get the dang thing to work. Ernie Luppert, dressed in a black-and-white striped referee's jersey – to augment the football homecoming theme, of course – elbowed Phil aside. Deftly, he fiddled with the knobby underside of the apparatus and, satisfied that it was now in working order, let loose with a two-fingered sailor's whistle that shot straight through the spinal column.

"Listen up," shouted Ernie. "Before we get to the main part of the program, which will culminate in the introduction of this year's Fightin' Bobcats who – I remind you – take on Haynesville tomorrow afternoon at Made Right Field, I want to give credit to just a few . . . "

Nick and Marie stayed close, swaying imperceptibly as if there was one final refrain audible only to them. Ollie McGuiness, pushing past, recognized Marie and briefly halted. Ollie was a former business partner with Marie's father Lou – not in Lou's current enterprise, the used car lot, but its predecessor, the machine and tool rental outfit. She swiftly nixed him away with a scolding forefinger from the hand still perched like a pet parrot atop Nick's shoulder. Ollie got the hint and moved on.

" . . . Larry's Lumber and Feed, Greenfield Savings and Loan, Law Offices of Diltz & Son, Shaw's Best Buy, and last but not least, Made Right Industries."

Scattered catcalls flew up from the audience like grasshoppers stirred by bounding deer.

"What's that about?" Nick asked.

"Rumors. That's what Jeremy says. Just rumors."

Mere rumors, of course, were not always to be dismissed, at

least not in Longview. The rumors that were most alive at this time had largely to do with Made Right's corporate intentions. The recent cutbacks gave rise to speculation that more were in the offing. Talk of modular manufacturing had everyone uneasy, as if it was a storm system sighted in the West Indies moving our way. The trip Jeremy Jr. took to Asia last spring – sightseeing and personal enrichment were his expressed motives – gave rise to rumors that offshoring was being contemplated. There'd been DHL overseas courier envelopes arriving from South Korea, three in one month, and rumors about an impending trade delegation visit. The hiring of a former Notre Dame football star as plant manager . . . well that was a very recent occurrence and the rumors it gave rise to were just beginning to take shape.

The stage was now filled with Fightin' Bobcat cheerleaders. Their outfits had not changed much over the years. The flared gold skirts with blue pleats were no skimpier than was fashionable in Marie's high school days, or Nick's. The navy sweaters were cut demurely high at the neck and, with one exception, were not so snug at the bust as to instantaneously excite impure thoughts. In fact, the cheerleaders – there were nine of them – did not appear to have been selected purely for their good looks or comely figures. Equal opportunity was how we liked to think of the composition of the cheerleading squad, a break from rigid sexist confines. We congratulated ourselves on that, in a joking sort of way.

These girls came in all shapes and sizes. There was even one, Cindy Delp, who was short and round and wore eyeglasses! And another, Sarah Bass, was gangly and, frankly, uncoordinated. A newcomer like Nick could be justified in wondering exactly what the selection requirements were. And it wouldn't take much for such conjecture to spill over to the football team. Truth be told, each year we had a lower and lower turnout for football tryouts and selection for the varsity was increasingly a function of that one primary and irreducible criterion, who's available and who's willing? Who wants to get off his butt and try to be something more than you are?

With the PA system reactivated, we were treated to the Preservation Hall instrumental recording of "When the Saints Go Marching In." This tune, a toe-tapping gem with rescripted lyrics, served as our official Longview High anthem. In recent years there'd been discussion about replacing the band's live renditions at Bobcat games with more a polished recorded version. So far the old guard (music teachers, PTA stalwarts, the school committee) had managed to forestall the implementation of this suggestion, but there was a general sense that, with declining school funds and youngsters' dwindling interest in learning to play instruments not featured in rock bands, it was only a matter of time.

The Bobcat cheerleaders, having arranged themselves in three rows of three, began to weave to and fro in a vaguely choreographed manner doubtlessly meant to be synchronized. The girls sashayed and smiled and looked to be enjoying themselves. This lasted perhaps a minute and then they regrouped into their basic 3x3 formation, keeping time with thrusts of their arms and clockwise hip gyrations.

Sarah Bass cut away from the group and stepped to the microphone. Marie had known Sarah Bass since she was a toddler, although it wasn't easy to connect this composed young woman to the chubby tike with a constantly runny nose. Sarah began to sing, "Oh when that kickoff/ Goes sailing high/ When that kickoff rises to the sky . . . "

These modified lyrics were essentially second nature to us. We'd been singing them, it seemed, our whole lives. "Oh when the Bobcats/ Take to the Field/ Oh When the Bobcats Take to the Field."

Nick noticed that Marie showed no interest in joining in. "What's a matter?" he chided. "Don't know the lyrics?"

"I wish."

Young men began to amass by the stage, this year's edition of the Fightin' Bobcats. To an outsider schooled on the Division 1 college game, they probably did not exactly look like football players. Only a few were large enough to look the part and many were legitimately small. And not just short and stocky. Some of these kids were short and thin. Others were larger yet pudgy. A handful had the type of handsome jaw and squinting steel eyes, augmented by military-style buzz cuts, that would allow them to pass for exemplary soldiers. But football players? Well, you would have to know the high school game, and you'd have to know our Longview talent pool, and you'd have to know the magic that can occur under a quality coach in order to accept that this shambling aggregation of guileless teenagers might transform into a gridiron squad capable of accomplishing very much. Yet we had our hopes. Always do early in the fall season.

Onstage, the cheerleaders were having problems forming their pyramid. One of the girls in the crucial middle layer was having difficulty balancing. Coach Pruitt, who'd been leading the team for over thirty years, was standing nearby, helping to orchestrate the gathering Bobcats. In his mid-sixties, small of frame with an improbably large skull and warm eyes, Pruitt was well liked. It was a measure of his popularity that a long string of losing seasons had not provoked overt calls for his resignation. Now he leaned over to give the toppled cheerleader a hand. Pruitt wore a blue and gold rugby shirt, our school colors, that did not flatter his bulging abdomen. He placed one hand on the faltering cheerleader's shoulder and the other closer to her skirted rear. Suddenly, as though he'd been shot from behind by a sniper, he lurched forward and lay jerking spasmodically on the rough plywood.

The cheerleader let loose with an ear-splitting scream. Sarah shrieked straight into the mike, launching a shrill audio zap that had some plugging their ears. Bobcat players rushed to see what had happened. Curious folk surged forward. The PA music abruptly cut off. Ernie Luppert in his ref's outfit charged to center stage and frantically announced, "Is there a medical doctor, or qualified nurse or EMT out there? We got an emergency."

A low rumble churned through the crowd. Two firemen stormed on stage.

"Please clear an aisle," Ernie Luppert beseeched us. "People, please. Please stay back. Give us room." Ernie bent over, cupping his hand to his ear. Someone in front spoke to Ernie. Ernie nodded, then stood to address the crowd again. "Yes, it's Ron Pruitt. Now please! Give us room."

Marie put her hand to her mouth. She was not alone in doing so.

"Who?" Nick wanted to know.

"Our coach."

Even as she said it, Marie was aware that there could be a contradiction between her professed lack of interest in football and the solemnity of her tone. So be it. To her, there was football – a game played by two squads of young men that held a disproportionate importance in the lives of people who would never set foot on an actual field – and then there was the Longview tradition involving Friday night and Saturday afternoon contests and this annual bonfire that she'd attended as a toddler, a cheerleader, and now a mom.

"He's been our coach," Marie explained, "ever since I can remember. Had a heart scare couple years ago. This could be serious."

Darkness had fallen. We were departing in droves through the smoky gloom. There would be no further celebration this evening.

"Football," Nick stressed, "is behind me. Done. I don't need it."

Only as she watched him limp proudly away, joining the flow of retreating townsfolk like a fallen leaf carried downstream, did it occur to Marie that she'd not said one single word to him about football.

And she certainly had not raised the subject of Nick's needs, whatever those might be.

CHAPTER

·····························

B y noon, the parking lot situated between the playing field and Longview High was swarming with tailgate parties. Yes, we tailgated just like fans at the major gridiron capitals, only with less overt hoopla. Like the big leaguers, we placed hibachis on the pavement and fired them up with deft squirts of charcoal fluid. We drank our brews from paper bags and kept radios (boom boxes for the younger crowd) on the station wagon's rear gate, blasting our favorites tunes. Oddly, there weren't very many actual high school students around. Many of us recalled the time when even the most cerebral students (your forensic club and math whizzes) would attend home football games as faithfully as they would Christmas service. But there had been a gradual shift through the years, as subtle as dripping water eroding a rock face. None of us were sure exactly why or what it meant, but these days you'd glance around the parking lot before the game and there was hardly a high school kid to be found.

Still, the aluminum grandstands at Made Right Field were reasonably full as game time approached, mostly parents, family relatives, younger siblings dragged along and their playmates, older townsfolk, plus the visiting team's entourage. The north flank of the grandstand was where the band, all ten pieces, sat in their blue and gold jackets. The band's repertoire had changed little over the decades: *Grand Old Flag, Sweet Georgia Brown, This Land Is Your Land, When the Saints Go Marching In.* Every couple of years, Larry Delp would introduce a new number meant to resonate with the kids' generation. This year it was "Bad Reputation", which Larry had done his best to transpose. Lacking electric guitar and bass, the music sounded like gargled mariachi.

The southern flank of the grandstand was where the hot dog shack was located. Younger children with no apparent interest in watching the Bobcats take on Haynesville hovered like starving pigeons at an outdoor café. A chain link fence ran behind the shack and we thought we spotted Nick on the other side, peering in. Why, we wondered, didn't he just buy a ticket and take a proper seat instead of peeking through the keyhole like some urchin? He'd been away from the game for a while, we reasoned, and probably carried some unresolved baggage. Most of us do.

From our earliest interactions, we detected in him an unusual characteristic, one that deepened our intrigue. Here was a guy who appeared to have a yearning to be one of us, to belong, to be a contributing member of the team, as it were. Yet from the piecemeal evidence, it seemed that he'd spent his adult life as a drifter. Three years with Hart, Schaffner in Chicago, three with Ransome Industries in Tennessee. Another four in Sacramento where, he let on, he would have stayed if only the investors had not chosen to relocate all manufacturing to Guatemala. The extended hitch in the Navy, we came to believe, was a partial cover, but less for anything scandalous than for the numbingly mundane short term employment stints. So much time spent packing up and starting over; it seemed a waste. Of course he'd managed to survive and that was nothing to sneeze at. Nor, however, was it the kind of accomplishment that made you leap up and applaud.

There were, to be sure, skeptics who suspected Nick wasn't all he was cracked up to be. Some, like Tuna (real name: Larry Fontune), insisted it was tantamount to a form of treason to rely on outside assistance when the town had so much untapped local talent begging for the chance.

"It's like cheating," Tuna asserted on more than one occasion, as though he was a paragon of moral rectitude. Tuna was Marie's former brother-in-law and it was often said of him, in reference to his hulking physique and sad, expressionless eyes, that he was not as dumb as he looked. Marie was always quick to add that neither was he as shrewd as he liked to believe.

Some argued, over a few cold ones back by the dart board, that even if hiring Nick was somehow "cheating," it was exactly the kind of so-called cheating that in the larger world simply constitutes competitiveness. Was it cheating for Duke to recruit the top basketball players? Was it cheating for the US military to be the best equipped in the world? Unlike Tuna, most of us took Nick at face value. Watching how he carried himself with a kind of stoic grace, heaving his thick athlete's torso forward despite the difficult hip, we found ourselves, without actually acknowledging it, beginning to root for him. Nothing blatant, mind you. He was too new here and his track record too limited to justify becoming heavily invested. But quietly, privately, inadvertently, subconsciously, we'd slipped into hoping for the best.

Each of us had our own interpretation of what brought him to Longview. Like angry callers to talk radio, ill-informed but hotly passionate, we had hunches. Escaping from a love turned wrong. A fugitive from a grave injustice. A tortured soul performing a strange penance. One explanation propounded by Mayor Luppert was that he'd been raised in a town much like Longview and secretly hankered to return to his roots. Another guess was that Nick was killing time until he got called up to his rightful place in the big leagues, metaphorically speaking. Mostly, though, we guessed he was like a lot of us, doing his best to stay afloat without the benefit of any great advantage. The vanquished luster of having been a football star thirty years ago was a condition we had no trouble relating to. A lot of us had enjoyed a youthful burst, only to have it wilt like a summer flower.

Gus Hoover reported he'd overheard Nick talking to himself in his room that first morning in town. Gus had gone upstairs to deliver some clean towels and paused outside the door to listen, baffled since he knew Nick was in there alone. According to Gus, it was the kind of talking-to a stern father would administer to a wayward son, warning him in no uncertain terms to knuckle down, do his best, give it his all. It was like there were two people in that shabby little hotel room, Gus said, one fiercely ranting, one sheepishly listening.

Nick's second week in town a postcard arrived for him at General Delivery, addressed to the other name, Remke. It was a Sierra Club postcard with a picture of an endangered gray wolf alone on a patch of snow. Of course, Helena Worthen, our postmaster, read it, but there wasn't all that much to be learned: California postmark; a woman's handwriting, small and neat; signed by "Norma," probably a relative. The correspondent wrote Nick that "Mom" was asking about him and begged him to please write to say he was fine, even if he wasn't. There was mention of a nephew enlisting in the Air Force and a new dog, a feisty mutt that had been hard to train, they'd named after him. "Still cheering for you," was Norma's sign-off.

When Nick came to pick it up, Helena told him it would be no problem to forward his mail straight on to the Ohio Hotel. Nick grabbed the postcard out of her hand and snapped, "That won't be necessary." And it wasn't. For whatever reasons, he never received another piece of mail.

Brad Zelk saw him once – this is jumping ahead a bit – placing a long distance phone call (the stack of quarters was the giveaway) from the glassed-in AT&T phone booth on the corner outside Wrenshaw's. Brad saw Nick slam the phone down, then bury his head in his hands. What the heck was that about? All we could think was that the guy had a complicated history. He'd had disappointments.

True to an earlier threat, Tuna did in fact conduct some "research," although exactly how he managed it was never made clear. Several of us were at the Riverview flinging darts later that evening when Tuna, a few sheets to the wind, swaggered in wearing a smile so wide you'd think he was happy. He wore a tan uniform of indeterminate law enforcement affiliation. We'd not seen it before. Tuna was known for alternating between vaguely official security attire and loose-fitting MVP jerseys bearing the surnames of his favorite pro athletes, Bradshaw, Bird, Canseco.

"Got some news, fellas," Tuna announced smugly. "Stuff you might want to know about."

Tuna waited until we were paying complete attention. He was the sort of half-cocked, highly opinionated fellow we took great delight in refuting. In that sense, he was kind of fun; otherwise, not so much. Begrudgingly, we gathered around.

Tuna wanted to apprise us of what he'd discovered. His presentation was so crisp and precise you would have thought he'd rehearsed it. Had he been this motivated and prepared back in his high school days, a "C" average would certainly have been within reach.

Tuna's background check had turned up several "disclosures." First, there'd been allegations that several unnamed members of the Notre Dame team had received "outside assistance" in their academic coursework and those allegations were never satisfactorily put to rest. More importantly, during Nick's playing days, the offensive line was a veritable steamroller, with three of the guys, each over 260 pounds, going on to the NFL. This line, according to Tuna, opened up holes big enough for a cripple to walk through, holes so humongous that even Nick's back-up averaged 6.1 yards per carry, that's how awesome those dudes were.

We were less than bowled over. "That's it?"

Tuna nodded, proud of his investigative coup.

"You're telling us he ain't exactly a saint?"

"Not even fuckin' close."

"Or hall of fame material?"

Tuna spat.

"Find out why he never went pro?"

"Too slow. Too small."

"Learn anything else?"

"Such as?"

"Like, you know, did he kill a man in Reno just to watch him die?"

"Fuck you!" Tuna stormed out again.

To be fair, Tuna was not the only nosey Parker. A lot of folk were itching to yank back the curtain, as though Nick's life was the subject of one of those maudlin TV docudramas where every person who ever knew the guy testifies in vivid detail about his emotional torments and smoldering lusts, about girlfriends who'd dumped him and teachers who failed to detect his genius. There were plenty in town who craved such voyeuristic details. But for most of us, the public face Nick chose to present, the cool customer in command of his feelings, the steadfast manager in calm control, was the one we were happy to accept even if it was not one hundred per cent accurate. It's how we would want to be received if we ever had the chance to start over.

A few minutes prior to kick-off, the Ziglar's black Lincoln Town Car pulled into a reserved parking space by the curb on Indiana Avenue. Junior climbed out first. Arch Robinson, one of our local business leaders who had been waiting for them, opened the passenger door to help the old man get out. Jeremy Sr. wore his Notre Dame jacket and a liver-brown fedora that would have been stylish in the Sinatra era. To us, he was in the mold of Ole Blue Eyes, dapper, classy, possessing a razor meanness that was crucial to his success.

The Ziglars followed Arch past the ticket booth, where they were waved through, no questions asked. The field had not always been named "Made Right." When the school was built in 1916, the field bore no formal name and needed none. But the next decade saw a string of winning seasons for the Bobcats capped by an undefeated team in 1924 that starred Jake Graf, later a teammate of the great Red Grange on his barnstorming New York Giants. Bleachers were needed for the growing number of spectators, and a donor was needed to pay for the building materials.

The Ziglar family would have cared about the fate of the
Bobcats had the company name not adorned the field. The town
was not separable from the company, and athletics were woven into
the fabric of the community. The football field, the company, the
team, the town, the school, the families whose children attended
and played here, the families who derived their livelihoods directly
and indirectly from the company – they were all part of a tightly
knit circular logic, self-referential and self-justifying. The Ziglars
definitely wanted the team to perform well. However, they did not
want victory appreciably more than the rest of us. And in many
ways, they needed it less.

Marie arrived just as the teams broke from the sideline in a neat
V-formation and scampered out to their respective kickoff positions. Hurriedly she climbed the risers to a middle seat saved for her
by Maddy Racklin, a long-limbed woman with a wild halo of black
curly hair. Marie had initially made little effort to fraternize with
the other parents, bypassing invitations to postgame pizza parties
and end-of-season potlucks. That was freshmen year. Back then,
she'd held out hope that football was less an athletic challenge for
Brian than a complicated form of psychodrama that would wear
thin soon enough. His dad had played quarterback, a fact that a lot
of older men in town felt the need to point out to Brian every time
they bumped into him.

Now Brian was a senior and cocaptain, his cleated stride tracing all too directly his father's footsteps. Her only consolation was
that Brian did not appear driven to eclipse the alleged heroics of his
lout of a dad or seek revenge through such psychologically tortured
means. Brian claimed he really liked the sport, liked the way it felt
to hit and avoid getting hit.

An announcement croaked from the PA system. ". . . a moment
of silence for Longview coach Ron Pruitt, who remains in serious
condition at County Hospital. Our prayers . . . "

Most of the parents, indeed most of the town, were already updated about Coach Pruitt's condition (the phone tree had that covered within hours of his bonfire collapse). He'd had a stroke. The prevailing belief was that Pruitt would bounce back but probably not return to coaching duties any time soon. The likely successor was his assistant, a veteran math teacher named Bertram Sherman who had trouble looking adults directly in the eye. Already he was being spoken of as a liability.

The school band, no longer a true marching band due to waning tolerance for the intensive drilling needed to effectively perform, launched the familiar intro to "When the Saints Go Marching In". Except for a couple of guys in the back row who were too busy finalizing the point spread and shoring up their bets, we dutifully rose to our feet.

Marie tapped the black vinyl casing of the binoculars that hung around Maddy's neck. "May I?"

Maddy handed them over.

Marie aimed first for the hot dog shack, hoping to find Nick still lurking outside the fence. Then she shifted her focus to the main gate and caught the Ziglars shuffling along the cinder track toward their honorary seats, five rows up at the fifty. Finally she settled on chalk-lined turf, twenty-four players in shiny helmets gleaming in the September sun.

"You got to adjust the gizmo in the middle," Maddy said. "Otherwise, it's just blurry."

Marie fingered the serrated plastic dial, edging it forward and back, before drawing a bead on the swarming huddle of Bobcats.

"Don't you love how they look before the uniforms get dirty?" Maddy gushed. "Like little soldiers. Except not so little."

Marie zeroed in on Brian, number 23. The field was not so large that binoculars were necessary, unless you wanted to see faces. Her son looked grim to her as he peeled away from the huddle and jogged towards the end zone. Among other duties, Brian was the team's kick returner. Marie knew enough about the sport to know this was considered a high status responsibility. Still, she hated to watch the two squads charge each other at full gallop with her son as the focal point of the impending collision.

The band ceased playing, though not all instruments at once. Marie handed the binoculars back to Maddy. The opening kick looped impressively high but not very far downfield. Still, we roared our approval, not so much of the performance as of the fact that the performance had begun.

Marie shut her eyes.

CHAPTER 9

....

The Ohio House of Pizza, or O-P as we called it, was situated just around the corner from the Ohio Hotel, a few doors up Mudge Street. During his first weeks in town, Nick ate most of his dinners there. The space was lit like a supermarket with hissing fluorescent ceiling lights. The walls were decorated with travel agency posters of Venice's Grand Canal, Pisa's leaning tower, Rome's sun-splashed Spanish Steps. There was a long serving counter, behind which squatted three large steel ovens. A half dozen yolk-colored fiberglass booths lined the wall back by the washroom. With judicious menu decisions (large cheese steak sub with a Greek salad), it was possible to satisfy one's rudimentary dietary needs at the O-P.

At particular times, especially long winter Saturdays when darkness came early, the O-P transformed from being a serviceable eatery to a virtual clubhouse for our local teenage population. The stuffy oven heat and stale lighting provided something close to a natural habitat for this set. Loud, irreverent, with scads of time to kill, these were kids we understood only too well, for we had been like that in our day. Teens laden with the imprint of all our shortcomings occupied a special niche in Longview. Observing them was like viewing home movies of one's own upbringing.

Brian Zanay often stopped into the O-P for a few cheese-and-sausage slices with his teammate, Will Racklin. Brian had his mother's cautious smile and trusting eyes, but with fairer skin and a natural blush that suggested, falsely, a perpetual enthusiasm. He had his father's build, muscular and lithe, and his father's habit of loping laconically when a brisker pace would be preferred. His hair was a close-cropped buzz cut, as was Will's (they were each barbered by Will's mom, Maddy, who'd briefly attended beautician school in Akron). After football season, they grew it long and their appearances morphed from that of Army boot camp recruits to heavy metal lead guitarists.

Brian and Will were considered "popular." They were nice-looking, amiable, good athletes, and on pace, barring accidents, to graduate in the spring. But neither gave a flying fig about it. To them, the "popularity" designation was a throwback to the bygone era of their parents and grandparents when, so they'd heard, teenagers took pleasure in the fairy tale belief that the world was their oyster, that high school was their launching pad. Brian especially believed no such thing. He was shrewd beyond his years when it came to detecting the falsehoods and mythologies promulgated by teachers, mentors, parents. Rejecting such hokum, however, left a lot of empty mental space.

The rear booths were teenage turf, a place to reliably meet up with friends who likewise had no place to go, nothing to do, yet energy, at least verbal energy, to burn. We were always astonished that these teens who were so notoriously monosyllabic and uncommunicative at home were never short of topics for conversation at the O-P.

"Grease is grease," Will might vehemently insist, dabbing his napkin at a coagulating puddle surrounding the pepperoni slices.

Brian would have none of it. "You're saying the stuff on this pizza's the same as the goop in a car engine?"

"Different flavoring, but yeah. On a molecular basis . . . "

"Molecular basis? What the hell you know about molecular?"

"Chem class. Grease is grease, man."

Kathy, the cute pixie waitress with the long blonde ponytail poking from her ball cap, was scurrying past on her return from a cigarette break. Brian waved her over.

"Kath, where's your pizza grease come from?"

"Phil's Auto Body," she answered with perfect deadpan. "Up by the bowling alley?"

Will flew into a flagrant touchdown celebration dance, gyrating in the aisle with mock sexuality and nearly colliding with Nick, who was on his way to the washroom.

"The new plant manager," Brian noted once Nick had passed.

"So?"

"Thought you like to keep up with community developments."

"You got that wrong."

On and on they would yammer, Brian and Will and Lenny Schulz and Tessa Babbitt and the rest, volume banter dished out with volume pizza, filling the gaps. Killing time at the O-P was nobody's first choice. But in the absence of other options, it frequently came in second.

It didn't take Nick long to figure out that the O-P was a good place to learn about us. And maybe that's the reason, and not simple loneliness, that he would linger longer than was necessary to devour his meal. He'd sit by himself in a booth, midway back, chomping on his sub and salad, the Longview Gazette spread before him on the Formica table, eavesdropping. For a newcomer with curiosity, there was a lot to be learned. Who's dating who. Which teachers you can't fake out. The stepmom reputed to have the olfactory acuity of a narcotics squad dog. Why a boy named Ace disappeared over Labor Day (hated his old man) and where they figured him to be heading (Nashville, because he was into that whiney chump music) and whether he'd return (yep, just like his older brother who'd made it all the way to Georgia but was now back working at the lumber yard). It amounted to a collage, a collage of conversation.

"Where's Melissa?"

"Doing that college prep thing."

"Geez, that's all she ever does any more."

"It's like a diet. You're never off it."

"Ain't for me," Brian chipped in. "No way."

Tessa playfully poked him in the rib. "You could use a diet."

"I mean college."

Nick probably thought he was being inconspicuous, hunched over his cheese steak, eyes fixed on the Gazette. Occasionally he'd flip a page and buckle it back for reading convenience, feigning fascination with the Zoning Board's approval of a former machine shop site for mixed use or an AP report on career women having babies later in life. But eavesdropping was what he was up to. Which we took to be a good thing. It meant that he cared.

There were other indications. He had a penchant for asking questions that were not your typical conversational fluff about, say, the weather forecast, short-range and long. He'd ask, what's Longview known for? Anyone famous ever live here, or come from here? What's unique, what makes this place special? Those were real head-scratcher type of questions, and that's pretty much what he got in reply, a lot of hemming and hawing and puzzled chin-stroking. He would pose such questions to just about anybody, Gus at the hotel, the cashier at Ramsay's where he bought his lunch sandwiches, even Arch Robinson the very first time they met. Arch was about the last person in town you'd expect to be stumped like a sixth grader hit with a surprise quiz, but he too came up empty.

Longview makes no appearance in any history books, certainly not in any of those sweeping panoramic surveys that confidently set forth the causes of America's ascent. No battles that turned any tide nor political confrontations that shaped the republic took place here. No technological inventions, at least none that ever emerged from the tinkerer's dingy basement, nor any works of art that ever sold for more than a song. It was unsettling for us to admit this. There was a tinge of embarrassment behind some of our long pauses following Nick's questions. For despite all our professed admiration

60

for the ordinary accomplishments of the common man, most of us prefer to be remembered for more than having simply persevered.

The closest thing to an "historic" event was the 1859 Manley House rescue. Nick only learned about this when Gus stopped him in the lobby, days after Nick had popped him the quiz, to say, yes, come to think of it, there was one notable situation that did occur in Longview. It took place around the time of the Civil War. Details escaped Gus ("only got a C-minus in that course," he chuckled at himself, "or maybe it was a D-plus") but he told Nick that if he was really curious he should go to the library where they kept a regular pamphlet on it. Coincidentally, a budget proposal was currently being considered by the town council to allocate funds (a few hundred dollars) for a revised brochure that would tout the educational and tourist benefits to be drawn from the incident. The Chamber, God love them for trying, was forever proposing improbable ways to bring in tourist dollars.

One evening, Nick did just that. He stopped by the library to read about it.

The Carnegie Library was a sandstone building built in 1902, high-ceilinged and carpeted, cool in the summer and cool in the winters too. Our collection included a leather-bound edition of "Tom Sawyer." The cork bulletin board by the entrance was always a good place to learn what was going on, and the librarian, Ginny Quint, was known for being able to fill in what the bulletin board left out. When Nick asked about the pamphlet, it took Ginny less than a minute to locate a copy in the periodical rack beside the empty tropical fish tank.

The pamphlet told the story of a Joseph Charles, an African-American carpenter, a master carpenter actually. He possessed exceptional skill at architecture and design, and was much in demand from wealthy home builders who were happy to pay professional rates for his services. Among the homes Charles designed was the Oliver Eastbrook House, a modified Victorian currently on the National Historic Register. Although our region had been sharply divided in its attitudes about the rights of Negroes (the Ohio River, after all, functioned as a border between slave and free states), Joseph Charles had been accepted as a peer and fellow citizen. He lived up the hill from the port in a settlement of several other free black families.

On October 4,1859, Mr. Hiram Bowman from Mason County, Kentucky, arrived in Longview by steamboat to offload and sell a dozen hogshead barrels of tobacco he'd grown and cured on his 9000 acre plantation down river. While in Longview, Bowman learned of Joseph Charles on a tip from a bounty hunter and came to believe – correctly, as it turned out – that this talented craftsman was his former slave who'd escaped five years previously.

The U.S. Marshall, William L. Mason, was summoned to pursue the matter with the full force of the law. Mason found Charles easily enough, as he was overseeing the completion of what would be one of the grandest homes along the bluff just north of town, the three-story Benjamin Manley House. Mason marched into the house (it was nearly complete), satisfied himself that Joseph Charles was indeed the former slave of Hiram Bowman, and announced his arrest. However, the Marshall's attempt to leave with Charles in tow was immediately blocked by several men – white men – who were also working on the house. Marshall Mason informed them that they were obstructing justice and violating federal law. The men did not budge. By nightfall, more than a hundred additional residents of Longview had arrived to surround the house and block the extradition of Joseph Charles. In effect, the U.S. Marshall was now being held captive.

Hiram Bowman showed up, accompanied by two men, said to be his cousins, who carried long Springfield rifles. A dozen more townspeople converged on the site carrying flaming torches. The illumination thrown off by the torches was said to light the bluff as bright as the stage of a New York theater. There was a heated argument. Shots were fired. Nobody was injured. The situation remained a standoff throughout the night. At dawn, with the house site surrounded by townsfolk, Bowman and his companions retreated back to their docked steamboat.

The U.S. Marshall departed, vowing to come back armed with a court order that the people of Longview would be foolish to defy. Joseph Charles fled north by horseback, intending to make his way to Ontario by means of what was starting to be termed the Underground Railroad. He was hiding out in a barn near Toledo with two other runaway slaves when a toppled lantern ignited a straw mattress and burned out of control. All were killed.

This incident would have been lost even to Longview history were it not for a former fourth grade teacher named Nancy Stearns who went on to become Longview's first woman Superintendent of Schools. She wrote this incident up in the pamphlet Nick found on file in the library. More importantly, Stearns managed to get the incident, and the pamphlet, included in our public school American History curriculum.

As a result, anyone attending public schools in Longview has had to memorize the names, dates, and political circumstances of the Manley House incident. High school students have had to answer "essay" questions about what the story meant. We're taught that it was not so much a story about mob justice as about mob virtue, mob morality, mob wisdom. A better word for "mob" was "community." At least under the right circumstances.

Our classrooms took field trips to the house, except for a period in the late 1950's when a crabby owner denied us access. Those trips to the hallowed rooms where Joseph Charles had helped plane and hammer the timber left an indelible impression. It was riveting, even for some of our, shall we say, less engaged students to stand with feet planted on the same turf where once upon a time a real showdown with guns drawn had occurred. We could, with a helpful nudge from a capable teacher, conjure the drama, replete with threats and gunfire and an epic clash of moral principles, that had unfolded on this very soil. With a little imagination and a little knowledge, we saw that history really could come alive.

Teachers loved to pose provocative questions. What if you had lived in Longview back then? What would you have done? Is it always right to obey the law? Could more have been done to keep poor Joseph Charles safely in town? What were the Civil War era societal constraints on the good people of Longview? How does that compare to today?

Folks who remembered absolutely nothing else from seventh grade, not the multiplication of fractions, not the Stamp Act, not the Spanish word for water, tended to remember these stirring classroom discussions. Too bad the knowledge never proved useful.

Late one Saturday afternoon at the O-P, as Nick nibbled at his meatball sub, the place was rocked by a thunderous blast of noise. It sounded like a gas main explosion. Nick dashed to the door, only to see a far more pedestrian source of the thunder. A defiantly un-muffered auto, a '79 Buick with jagged flames spray-painted along the chassis, had pulled in front and was gunning its engine for the raw pleasure of causing so much disruption. After an agonizing minute, the engine shut off and the car's occupants loped into the O-P.

Three teenage punks, new to Nick but old hat to us, strutted in and plunked down in a booth abutting where the high schoolers sat. They wore ripped jeans with butt patches and sooty leather vests.

"Hey, my heroes," saluted the taller one with a dapper tip of his imaginary cap. This was Fritz Bolton. He had been the quarterback on last year's Bobcats until being disqualified either for being too old or for failing grades (there'd been some controversy about the true cause). An apple-cheeked young man, he had to work hard to appear even a tad grungy. He did, however, have the vaguely malevolent air of a kid who might go to radical lengths to prove he was grittier than he appeared. "Who won the big game this week?"

When nobody answered, or even dared look him in the eye, Fritz snorted, "Ain't whether you win or lose, kiddies. Don't never forget that. It's whether you get laid."

His pals got a good yuck from that. Nobody else did. Nick undoubtedly had seen this act before. We all had. Even this particular pairing of a wise-guy stud with two admiring trolls was almost traditional. These kids were not substantially different from teenage outcasts of generations past. Only a few years out of high school, if they'd even graduated, their resentment of Brian and Will and the rest was no deeper or more complex than jealousy. They resented anyone who was still buffered, however briefly, from their own bleak future.

Fritz was essentially a latter day version of Will and Brian if they didn't watch it. Leaning across the back of the booth so his face almost grazed Brian's, he taunted, "So how's your, ah, what do you call it, yards per carry?"

Brian knew better than to get sucked in. "Fine. How's yours?"

"Never been better." Fritz grabbed his crotch. However, as Brian couldn't see the gesture, it lost its comic impact. "And those cute little cheerleaders? Giving them something to squeal over?"

Brian didn't answer.

"Hey, Fritz," said Will. "True you almost joined the Army?"

"Fuck 'em. What do they know?"

"Guess it's true."

"Fuck you." Fritz jabbed a threatening paw over the back of the booth. Brian slapped it away, causing Fritz to bang his funny bone on the sharp corner of the booth. "Sonofabitch," he yelped. The shorter of his companions popped up like they'd heard the opening gong. Will stood, ready for the snap.

"Hey, hey, hey. Cool down. Cool down, kiddies," chided Fritz, massaging his elbow. Will slumped back down, as did Fritz's pal. This wasn't going any further. Getting banned from the O-P, the certain penalty for an altercation, was simply not worth it. Not with another long dreary winter looming a few months away. Besides, none of these boys, not the punks, nor Brian, nor Will, were into fighting for fighting's sake, certainly not as a means of strutting their stuff for the benefit of female onlookers, even cuties like Tessa and Kathy. That too was a bygone era. Let the chicks duke it out, was their attitude, if they really like fighting so much.

Once everyone had settled back down to their oily cheese-and-sausage and aimless snarky banter, Fritz leaned over the back of the booth and for no good reason threw a sucker punch at Will. The blow made an ugly smacking sound when it landed on his cheekbone. What the . . . ? Best guess was that Fritz was doing uppers that got the better of him.

Brian bolted up and drove his shoulder hard into Fritz' sternum, pinning him against the coke machine. In an instant, Nick was on them both, one hand on each of their throats.

He flung them apart with enough force to discourage retaliation. The boys snorted and cursed a barrage of fuck-you's. Will leapt into the aisle, facing off with Fritz's comrades. Staying between the lot of them, Nick performed a steady 360 rotation, like a lighthouse beacon. The message was: any additional skirmish would have to pass through him. A minute went by. Nobody was up for it.

"Peace?" Nick said it like it was a question but it wasn't.

Joey Khouri, the O-P's owner, raced over, wiping his large hands on his stained apron. The teens dropped sheepishly back to their seats. That's all Joey needed to see, and he went straight back to the ovens.

Brian and Will grabbed their jackets and left. Nick returned to his meal. When he was finished, he carted the brown plastic tray with its sauce-stained paper plate to the counter.

"Hey, pops," Fritz cackled after him. "You forgot your newspaper."

"Thanks. I'm done reading it."

"Oooh, wow. Even World Events?"

"Even that."

"Any wars we should, like, know about?"

"Just the big one, sonny."

Fritz had a sneer copped straight from tough-guy TV posturing. "And that is?"

"You know, the one right here at home."

Fritz opened his mouth as though formulating a stinging smartass retort, one that would put Nick in his place and announce who was the master of this domain. But if he did think of something to say, it did not come quickly enough. Nick left the O-P without bothering to look back.

Nick arrived each morning around 5:30 a.m. He wanted to be at the plant well before workers arrived (Made Right had long ago abandoned its overnight shift except for emergencies) and before the Ziglars. For all our grousing about them – too cheap, too inflexible, too remote – we never faulted the Ziglars on their work ethic. Junior and the old man put in very long days and rarely took vacations, although the ones they did take tended not to be your Six Flags or Cedar Points.

The day shift began formally at 8 a.m. Whenever possible, Nick positioned himself at the Arrowhead Street vestibule to welcome us, like a school principal eager to win over the students. He tried hard to learn everyone's names, although this was not his strong suit. Early on, he'd embarrassed himself by greeting one of the stitchers as "Opal." She was short and quite round and no doubt her shape reminded him of an oval. Eloise was her name, and we had a good chuckle as the anecdote circulated.

Brenda Smokavich was no oval. She was a trim, voluptuous sleeve-stitcher in her early thirties, and nobody, not even Nick, forgot her name. This lady was memorable. She had a dark-eyed four-year old son whose picture she kept taped to the base of her Union Special like it was one of those missing children posters.

Brenda wasn't married, which made her an item of some interest on the floor. Last year she'd broken up with a mysterious hillbilly sax player who went by the name of Flash, and that only heightened our interest. A number of guys were hoping to be next. Among other impertinences, she had a knack, much admired, for needling management. Nick was not exempt.

He'd greet her merrily as he made his rounds and she'd either shoot him her trademark sultry smile and leave it at that or, depending on her mood, give him a dig about the Korean rumors or lodge a complaint about the overnight clean-up crew.

"Well . . . ah, well," Nick would stammer.

And before he could say more, she would cut him off with a mocking rendition of his anticipated response.

"I know, I know, I know," she'd sigh, lifting a dismissive hand. "Can't do what can't be done. Can't go where no one's gone. Same old same old."

In his pocket-size spiral notepad, Nick jotted a furtive note. Brenda craned her neck.

"Just notes to myself," he assured her. "Always looking for ways to improve."

"Restore them layoffs. That'd be improvement."

An effective plant manager had to be attuned to the needs of the work force, and not all of them were directly related to productivity. He was responsible for the plumbing in the washrooms, maintenance of the cafeteria, ventilation in the heat, heat in the cold. He needed to be respected but not necessarily loved. The analogies most often used to describe the job – sergeant, general, orchestra conductor, expedition leader, head coach – were inexact yet helpful. It was not a theoretician's job. Plant managers didn't go to graduate school to learn the trade. Guys like Nick, and all his predecessors, knew how to set sleeves and punch buttonholes, how to operate the cutting and stitching and overedge machines and how to perform rudimentary repairs on them. He'd learned to do the job by doing all the jobs.

Nick first worked in manufacturing the summer before his junior year in high school at a small company that made men's dress shirts. His tasks consisted of sweeping clean the vast floor space that was constantly littered with fabric scraps, folding, and occasionally helping with inspections. His day was broken into four unvarying segments: morning until break; morning until lunch; after lunch until break; after break until quitting time. Every time he'd glance at the big clock suspended above the salt pill dispenser, he was shocked to realize only a few minutes had elapsed since last he'd checked. It was surreal, as though time had literally stopped. It had seemed unimaginable to him then that any person could endure such monstrous tedium without screaming out from psychic pain. Yet some thirty years later, here he was, and grateful for the chance.

Having escaped a possible confrontation with Brenda, Nick was heading back for coffee when Marie suddenly intercepted him, walking briskly. She wore a bright floral blouse that highlighted her natural glow. Thirteen years working at Made Right and she still dressed like it was her first day on the job, hoping to make a great impression on an imaginary somebody.

"Jeremy wants to see you."

"Now?"

Marie nodded.

"Know what it's about?"

"No. But his father's there too."

Nick trailed Marie past sleeves and lining. Heading upstairs, Marie glanced back. "How's the knee?"

"My hip. And it's fine."

Jeremy Jr. pushed back from his desk when Nick entered, waving him in with the forced bonhomie of a head waiter. His father remained in the leather recliner.

Junior gestured for Nick to take a seat on the sofa facing them. "Get you anything? Coffee? Juice? Coke?"

Nick did not sit. There was something worrisome in Jeremy's

demeanor. This was pretty soon to get fired, and he could think of no good reason. Yet he was alert to the possibility that rumors may have circulated, ones that were beyond his capacity to discover or to refute. Accusations could be swirling, and not all of them would have to be complete fabrications. He'd not lived the life of a saint. Nor, however, was he running for office.

Junior began somewhat nervously. "So . . . Made Right, and there is no way for you to necessarily know this, Nick . . . we have policies and procedures that have been in place a long time. Our longevity, our success, we owe in no small part to our adherence to these procedures. I, and my father, we're both firm believers in adherence to the rules. A company this size, well, you make exceptions for one and pretty soon you're besieged with requests to make exceptions for all. Understand?"

Nick only understood he should say nothing.

"So it is not without giving this matter considerable thought that we, my father and I, have come to the conclusion that, well . . . "

Jeremy Jr. turned to his father for help but the old man was suddenly beset by a fit of coughing. He gasped for air, his cheeks turned scarlet, drool leaked from the corner of his mouth. It was Nick who had the presence of mind to grab a water glass from the desktop and hand it to him.

Finally calmed, Jeremy Sr. got to the point, "We want you to coach the Bobcats."

Nick had been braced for worse.

"The Bobcats mean a lot to this town," Jeremy Jr. pointed out. "I don't have to tell you. It'd help if they had a good season."

The old man grumbled, "We've never had a coach who really knows the game."

"Like you," added Jeremy Jr.

"Pruitt's a good man. But he wasn't all that good when he played. And he never played past high school."

Nick wrung his hands, in no hurry to reply. He'd once told Ashong about a work place flare-up that had cost him a promotion.

Apparently he'd lashed out, verbally but with a not-so-veiled physical threat attached, at the wrong guy in the pecking order. This little anecdote confirmed our hunch that Nick had been a swaggering young buck with a chip, and that the even-tempered mediator we now experienced was a fairly recent development. He had the carefully composed demeanor of an anger management graduate, possibly court-ordered.

Nick finally squared up to address the Ziglars directly. "Listen, I'm flattered. Really. But I simply don't have the time. My job, as you well know, demands two hundred percent."

"Understood. But we're prepared to let you off a bit early and pay standard overtime for your efforts, possibly a bonus. Now through Thanksgiving. That's when the Superbowl game takes place."

Jeremy Sr. added, "We haven't been in it since what? '82? Town could use a boost, and what better way?"

From Nick's perspective, the proposal was a hornet's nest, plain and simple. And the Ziglar's obvious zeal only reinforced his apprehension. It meant too much to them.

"Isn't there a regulation that you need to be a teacher at the school, or be affiliated with it to coach?"

The Ziglars eyed each other conspiratorially. "That's fixable," said Junior. "The school board knows the situation. Couple members have kids on the team. I've already spoken with the principal. We'll make it work."

"Like my son was saying, we believe in firm rules. Occasionally," the old man winked, "we make an exception."

Nick went to the picture window and gazed at the grand vista across the river. On the far bank, leaves were turning fall colors, splashes of orange and yellow in the upper branches.

"I came here to run your shop," he finally said. "That's what I do best. Football . . . it's only a game that I played a long time ago."

Jeremy Jr. chuckled. "You're humble. The good ones generally are. But in this town, Nick, you'll be happy to know we don't think it's only a game."

The old man rose with difficulty. "If you can teach those Bobcats a fraction of what you know . . . "

"Just because a guy played doesn't mean he knows diddly about coaching. That's like saying because a guy looks sharp in a suit he's . . . "

"We'll take our chances."

Jeremy Jr. also stood and moved from his chair. The Ziglars had him surrounded.

"What if I decline?"

Jeremy Jr. and his dad exchanged self-satisfied grins. In Longview, when the Ziglars made what they considered to be a generous offer, it was simply never declined. Certainly not by somebody they employed.

....

Nick was driven straight from the plant to Made Right field by Leo Heston, one of the guys in shipping, getting there just after 3:15 p.m. Bobcat players were expected to be at the field fully uniformed no later than thirty minutes after the last bell. To get to the field from the basement locker room on the opposite side of the high school, players generally took a shortcut through the school's central corridor, clattering in full battle gear across the waxed linoleum. They sounded like an out-of-synch tap dance troupe. Students and teachers involved in after-school activities – science projects, the yearbook committee, makeup tests – resented the disruption and would slam shut the classroom doors in a show of complaint. Coach Pruitt had managed to fend off administration pressure to make the players take the long outdoor traverse from the locker room, but in his absence the balance of power could shift.

Nick looked on surreptitiously from beneath the bleachers before coming directly onto the field. Sloppiness had begun to set in, and you wouldn't have to be a Notre Dame veteran to detect it. Bobcats in yellow helmets and grass-stained pants horsed around like unsupervised kids at the beach, jabbering, laughing, munching snacks, jabbing playfully at each other. Near midfield, Brian was tossing lazy passes using his left hand, his wrong hand, to Will Racklin. The passes had the precision of orange peels flung by a gorilla.

"Dive, you wimp. That's what we got to do with the slop you throw."

"Shit. My passes ain't nowhere that bad," Will was the Bobcat's QB. Under Pruitt, they only threw the ball once or twice per game, and there was a reason.

"Oh yeah? Check the video."

The Bobcats had no videotaping capability. It wasn't in the budget and even if it had been, Pruitt did not believe in such technology-driven shenanigans. Our regional cable access Channel 68 did occasionally broadcast, or tape for broadcast, some of the games, but the camerawork was far too unsteady and unreliable to be of much instructional value. Or entertainment value, for that matter.

Brian's errant pass tumbled toward the grandstand overhang where Nick still lingered, keeping his distance.

Spotting Nick, Bertram Sherman sprang from the bench where he'd been grading papers. "Just in the nick." Sherman halted, amused by his near brush with a pun. "We've been waiting for you."

A veteran math instructor with a crown of curly gray hair, Sherman was not a Longview native, but his aunt and uncle were and that's what brought him here, straight from Miami U's School of Education. He'd been with us for twenty years. His hefty build might indicate a former offensive guard or tackle, but his knock-kneed waddle and his severely slouching shoulders gave him away. He'd served as Pruitt's assistant out of obligation to the school, not because he knew much about the sport. Pruitt needed a numbers guy on the sideline (every NFL telecast these days preached about how indispensable the stats and prognostics had become) and who better than a math teacher? Sherman was deft with a clipboard and spreadsheet, didn't mind compiling data far from the action as the game unfolded, and further qualified for the role by posing no threat to the hierarchy since he had zero interest in taking over. He was not head coach material. The players knew it and demonstrated this knowledge in the inimitable way of teenagers. By screwing up and slacking off.

"Kids sure look like they're enjoying themselves," Nick drolly noted. Sherman fingered the silver whistle that hung from a shoestring around his neck, as though itching to hand it off. "I'm math. And a little science. Coaching's not my thing."

"Nice win you had on Saturday."

"That was Haynesville. This week's Gladstone. It'll be different."

"Pretty focused on winning?"

An odd question, and it was Sherman's first indication that Nick might be more complicated than the stereotype of the hard-nosed, drill sergeant ex-jock recruited by the town fathers to whip the team into shape. As a math instructor, Sherman had what you could call a professionally trained eye for the pitfalls that result from false constructs. He tried to instill in his students a resistance to the temptation of quick assumptions and make them aware of the seductive traps posed by first glance solutions. Or something like that. At any rate, the concept of a former football hero returning to the sport at which he'd excelled had all the earmarks of just such a trap.

"Focused on winning?" Sherman mulled it over a moment.

"I mean, is this a win-at-all costs operation, or a do-your-best-and-let-the-chips-fall?"

"Little of each, I guess."

"What if I asked Jeremy Ziglar?"

"Probably say the town needs a winner."

"Does it?"

"Few more wins would be welcome."

On the field, the players were having far too much fun, tripping each other from behind, playing keep-away with someone's mouth guard. Sherman blew a long shrill screech on the whistle. Slowly, the Bobcats began to gather around.

"I'll just hang back," Nick said.

"They all know who you are."

"I'll be here. You're the boss."

Pruitt was a proponent of doing the same drills over and over with only minor variation, regardless of what had occurred in the previous game or who the opponent was coming up next. Pruitt's squads didn't always win (to put it mildly), but they always displayed nifty warm-up drills. Coach was an ardent believer in conditioning not just muscles but muscle memory, instilling through an ordeal of repetition something like an automatic response system in each player for each type of contingency that the chaos of a game can produce. It was an okay theory, and since nobody had come up with a better one to supplant it, it remained in place. The emphasis in each practice was usually evenly split between offense and defense, and the Longview line-up invariably featured many who played both ways. In truth, the squad contained no more than six or seven skilled athletes, and only a fool of a coach, which Pruitt was not, would parcel them out exclusively to the offensive or defensive units. Thus, the handful of talented kids played nearly every minute of every game, except for blowouts.

Sherman hovered a few yards behind the backfield, as Pruitt would do. Nick stayed tucked to the sideline, hanging back like a trainee on a sales call with his boss. A cloud bank moved in from the west. Dusk was coming early and with it a touch of gloom.

Brian, running a sweep from a pitchout, got no blocking and raced clear to the sideline before being toppled by the entire right side of the defense, who threw him to the ground directly in front of Nick. Scrambling to his feet, Brian was nearly face to face with the new assistant.

"Know what you did wrong?" Nick asked.

Brian spat. "Got tackled too soon."

"Exactly! Correct that, son, and sky's the limit!"

Brian shook it off and jogged back to the huddle.

"What the heck kind of advice is that?" Sherman asked.

"It just came to me. You disagree?"

It was getting too dark to see. Players began heading to the locker room on the assumption that Sherman, if he had better sense, would have dismissed them anyway. Three remained. Timmy Hudson was a plump, pleasant boy who Pruitt had named our designated place-kicker. It was a role that was mostly honorific, since Pruitt did not believe in field goal attempts – it had been nearly three seasons since the last one had been tried in game conditions – and preferred to try for two-point conversions after touchdowns. Sherman, the numbers guy, had worked it out in a chart that demonstrated the probability of the extra point conversion succeeding versus the odds of pushing the ball over from the three. Based on the numbers, conversion by kick was the inarguable conclusion. Pruitt didn't buy it.

Nonetheless, Timmy liked to stay late after practice with his designated holder, Artie Kranz, a back-up receiver (on a team that never passed). Nick watched them set up at the fifteen yard line. Vince Wilkins, our center, was surrounded by footballs and he would bend over and hike them, one after another. Art snagged the hikes, placing them instantly on the turf as Timmy swung his right foot, the balls arcing higher, higher . . . but never passing between the uprights.

Nick limped onto the field. The kids watched him make the long walk across the grassy expanse.

"Know what you're doing wrong?" he asked Timmy.

"Plenty."

"Actually not. Just some mechanics."

With a groan, Nick knelt on the ground. Artie obediently stepped away, allowing Nick to show him how. The snap rifled into Nick's outstretched hands. Nick spun the laces a quarter rotation of the ball, planted it firmly on the turf, balanced it with his forefinger. Timmy's foot swung through. The ball lifted like a heron off a tranquil pond, in a perfect trajectory over the crossbar.

Nick did his best to remain deadpan, although we had to believe he was pretty pleased to have his inaugural piece of advice produce an immediate and irrefutable result. His reluctance to show emotion would normally be a quality that might make us wary. People who conceal their emotions tend to be a bit too crafty for our tastes.

Of course there are some who simply are not in touch with their feelings, and that too is a type we're familiar with.

The players jogged off. Nick tagged along with Sherman while he prowled the sideline picking up discarded water bottles and stuffing the litter in a large garbage bag he slung across his shoulder, a dour Santa.

Sherman asked Nick if he needed a lift home and Nick accepted without letting on he had no other way of getting there. They took a shortcut beneath the grandstand to the parking lot.

Sherman gestured to Nick's uneven stride. "A football injury?"

"Just wear and tear. And time. Nothing sexy."

"Should invent a better story. Definitely should say it's football-related."

"Why's that?"

Sherman had meant the remark as a caustic nod to our local penchant for heroes wounded in the line of fire, of which football was thought to be an example. But he saw right away that Nick was too new to Longview to comprehend. "Forget it. Just be yourself."

They deposited the trash bag in a steel dumpster outside the stands and crossed the street to the parking lot. A few football parents were standing outside their vehicles, waiting to pick up their sons.

Peggy Talbert, a gaunt woman with white-blonde hair, cut away from the group. "I'm Josh Talbert's mom. My husband wants you to know that his uncle Sammy played for the Spartans against you."

Others gathered around.

"Good to have you aboard."

"What's it's like, coming back to the game?"

"You'll see, we got good kids. Just need coaching."

"Welcome to Longview, Nick."

Nick nudged Sherman to keep moving. "Nice meeting you'all."

Sherman's rust-pocked station wagon was crammed with accordion files and an unoccupied dog crate. He swiftly cleared the passenger seat and Nick squeezed in.

"They're just being friendly, the parents."

"I was friendly back."

"Could do better."

Pulling out of the lot, Sherman steered past a gaggle of players hanging with a few girls and showing more alertness than they had at practice. "You must have been quite the high school hotshot," Sherman coaxed.

"I guess."

Sherman drove the more scenic route, avoiding the strip malls along County 12. He didn't know how much of the town Nick had seen already, but he didn't want to be the one to introduce him to the tasteless commercial zones with their bull-dozed vacant lots that advertised not only our failures but the smallness of our aspirations. Sherman looped down Flint Road to where it intersected Bluff Parkway, then cruised by Riverside park circling back toward downtown.

"Nice place," Nick mused. "Time kind of stands still."

"Trouble is, it doesn't. These kids still think it's the old days, you know, goof around high school for four years then on to Made Right for a decent wage until it's time to retire."

"Not the worst life."

"These kids got a better shot at a career in the NFL than they do in manufacturing. And that's a fact. It's all computers now. Either they don't get it or – and I'm sorry to say this – or they're too much like their parents, clueless. It's like they think they're in a wildlife sanctuary, protecting them because it's always been this way. Well, guess what? No gate's keeping them in, and no gate's keeping the predators out. I try, but a teacher can only do so much."

It was dusk tinged by an Indian summer softness. Along High Street and Mudge, a few street lamps came on. The western sky was darkening, the last wisps of lavender fading to night. At the Ohio Hotel, Gus was cleaning the lounge of leftover Styrofoam cups with their slosh of stale coffee and extinguished butts.

He cheerfully greeted Nick soon as he came through the door. "Evening, coach."

Nick wheeled on him. "Who told you that?"

"Nephew Petey, he's on the team. Short, skinny kid and fast? Should definitely not be offensive guard, but that's where they got him. Ask me, he's cornerback material."

"I'm just helping out. That's all." Nick started up the stairs.

"We could use some wins, coach."

Nick was paying $118 per week including state tax for his room at the Ohio. There was speculation concerning why the new Made Right plant manager, hired at a reasonable salary with long-term prospects, would be rooming at a weekly rate in an establishment that quite a few of us, including Gus, considered to be little more than a glorified flophouse.

What people didn't know, what we didn't know, was how comfortable Nick was at the Ohio, glorified flophouse or not. He had a room that was familiar and safe. If he awakened, say, at 2 a.m. in a frightened sweat from a nightmare about being swept down a rampaging river through a steep canyon, he had the comfort of knowing precisely where in this modest rectangular space his bed was located, and the nightstand in relation to the bed, and the bathroom in relation to that. He'd taken a few steps to make the room homey. He'd bought a clock radio with an aqua neon face that he placed on the nightstand. Across the top of the bureau, he'd draped a small Navajo throw rug bought at Benson's, same place he'd bought the radio. On top of that he'd placed a carved wooden picture frame. No photo to insert, but that could change.

Anything could happen. That's the message Nick would preach to himself, according to Gus, late at night, alone in his room, his voice a low steady monotone, vehement, stern, firm. Stay cool. Stay focused. Time still left on the clock. Don't panic. Third and long. Anything can happen.

....

Nestled in the bend of a great river on a protrusion of land contoured like a gnarled thumb tip, we're a long distance from any commercial airport and the passenger train only stops here twice a day in each direction. In olden times, riverboat was the main method of arriving. Today, it's auto.

Driving south on County 12, the terrain is as flat as Nebraska and similarly given over to vast acreage of soy and corn. The homes out this way are mostly weather-beaten farmsteads, with an occasional house trailer. Nearing town, the landscape starts to rise and dip, sometimes precipitously, but the road itself remains ruler-straight. There's a half-built subdivision on the outskirts, not quite a ghost town but a far cry from the envisioned dream. It was begun in the late 1960's by an ambitious developer named Rolf Chaney (he later ran for Congress and lost). With spacious ranch houses and picket fences, new streets sporting names like Jupiter Drive and Echo Lane with sparkling granite curbs, Heritage Hill was intended to grow in size as our reputation as a hotbed of economic activity became evident to the thriving businesses that would settle here. Guess what didn't happen?

County 12 is a straight shot into Longview proper where it routes around a sequence of residential neighborhoods that haven't changed much, in character or housing stock, in sixty years. This is where Marie grew up and still lived. It was a Made Right neighborhood. The homes on these pleasant, tree-lined streets shared basic design characteristics: center-entrance, 2-3 bedroom, front porch, detached garage, two-story, aluminum or vinyl siding, asphalt roof, gravel driveway.

The median home price in 1990, the year of the most recent census, was classified as "below the state average." A third of us were renters, with the median apartment rental fee being $254 per month. Whereas nearly 70 per cent of our adults had a high school diploma, only 14 per cent held bachelor degrees. Homes routinely sold, when they sold (our turnover was low enough that all local realtors did it as a sideline, not a full-time vocation), for approximately what a parking space would cost in Boston or New York. In fact, a news item to that effect appeared in the Gazette last winter and it gave us an odd sort of boost. We preferred where we lived to a cold gray concrete warehouse for cars. It made us feel like we had a choice, and that we'd chosen wisely.

Those are some of the "facts" about Longview. They conveyed meaning, however, only in a generalized way. They didn't tell anything about what occurred, or was likely to occur, to individual people on the ground. Regarding the joy and heartache of any one person's life, statistics were no more predictive than an astrological reading. Nick was a Leo. Marie a Virgo. Our local hospital records showed an almost perfectly even distribution of births among the Zodiac signs. Our fortunes were anyone's guess.

Marie lived less than two miles from downtown, on a street of tightly bunched beige and mustard bungalow-style homes. It was the same house on East Hunter Road where she'd been raised, a two-bedroom with an alcove dining room off the kitchen and a narrow living room with a picture window that looked over a front lawn layered with fallen leaves that should have been raked. Her father Lou benevolently leased it to her at a favorable rate; he now lived in a side-by-side one block away.

She was prickly about still residing in the very house where she was born. She did not consider it charming. Fleeing Longview for the wider world had been a solemn promise she'd made to herself as a girl. Her downfall came in an ordinary way. At the age of eighteen she fell hard for Rafe Fontune, the Bobcats' quarterback. A carefree, wily boy who liked attention, Rafe was voted most likely to succeed and in a perfect world, a world that roughly emulated high school, he just might have. Marie, however, should have known better, and by the time she did she had a baby. After her divorce, which was not entirely amicable, she felt almost lucky to still have a home at 845 E. Hunter.

Many in town held mixed sentiments about Marie. As a teenager she'd been just uppity enough that some people wouldn't mind seeing her knocked down a peg, and not all of those were sour grapes high school boys who failed to catch her eye. She was good-looking and perky and accomplished (cheerleading, drama club, young nurses), a member of the National Honors Society and ranked #3 in her graduating class. Accepted for admission at Ohio State University and College of Wooster, she was unabashed in proclaiming her designs for a bigger life that would not be located anywhere near Longview.

Her local prominence, and the envy it generated, was further enlarged when, starting junior year, she became Rafe's girl friend. He was no academic achiever nor was he exactly a model citizen. But he was the quarterback and baseball shortstop. He was handsome in that windblown, devil-may-care fashion that peaks around the age of eighteen. He was mentally agile, quick with deft quips, and good with auto engines. Guys like Rafe dominated the world from what we could tell.

For a while they were our golden couple, Marie and Rafe, the pair that everyone stopped what they were doing to ogle on the dance floor, marveling at how exquisite they looked together. Towns like Longview occasionally produce such radiant young couples, seemingly the distilled essence of the very best the community has to offer. We were infatuated with them, especially the older folks who observe life like fans in the bleachers, longing to see their hometown kids finally bust out and take the world by storm. Which is what, in our myopia, we thought Marie and Rafe capable of. We yearned to follow their progress with field binoculars as they promenaded gracefully into the distance like winged gods twirling up from the varnished floor of the high school gym straight into the scintillating stratosphere. We could imagine, we did imagine, how they would return every few years to shower us with romantic tales of their triumphs, and of course thank us profusely for all we'd done to properly launch them.

When Marie did not go on to college but remained in Longview after graduation to get married, we assumed, based on too many prior examples, that she was pregnant. She wasn't. They rented an apartment in town above Forrester's Shoes and decorated the place in hip, counter-culture aesthetics, rock star posters and madras wall blankets and a sofa fashioned from the back seat of a Corvair. On weekends they threw loud parties attended by high school pals who lived at home. Rafe was still the life of the party, as he'd always been. The parties, however, were not so glamorous.

Rafe was never college material, not intellectually or athletically. On the face of it, he was a perfect candidate for the armed services, any branch. Except that he wasn't much for discipline or routine or taking orders. What he was good at was having fun and enlisting others to join in. Those can be valuable assets in this life; they just don't pay very well. Rafe got an entry-level job as a sales support person with a sporting goods concern that had outlets throughout the region. It was not a bad situation for a young man determined to work his way up. Rafe was not that young man.

Marie initially found work in the billing department at the hospital but soon switched to Made Right, doing roughly the same. She'd lost a little luster and was a lot less perky. We no longer speculated about the mountains she might climb. Then she got pregnant. The one-room apartment above Forrester's wouldn't do, and they couldn't afford a house. Her father Lou was fond of Rafe (best QB in the past decade, Lou claimed at the time, maybe the past two) and was sympathetic to their predicament. Anything he could do to give them a cushion, he was willing to do. That turned out to involve Lou having to relocate down the block and letting Longview's golden couple inhabit his home for as long as they needed in order to solidify their situation. Little did anyone guess.

Marie was still here, same street address. Like the rest of us, she was engaged on a full-time basis in getting by. We wondered if by now she'd finally accepted that she was irrevocably one of us. Did she fantasize that Brian might yet live out the fulfillments that she had failed to achieve? Or did she still harbor notions of busting out? Was it that kind of silliness that explained her pretentious clothing and standoffish ways? It amused us to think so. And pained us too.

Because we couldn't altogether forget that Marie had once been our golden girl, half of a golden couple that we'd privately hoped would set the world on fire.

This particular Saturday, Brian was on the sofa in his underwear, watching Sesame Street when Marie flew out of her room. She had on a knee length, scalloped hem skirt, which was not typical for a Saturday and especially not for a football Saturday. Her jade V-neck top was a color she didn't normally wear.

"Where to, Mom?"

"Shopping."

Brian returned his gaze to the TV. "Coming to the game?"

"You bet."

Her Taurus station wagon was parked in the drive. They had a garage but it was too stuffed with junk to be available for the car. Cleaning the garage was another chore that needed to be done before winter set in. Marie drove down Arrowhead, turned left at Neptune, then onto High. It was, almost literally, a drive she could perform with her eyes closed, assuming no errant traffic interference. She supposed it could be a metaphor for her life, this capacity to blindly navigate nearly any route so long as she remained within Longview's familiar confines. There was comfort in that, but with every passing year it was a comfort that mattered less.

Nick was waiting for her in front of the Ohio, basking in the morning sun. His face was tilted to the mild rays as though he was relaxing in a deck chair on a Princess cruise ship.

He squeezed into the passenger seat, and Marie asked, almost instinctually, "How'd you sleep?" It was a question she might ask Brian.

"Fine. And you?"

"Waited up too late for Brian."

"Team doesn't have a curfew on game nights?"

"He wasn't all that late. But once I start to worry, it's hard to get to sleep."

Marie drove away, toward River Road. On River, she turned right. They were heading to Lou's Used Autos.

"Seems like a good kid. Brian."

Reflexively, Marie switched on the radio. A musical commercial for bargain rate refinancing came blasting out. She turned down the volume. "Thing is, he needs to be more than that. Otherwise, he'll end up like his dad. A fun-loving guy who has less and less fun."

"I know the type."

"Because that's the way you were?"

Nick looked at her hard. But he let it slide.

Lou's Used Autos, euphemistically referred to as "Loosed," was a 20,000- square-foot lot of buckled asphalt, surrounded on three sides by a chain link fence. A mobile PacVan functioned as Lou Zanay's office. Lou did not like it when anyone referred to it as a trailer, which some of us did just to annoy him. "Headquarters" is what he called it.

Lou's Used was nearly always adorned by the gaudy trappings of a special promotion, and today was no exception. Red, white, and blue balloons were fixed at regular intervals along the fence and adorning the two utility poles. A large sheet of plastic with block lettering in patriotic hues served as an advertising banner across the entrance. "Columbus Day Sale!!!" Lou was a traditionalist when it came to marketing.

Her father was outside waiting as Marie pulled up. Lou was fairly fit for a man of seventy, despite the fact that he did no exercise and spent several nights a week drinking beer and wolfing down chips with his buddies at the Legion Hall. He was balding but managed to keep much of his scalp covered with the remaining strands. On this day, he wore a suit of shimmering canary yellow fabric and an open-necked purple shirt with a high starched collar.

He gave Marie a quick hug and bustled around to the passenger side as Nick emerged. "And this must be?"

"Daddy, I'd like you to meet Nick Nocero."

Lou already had his hand out. "An honor. A real honor."

Nick accepted the handshake.

"I was a fan of yours. Big fan."

Nick said nothing.

"But don't go taking advantage." Lou shot a theatrically exaggerated wink, a narrowing of one eye and a bulging of the other. "When we get down to talking price."

"I would never . . . "

"Just kidding. Nick Nocero's gonna walk out of here – or shall I say drive out – with the best buy anybody could possibly get in a quality used automobile within a sixty-mile radius."

As Marie feared, her father was going overboard. "Nick doesn't want any special treatment."

"You're one to talk."

"What's that supposed to . . . "

They followed Lou down an aisle of cars. Some had dented fenders or rust along the doors. Some bore decals or bumper stickers. "Humpty Dumpty was pushed!" was one that stood out. There were Fords, Toyotas, Chevys, Hondas, each with its rear window marked by the classic sales device: a sales price scribbled in magic marker slashed through and replaced with a crudely numbered lower amount. All cars were washed and waxed, but some were doomed to appear irretrievably used. On the other hand, a few looked so spiffy you had to wonder what twist of sheer bad luck had steered them into Lou's possession.

"Something catches your fancy, let me know. Don't forget – holiday discount."

"Columbus Day is not for another week," Nick pointed out.

"Every day is Columbus Day here . . . Except Veteran's Day, New Year's, Valentine's Day, Memorial Day, Independence Day, Labor Day . . . Let's see, am I missing any?"

Marie had heard enough. "You got the major ones."

"Anything you see's on sale, Nick. Shoot, there was a time I'da paid for your autograph."

"Can't live in the past, Daddy."

"Says who?"

Nick was admiring a candy-apple red '93 Pontiac Grand Prix. He smoothed his hand across the hood, walked around it, peered in the side window.

Lou was at his elbow. "Like it? You can take her for a spin."

"Well . . . "

Lou held the driver's side door open for him like a valet.

"Someone from the dealership needs to go with." Lou announced with a devilish wink. "Company policy. Might even be a state law, for all I know. Marie?"

They eased into the Grand Prix as Lou went to fetch the key. There was a whiff of the lanolin and leather freshness of new upholstery, and it was clean. Either Lou had taken special pains to spruce this baby up, or the poor soul who'd owned it previously had been forced to unload the car at its peak.

"What do you think?" Nick asked.

"I don't know, it's kind of a young person's car."

"I heard that!" Lou was back. "Maybe that's how Nick here feels. Right, Nick?"

Nick hit the gas and the Grand Prix shot forward. Soon they were sailing along River Road. Nick was like a kid on a go-cart track, pulling up close to the car in front then zipping around it with a kind of taunting panache. Marie had a strong urge to yell at him to slow down. It's how Brian drove before she yanked his license away. It's how her ex drove . . . until one fall afternoon a dozen years earlier when he just kept going, or so the story went.

Nick hit the radio button. Loud static burst out. He scanned the panel – Marie wished he'd keep his eyes on the road – and quickly found the Seek button. A classical music standard – Dvorak? – came on.

"No rock and roll stations in this town?"

"Yeah, right."

He hit Seek again and was rewarded with the Rolling Stones' raucous *Tumblin' Dice*. Nick turned up the volume, zipped down the window, and threw his right arm across the passenger seat. Yet another instance of muscle memory. Like the deft spin away from the pressure to avoid a tackler . . .

At some point, Marie became aware that Nick Nocero, driving 50 mph in a 35 zone, had slipped his arm around her. The prudent gesture would have been to scold him to slow down, as she might have scolded Brian. Instead, she leaned closer, her shoulder touching his, the fall of her hair grazing his neck. Muscle memory at work again.

When they returned, Lou was in front of his trailer – er, headquarters – haggling with Jerry and Ruthanne Martinson, an elderly couple whose grown-up daughter had just moved back from somewhere near Detroit to live with them. Lou promptly excused himself and bustled over to where Nick had pulled the Grand Prix back into its original space.

"What d'ya think?"

"It makes him crazy," said Marie, climbing out with a smile she could not conceal.

Nick took his time climbing out.

"She's a beaut," Lou pointed out. "Nearly new."

"The odometer says . . . "

"Ignore it. This car's had one owner, an elderly lady with severe diabetes. Most of the miles were going to the pharmacy for her Coumadin."

"Insulin. That's what diabetics take."

"Whatever. She was elderly and infirm and a super cautious driver, the way the elderly and – did I say infirm? – should be. Drove this like it was a baby buggy."

Marie said, "Odd choice in cars for an old lady."

Lou scowled. "In her final months she was desperately trying to recapture her youth. You got a problem with that?" Lou added, "Don't forget, our Columbus Day special discount pricing."

"Daddy!"

He was too far into his sales pitch mode to stop now. "Make that our year-round football star discount."

"Daddy!"

"That's right, folks! Year round, all-American football star discount brings this good-as-new, perfect working order 1990-something Pontiac Grand Prix in at an impossibly low $3499. No money down. Payable in monthly installments. Or whatever we choose to work out."

Nick circled the car, gently but methodically giving a toe kick to each tire.

"No!" Lou hollered. "Don't! Stop!"

Nick froze.

"Just kidding, just kidding. Believe me, you could get what's his name, your old punter, to whack these babies and he'd probably crack his toe, they're so firm. $3299. That's as low as I can go without compromising my daughter's financial future."

"You never give me even a nickel," Marie protested with exaggerated indignation.

"Some day. Someday I just might." He turned to Nick. "$3199. A deal?"

Running his palm across the glistening cherry finish, Nick moved to the other side of the hood.

"What this is, frankly, is an opportunity," Lou stated enthusiastically, as though he'd just discovered an important and previously missing piece of wisdom.

"Please," Marie snapped. "Do not go there."

The dreaded "there" was Lou's penchant for dispensing unsolicited motivational advice. He was a lifelong devotee of self-improvement books, starting with Napoleon Hill ("Think and Grow Rich") right up through Tony Robbins. He regularly watched those late night infomercials on TV that advertised videos guaranteed to produce seven-figure incomes from real estate investments. Lou was less interested in the get-rich-quick aspects than he was the psychological techniques of the slick pitchmen. Anyone who knew Lou even casually had at one time or another been on the receiving end of his second- hand pearls of wisdom. He'd recently been absorbed in "When Opportunity Knocks: Six Groundbreaking Steps to a Brighter Future," by the Australian psychologist Clinton Gantt, whom he'd seen on the Jay Leno Show. Lou did not agree with all Jay's selections when it came to special guests, but he admired Leno's overall generosity of spirit, especially compared to the snippy Letterman.

To anyone who would listen, and some who would not, Lou had touted what he believed to be the book's most remarkable insight, namely that opportunism was a complex concept often given short shrift by the listless and lazy types who preferred to call it "luck." Opportunism, according to Lou's synopsis of Gantt's thesis, was in actuality a precise discipline that, if diligently and methodically practiced, could absolutely transform one's fortunes, and always for the better.

"Ask me, Nick here could use a dose. See Nick, opportunism – you know the word, don't you? – opportunism is the overlooked ingredient in what makes men successful. This book I been reading tells you how to survey for opportunities, kind of like gold miners in days of yore. You can make a science of it. Like coach Lombardi always said, gotta create your own good luck."

"Wasn't that Henry Ford, Daddy?"

"Ford and Lombardi, and probably a few others. When something's dead-on true, no one person thinks it up. I look at Nick and I see an immense talent who could maybe use a sharper approach to opportunism. A car like this . . . "

"What kind of down payment?"

Jerry and Ruthanne Martinson were waving their arms to get his attention.

"For Nick Nocero? Just your signature will be required."

They shook.

"I'd say good luck in the game today," Lou added. "But what I mean is . . . don't be afraid to be an opportunist."

CHAPTER 13

T he stand of Norway maples and pin oaks behind the football
field were so brightly colored they might have been splashed
with buckets of primary paint. The yellows and oranges were
intense in the upper branches, tapering to varying muted
shades lower down. There was a breeze and when it kicked up, a
great flurry of leaves would sweep into the sky. It was an afternoon
that twirled with dancing golden light.

Throughout the first quarter, Nick did not waver from his sec-
ondary role as dutiful assistant. He'd declined Sherman's pleadings
and the Ziglars were reportedly okay with that. We watched him
plod along the sideline, waiting for him to assert himself. He did not
interact much with Sherman, even on a very questionable decision
to punt the ball on fourth and one from midfield. Nick must have
understood, in a way that Sherman the math instructor could not,
that our punter, Denny Vranek, was completely capable of kicking
one that went nowhere. Better to go for the first, we thought. But
Nick made no effort to intervene. Sure enough, the punt traveled a
mere fourteen yards before careening out of bounds.

In the second quarter, several plays sent us howling in disgust
at what looked like blatant unfairness on the part of the refs. But
Nick did not flinch. There was one obvious – yes, obvious! – pass

interference that went uncalled even though the Upham wide receiver essentially stiff-armed our defender before grabbing the ball. Another time, our sweep left was executed to perfection only to be curtailed by a deliberate and illegal yank on Brian's face mask when he had clear sailing ahead. At half time, it was 7-6 Upham.

Since the locker room was not big enough for two teams, neither team was allowed to use it. Instead, the squads retreated to their respective patches of turf behind each end zone. On the south side, the Bobcats slumped on the grass, sipping Gatorade like parishioners at a church outing. Sherman stood in the center, lecturing as though it was an SAT prep session. He reiterated the need "to focus on fundamentals," then turned to Nick, who was standing at the periphery. "Anything to add?"

"Naw. That's fine."

"Sure? Anything you pick up that I might have missed?"

"Naw."

Upham ran back the second half kickoff for a touchdown, and the score stayed that way, 14-6, until late in the third when, with several scrambling QB keeper plays by Will, we scored. That made it a one-point game again after Timmy managed to convert the extra point (he'd missed badly on his attempt after our first TD).

The breeze from the south was sweet and summertime humid. There was music in the air, the mariachi clatter of rustling leaves, sharp brass notes from the school band, the synchronized eruptions of cheers (and groans) from the bleachers, crackling vocal bursts from the antiquated PA system. At the start of the fourth, a red-tailed hawk sailed majestically over the field. We lifted our gaze like avid Audubon enthusiasts. For several minutes, the hawk continued its high, lazy circling. We pointed and stared and traded tidbits of half-remembered fragments of information about the bird and its habits. And we wondered, did it detect some promising prey down here in the grandstand?

An Upham lineman, pulling out to lead a sweep to the right, flattened our linebacker from behind in a flagrant clip, opening the way for a twelve-yard gain. The play was a culmination in our minds of the sort of sneaky, reprehensible tactics Upham had employed, with considerable results, for the entire game. Losing fair and square was one thing, and we'd done a lot of it. But being defeated by an unethical foe who figured they could get away with cheating so long as it was invisible to the referees left a bitterness that was not so easy to shrug off. The grousing was getting louder. That's when we noticed that Nick had inched beside Sherman.

His bellowing voice was audible, even above our own escalating roar of complaint. Nick stomped to where the ref was marking the ball along the sideline. "That's a clip! They've been doing it all day. Call it already!"

The ref ignored him.

"You saw it! Call it!"

The ref was not contrite. "Off the field," he barked. "You hear me?"

Already this season had witnessed a number of ugly incidents at school football and soccer games, not just in our area but around the country. It seemed like there was a whole new section of the sports page devoted to parents assaulting other parents, coaches pummeling players. In Middleton, a mom had pulled a knife on a ref. The Ohio Association of Sports Officials had disseminated a series of guidelines to referees for handling "difficult" situations. Try to ignore, keep it brief, don't antagonize, report to the police.

Hiram Felt was the referee. A few of us knew him from his work at a custom pipe operation, and we'd been wondering what in the world he might have against us that he was doing such a lame job of policing Upham's treacheries. "That's enough, fella," Hiram said to Nick and walked back to midfield.

Sherman put a calming hand on Nick's shoulder. Nick knocked it away.

The clock showed a little over a minute remaining. Upham had the ball on their own twenty. Their quarterback took the snap from center and darted backward, not to pass but to run an almost preposterously wide and self-defeating reverse. The boy was tackled for a six-yard loss, and when he got to his feet he was congratulated by his teammates as if he'd scored a touchdown. We were befuddled.

Nick was not. "They're running down the clock," he screamed to Sherman. "Call time."

"We only got two left."

"Use one!"

Sherman signaled frantically to the ref. Time-out. The Bobcats came to the sideline for a quick huddle.

Sherman informed the players, "It's not over yet." It was a remark as likely to inspire them as a homework assignment. Nick nudged Sherman aside.

"They're just running down the clock," Nick told the kids. "Next play, let the ball carrier – probably their QB again – just let him go upfield. Just let him. Give him five, ten yards. Linebackers, drop off. Let him get some speed. Seduce him. You know what that means, don't you? Let him feel he's got a shot at going all the way. Then come at him full bore. At his hands. Don't want to tackle him. We want the ball. But first let him get some speed."

Their uniforms were grass-stained and soiled. The players looked like weary veterans of a military battle gone wrong. Our hearts went out to them. They'd played tough and they'd played smart and they'd played fair. And it was too bad that the score, which by rights should have honored such a noble performance, showed only that they were trailing. "Sports are like life" was a statement you heard a lot. Well, there were times when sports imitated life only too well, and we wished it wasn't so.

"Okay?" Nick asked.

The kids waited for him to say more. Pruitt usually got so long-winded in these tense sideline pep talks that the officials had to trot over and remind him there was a game that needed to resume. When it was clear that Nick was done, that he'd said his piece and it was not a prelude to the Gettysburg Address, they clapped their hands and shouted, "Okay!"

The Upham QB took the snap and made the same backward sweep he'd made on the prior play. A Longview lineman ran at him and missed, then another. The QB had little choice but to turn upfield. He cut back to the middle where there was ample room. His stride lengthened as he sensed the golden opportunity every runner craves. The field before him was ridiculously unobstructed. He accelerated to a full gallop. In the bleachers, we were mortified that the Bobcats would commit such a monumental defensive lapse at such a crucial time. As we were moaning and whining in one final orgy of lament and self-pity, Grant Rustich sprang from behind at a blind angle and slapped furiously at the QB's arm. The ball sprung loose and cartwheeled spastically backward to where it was kicked twice more before we recovered on the Upham nineteen.

The sun had dipped. Shadows from the nearby trees were creeping onto the field. We cupped our hands over our brows to shade the angled light. The electronic scoreboard with the Made Right logo – a cursive M and R, tightly back-to-back – was difficult to see.

"How much time?" Marie asked.

"Enough," we instantly replied.

Twenty-two seconds, to be exact.

Nick stood directly before Sherman. The clock had stopped after the fumble. We had one time-out remaining. "Go for the field goal," Nick instructed.

"We haven't tried, much less made one, all year." complained Sherman. "Or last. Plus we got time for another play or two."

"This is gonna come down to a field goal any way we cut it. Better now, when the kids are fired up. Timmy?"

Nick strode hurriedly along the bench. Timmy Hudson was seated where he always was, with Josh Hulbert and Chris Furness and the others who rarely got to play.

"Give it your best," Nick told him.

Timmy managed a terrified smile and trotted gamely onto the field.

We'd grown boisterous during the time-out, roaring with a mixture of relief (the game wasn't lost yet!) and unexpected hope (anything can happen!). Now a taut hush swept over us as we watched poor Timmy measure off the steps to his approach. It wasn't exactly that we feared the outcome; deep down, we were always braced for a letdown. The quieting had more to do with the solemnity of the occasion. One fragile teenager, somebody's skittish son, now bore the weight of the team's fate. It was okay to watch this stuff on TV and holler your lungs out at paid professionals. But poor Timmy Hudson had the look of a condemned man, and at such a young age.

Unlike some other kids on the team, Timmy's experience in sports had hardly been a parade of triumphs. He was heavy-legged and slow. Like most sports-minded children, he had a few gleaming plastic trophies on the shelf in his bedroom, largely the result of everyone-gets-one situations. Why he had not quit sports by this age was the big question. Even his mom didn't know the answer.

Irma Hudson was one of those hard-working, common sense, perpetually upbeat women that probably should run the world. She had moved here in junior high from Tennessee when her father came north for work. Her ex lived up by Akron and supposedly sent support payments, though you'd never know it by the family's lifestyle. Irma worked two jobs, admin with the chiropractic group over in Tunbridge and two nights a week cashiering at Walgreen's. She did everything that an overworked mother could to make certain Timmy stayed clear of the troubles that drew other boys like metal filaments to a pocket magnet.

Irma closed her eyes as the teams lined up. Beth Pradlund, seated beside her, mother of number 61, the left guard, held her hand.

Artie Kranz knelt in position, licked his fingertips, and awaited the count. The wobbly hike managed to travel the full seven yards. Artie nabbed it chin high, placed it perpendicular to the ground, spun the laces as he steadied the ball with his outstretched index finger. Like Irma, he closed his eyes. Timmy's right foot swung through.

We held our breath. The ball rose in an elongated pop-up. Timmy's aim was true, but was it long enough? That question hung like a wobbly soap bubble and was not answered until the ball descended, nicking the cross bar, then bounding up, up . . . and over!

"Nice job," was all Nick said to the kids afterward. Nothing more, not even to Timmy. He had a way with silence, perhaps more than he did with words. He must have been feeling exuberant, yet there was no visible sign of it.

It was left to Sherman to provide the standard postgame wrap-up for the team. He told the team how proud Coach Pruitt would have been of the guts they'd showed out there today, how they had confronted a daunting crossroads and navigated it with admirable aplomb. It was as though Sherman were speaking in tongues, saying stuff he was known to privately scorn. Magic was in the air.

We were overjoyed for the kids, of course, but there was something more. With the miracle of Timmy's kick, it was as though Nick himself was sailing upward, hurtling across the goal post. What a great way to return to the gridiron, we thought. And to think the Longview Bobcats had provided him this chance. He didn't say much, he didn't punch the sky like triumphant jock celebrants do on TV. But as he crossed the parking lot to his Grand Prix, he looked like a man gliding on air, and for an instant it seemed that his limp had all but vanished. A golden fall afternoon of come-from-behind football could do for a man.

The parking lot was mostly empty. Half a dozen cars remained and some discarded plastic water bottles. As Nick poked the key into his car door, the door of the car beside him popped open and Earl Muntch hopped out. Earl was the Longview Gazette sports editor and twice-a-week columnist. He was a moon-faced man with no discernible eyebrows and a vaguely Asiatic slant to his eyes. A tight skittish bundle of nervous energy, barely over five feet tall, he had a beach ball torso, short arms and legs, and a wispy moustache that he believed made him look rakish. He wore a tan blazer over a black knit shirt, a look currently in fashion among commentators on ESPN. On Earl Muntch, the outfit simply announced that he was trying very hard to look presentable.

"Nick Nocero? Earl Muntch, Longview Gazette." Earl had a high voice, which he attempted to fortify with the biting enunciations of a wise guy. "You might've read my column?"

Nick shrugged. "Don't pay much attention, not to by-lines."

"You should. Definitely should."

"You say so."

"Town's taken an interest in you, Nick. What brought you here, that sort of thing. I'm thinking a sit-down interview. And I'm the writer to do it. Check my column. Yesterday's, don't know if you saw it, was about paying huge salaries to superstars."

"Pro or con?"

"Nothing's that simple. Not to Earl Muntch." He began fishing through the inner pocket of his sports coat and managed to extract his business card, which he handed to Nick. "Let's put it this way. It's a story that deserves to be written. You want to call me?"

Nick settled into his car. "I'll think about it."

Muntch stayed right there, like a hotel valet patiently awaiting his tip. "If you want, I'll call Ziglar to set it up."

Nick scowled. "I said, I'll think about it."

Nick stopped by the Riverview before going back to his room. The bar was too conveniently located to resist forever.

Autumn weekend afternoons were not prime time at the Riverview and Blanche was alone at the bar. Nick took a seat a few stools down but knew that this buffer zone wouldn't last long.

"Well if it isn't . . . "

Blanche greeted him enthusiastically. He'd not seen her since that first encounter. In fact, he'd avoided the bar since then.

The Captain poured Nick a drink before he'd even ordered and set it down. Old Grand Dad, double shot. "How's the weather forecasting business, my friend?"

"Fair and mild," Nick good-naturedly replied in character, deep of voice and quite earnest. "Until, of course, she turns nasty."

The weather report was Blanche's chance to scoot closer. She did not appear drunk or depressed. You had to wonder about an intelligent woman who could pass time in a dingy bar on a lovely Saturday without succumbing to either of those conditions.

"Been hearing a lot about you," she told Nick. "Turning things around. Lord knows we need it." When he didn't immediately say anything, she continued, "I've been thinking about that boy. The one you told me about?"

"Yeah, well." He didn't need to be reminded.

"You ever wonder whatever came of him? I know how young people are. Something that intense happens, it makes a lasting impact. They become driven. One direction or the other, they become driven."

"Well," Nick sighed, "It's a long story." Maybe he thought this would discourage his listeners.

"Should be possible," suggested the Captain, "to track him down. You know, if you remember his name . . . "

Nick slapped the bar. "Okay. Short version, then don't ask again. Kid paid his price. You know, his debt to society. Became his own judge and jury and the trial went on a long time. He was his own worst enemy. That's all I know."

The Captain wasn't buying it. "No biographical details?"

Nick took a long sip, as though buying time to formulate an escape. To our surprise, he complied. "Kid served his time. Twenty hard years. Not literally, in his mind. Then he got paroled. Paroled himself, that is. Reentered normal society as a productive citizen. And then . . . "

Blanche and the Captain waited for more.

"That's where he is today, living his life." Nick downed his drink with a flourish and abruptly stood. "Living happily ever after."

"Seems," said the Captain, "there's got to be more."

"Probably is," said Nick. "But I don't know it."

．．．．．．．．．．．．．．．．．．．．．．．．．．．．．．．．．．．．．

Before he was hospitalized, Coach Pruitt would give an annual talk at one of the regular Chamber of Commerce luncheons. It was a tradition, as was the content of his talks. He always declared what a fine bunch of young men this year's team was and pointed out, in virtually the identical words he'd employed the prior year, how win or lose these were kids who would go on to accomplish wonderful things in "this game we call life." We nodded like appreciative church-goers at another retelling of a satisfying Bible parable.

The Longview Chamber of Commerce ("serving the interests of the lower Greenfield County") was not an entirely cohesive group. Participation in monthly luncheons was way down and it was no great mystery as to why: the number of businesses who considered themselves solvent enough to actually contemplate a future, much less strategize in concert with other like-minded businesses for the purpose of upgrading broad aspects of the local civic and economic environment, was rapidly dwindling.

Recently, we'd embarked on a number of recruitment schemes – cutting the membership fee to $50 for sole proprietorships, permitting payment on a flexible installment plan, extending participation in our Humana group health plan, providing a free one-hour computer technology consultation. All to no avail. As recently as 1990, the chamber had 78 member businesses. These days, it was down to 41, and that included several – like Betty's Big Wardrobe, the new clothing store for "large-figured" ladies – that had joined on a trial basis and nobody expected to be around a year from now.

The Chamber was a two-tiered entity, run by a handful of the old guard businesses that were more or less stable and had a history of striving, not always selflessly, to enhance the image, and to a somewhat lesser degree the reality, of greater Longview. Made Right and the Ziglars were charter members of this tier, as were Farmers National Bank, Stevens Funeral Home, and the Longview Gazette. The second tier consisted of enterprises that had started up in the past few years and had futures that were hard to contemplate more than a few quarters out. The primary reason they'd joined the Chamber was that they had been strongly encouraged to do so by our aggressive new director, Todd Whelton. Todd was a Longview High alum who'd majored in Business Administration at Bowling Green where he'd been president of the Delta Upsilon fraternity. He had a salesman's smile and a pitchman's zeal. We wanted to like him so much, being one of our own, that we nearly did.

With Pruitt sidelined, it had been assumed that Bertram Sherman would fill in as the guest speaker, a not entirely welcome development. The notion that the insider's perspective on this season's edition of the Fightin' Bobcats would be furnished by a math instructor who knew less about football than some of the alcoholic vets hanging around the American Legion hall struck many Chamber members as a bit like having a Jew preside at Easter services. Plus, it was bad box office. It was the brainstorm of Todd Whelton, our new chamber director, to enlist Nick to pinch-hit for Pruitt. "Renewed Hope for a Bright Tomorrow" was this year's chamber motto, and who better to put a human face on the concept than our new Made Right plant manager and former Notre Dame tailback, Nick Nocero?

Nick had reluctantly agreed to appear on the condition that he only be obliged to make brief remarks.

"Speaking's not in my skill set," he'd complained to Jeremy Jr.

"People just want to hear you," Jeremy had responded. "They don't care if you're any good."

"I care," said Nick. "And I'm not."

"Fifteen minutes. That's all."

"Fifteen minutes with nothing to say? That's an eternity."

"OK, ten."

The football luncheon was held in the Taft conference room at the Holiday Inn on County 12. That too was a tradition, holding the football luncheon at the one facility in town large enough to accommodate a sizeable turnout, just in case. There was a consensus that chamber expectations should be as lofty and ambitious as Bobcat expectations, or even exceed them.

Nick came dressed casually in a powder blue button-down shirt and tan sports coat with creased slacks. He looked about as comfortable as an inmate at a parole hearing. The standard agenda was for everyone to assemble at noon, spend fifteen minutes schmoozing, sit down to eat, then listen to the scheduled talk plus whatever business items needed to be aired and addressed. Nick had managed to arrive late enough to entirely miss the social interlude and had been escorted straight to his assigned seat at the head table, between Arch Robinson, head of our Mutual of Omaha office, and Jeremy Jr. He busied himself chowing down on the chicken marsala with mash potatoes and local greens, probably eating more than a person should prior to a public talk. But there were advantages in having a mouthful of food whenever Arch or Mayor Luppert wanted to engage him. He could nod in amiable agreement at whatever was being said.

Once dessert – pecan pie and vanilla ice cream – was cleared away, it was time. Ten minutes is what he'd agreed to and that is what he'd prepared. He spoke about how much he liked our town, how we exemplified the can-do spirit and community values that were what was best about this nation, and how grateful he was for the opportunity to pitch in, both at Made Right and with the Bobcats. He did not speak with polish or bravado. Even his pauses, which he had the self-confidence to indulge without embarrassment or panic, struck us as worth heeding. In truth, the pauses probably caused us to pay even more attention. He declared that this Bobcats squad – he could not speak about past years – was the embodiment of what's good about sports, and for this remark, although we'd heard an approximate version of it every year from Pruitt, he received a warm round of applause. The applause seemed like the right cue to quit. Which he did with a humble thank-you.

From the viewpoint of the nearly thirty attendees – the best chamber luncheon turnout in four years – it was a talk that could have stretched a good deal longer. We'd only applauded at the hackneyed line about the embodiment of sporting virtues in order to bolster his confidence, to urge him to keep going, to say more. People had hoped that Nick would speak autobiographically, as ex-athletes were known to do. We'd hoped he'd recount a few old war stories, tell us about some big plays in big games, drop a few names of legends he'd played with or against, give us something a little personal and unique, some tidbits we could take away and cherish as special. It wasn't that we felt disrespected by the relative brevity of his remarks. Audiences only get aggrieved in that way when they've paid a steep ticket price. But we did feel let down, and that was not the mood Todd Whelton and the chamber were hoping to achieve.

Before any real disgruntlement set in, Jeremy Jr. stepped to the rostrum. As a wrap-up, he'd prepared one of his periodic "our niche in the global economy" briefings. Between the heaviness of a rich midday meal and the letdown over Nick's anticipated gridiron yarns, we were not an ideal audience for Junior's macroeconomic theories.

" . . . as our forefathers in days of yore pushed onward, upward, westward to explore the frontier . . ." Jeremy Jr. could have been an effective anchorman at a local news station. His voice was deep and commanding and conveyed an authority disproportionate to his true expertise, which was pretty much limited to the clothing industry, southern Ohio politics, and Notre Dame football. " . . . so we must, all of us here, as community leaders and concerned citizens, we must approach with the same bold sense of challenge this exciting new frontier of computers and technology."

It felt like being trapped in Sunday school.

" . . . As our very own Senator John Glenn said when he was orbiting our fair earth in the tiny space capsule, looking down from above at the small comings and goings of the human race . . ."

Mercifully, it came to an end. As the waiter came by to collect our plates and silverware, Nick stood to leave. Jeremy, down from the podium, quickly intercepted him, as if to say "not so fast."

"Todd here has an idea," Jeremy stated.

Affirming this, Todd Whelton proudly threw an arm around Nick's shoulder and steered him towards the lobby. Arch Robinson hopped over for support, his shock of brilliant white hair like a bouncing ball. Nick was cornered.

"Wednesday before Thanksgiving," Todd began, "that's our annual Christmas tree lighting. Sort of a tradition. You know, the days are getting dark, winter's coming on. Gets the town in a holiday mood. Spending-wise, that is."

"It's our chance," Jeremy chipped in, "what with the layoffs and all, to say to the community: we care."

The Holiday Inn lobby was vacant except for a young cleaning lady in an ironed yellow blouse vacuuming the area behind the sofa. The machine noise made it hard to hear.

"My idea," Todd nearly shouted, "is to get a celebrity to preside. At the tree lighting. It'd sure be a boost. One year . . ."

"Eighty-one," Jeremy said. "Year we went to the Superbowl."

"Denny Moose, the weather forecaster. The one always dressing up in costumes?"

Nick stiffened.

Todd pulled a piece of lined notebook paper from the inside pocket of his plaid sport coat. The vacuuming blessedly stopped.

"Just a wish list, mind you." Todd explained. "John Madden, the color commentator. Dan Marino, no explanation necessary. That blonde gal, Bonnie something, who does the reports from the side-line during time-outs. You know, with the tight sweaters."

"Plus you might have suggestions of your own," Arch added. "Guys you played with who made it big and might want to come out for a visit. Sort of a reunion, for old time's sake."

The foursome exited the motel lobby. In the parking lot, the last of the luncheon goers were bidding good-bye to each other, shaking hands, shooting thumbs-up, cackling after one last wisecrack.

Arch continued, "Whoever you get, he wouldn't have to do much, just say a few words, then flip the switch on the lights."

"And get his – or her – picture taken."

Nick was a runner trapped in the backfield, glancing around for an exit. "Celebrities," he asserted, "want money for public appearances."

"Yes," responded Todd, "and that's where you come in. That's my idea! We don't have a budget. But if you could use your connections, make a few calls . . . See where I'm going with this?"

Nick saw only too well and he was irked. "Guys, let's get this straight, once and for all. You want a carnival magician, some faith healer, go get yourself one. Be my guest. But that ain't me. One job at a time. That's my style. See where I'm going with this?"

That should have been the end of it, but Todd was a bit thick that way. Or crafty; take your pick. "That's great, Nick. Just do what you can. Can't ask for more than that."

Nick faltered in the face of Todd's seeming obtuseness. "I'm not . . . I mean, what you're asking is, well, it's way beyond a long shot."

"Hey," Arch chimed in, "long shots are what we live for. Right, fellas?"

Nick winced noticeably. Compared to most of us, his life had been a high wire act, no safety net in sight. We, on the other hand, awakened every morning knowing exactly where we'd be lying down to sleep at night, and with whom. Who were we to employ the concept of "long shot" in begging for his help?

"So you'll try?" Arch pressed.

The sky was thick with clouds. The vacant field behind the parking lot where a decade ago a mini-mall had been planned was overgrown with tall weeds. Along County 12, you could hear the loud hiss from the tires of passing trucks. It must have drizzled during lunch.

After an awkward pause, Nick was compelled to say something. What he said was, "Sure, I guess I can try."

Before returning to work, Nick made a quick stop at the Ohio to change shirts. He slipped a dime into the parking meter across the street, good for an hour. Other municipalities had switched exclusively to quarters for revenue purposes, but we really didn't have enough metered spaces to justify the cost of transitioning.

"Nice wheels."

Tuna stood lurking beneath the awning of Eddie's Smoke Shop, a cramped two-room storefront that carried tobacco items but specialized in lottery tickets and shrink-wrapped magazines. He was wearing his traffic cop uniform. The short-brimmed cap and the epaulets on the shirt differed from the official police uniform, but you had to look closely to detect it.

"Thanks," Nick said, easing away.

"Girl friend buy it for you?"

Nick would likely have encountered Tuna before this, as he was employed part-time, usually nights, as a security guard at Made Right. Tuna had been a lineman back in high school and a big disappointment to Coach Pruitt, who'd expected more of someone that large (240 pounds as a sophomore) and that surly.

"You want a conversation?" Nick asked pleasantly. "Or you just doing color commentary?"

Tuna scuttled from beneath Eddie's awning. "Stay away from Marie."

"This an official police department warning?"

Tuna glanced down, as if to check which uniform he was wearing today. "You heard me."

"You have a name?"

"Tuna."

Nick stifled a laugh. "Last name?"

"This ain't a last name kind of town, Mister ah . . . Remke? That is the name, isn't it?"

Nick did a swift appraisal. This was not the occasion for a fuller explanation and Tuna seemed like a person who could be counted on to mangle the truth.

"Nocero," Nick replied crisply. Then, sensing that Tuna was contemplating a rejoinder, he added, "Thought you just said this isn't a last name kind of town."

"It ain't. But I guess you wouldn't know that."

CHAPTER **15**

....

At one time, Made Right enjoyed a thriving overseas export
trade that accounted for nearly forty percent of its gross
revenues. Old Ziglar had a repertoire of risqué stories from
those days, tales of sales trips to Buenos Aires, Prague, and
other exotic locales, anecdotes about coltish frauleins and buxom
senoritas complaining about the tight fit, pleading with him to
correct it. Nick, we'd noticed, wasn't all that amused.

For him, Made Right's glorious past, including the old man's
ribald accounts of foreign conquests, had scant relevance to our
possibly less glorious future. He could no more benefit from knowing production and sales figures dating from our Eisenhower era
zenith than he could from that inspirational movie "Rudy" everybody was urging him to see. The past, to Nick, was decisively past,
and the only reason to dwell on it was for purposes of diversion.
He never actually stated this in so many words, but that was the
message we gleaned from his persistent refusal to indulge our
curiosity about his prior exploits. You would think this might
engender some resentment, but, oddly, the opposite was the case.
We felt tacitly scolded, even rebuked, for this penchant for looking backward. It was as though Nick was striving to redirect our
attention to the more pressing need to focus all energies on the

immediate tasks at hand. The message was: we did not have the luxury of wallowing in the past.

Still, we couldn't restrain ourselves from urging him to see "Rudy." "Can't believe you haven't seen it yet," we'd say every time the topic arose (raised by us). "This no-talent kid working his butt off at practice? You'll love it. You will absolutely love it."

Why he'd not seen it was perplexing. An inspirational story set in the very surroundings he knew so well, University of Notre Dame football and environs, it had been both a smash hit in the theaters when it came out and an equally successful video rental. You'd think that it would have come to his attention before the good folk of Longview recommended it en masse. Indeed, the real life Rudy (the film was supposedly based on, or inspired by, as they like to phrase it, a real person and real incidents) would likely have overlapped with Nick in South Bend. Maybe he didn't like the guy. Maybe the guy was not quite the paragon of work ethic virtue that the movie portrayed him to be. Maybe Nick was rankled by all the melodramatic Hollywood fabrications. That would make sense. Still, it would have been nice to have that conversation with him, to hear him explain why he was so reluctant, if reluctance was what it was. Hearing it from him straight might even reverse our fondness for the film. Our opinions were not set in stone.

The reasons people kept urging "Rudy" on him were obvious. We wanted him to talk football. We wanted his outlook on the matter of gutsy underprivileged long-shot underdogs persevering against all odds. Yet even as we prodded, however unproductively, we privately acknowledged there could be a valid reason beyond mere obstinacy behind Nick's desire to avoid such discussions. He'd been around. He knew the ropes. He knew that the effect that fantasies can have on people was as likely to be insidious as inspiring. Especially with crunch time hanging over us.

Making the rounds early in the morning, methodically wending his way work station to work station, he was like an officer among the troops, dispensing encouraging words. Each interaction was punctuated with handshakes and back slaps and thumbs-up signals. He was a performer. The factory floor was his stage.

He made his morning rounds roughly in the sequence in which the garments traveled, beginning in the southwest corner, in the dingy recess lit by the glow from the vending machines, and culminating at the steam tunnel where the finished coats, hundreds of them, waited on hangers for the final inspection before being wheeled out to the loading docks for shipping, primarily to New York, but also as far south as Atlanta and as far west as Denver.

Early in the morning, when the machines began chomping and buzzing, when the human energy kept pace with the machine energy, the plant surged with vitality. The sheer fact that it was a brand new day held out the brightest hope, if only because so much unexpired time remained on the rust-colored punch clock. Anything could happen. Nick clearly felt that way first thing in the morning, and that's how he wanted all of us to feel.

First shift started at 7 a.m. By then he'd already gone over any memos that might have been left from the overtime crew, checked the shipment logs as well as any new manifests, swallowed several bitter cups from the failing Mr. Coffee in his office, and paid a visit to Isaac Ashong, the union rep (Made Right workers were members of the Amalgamated Clothing and Textile Workers) who had his own private office, decreed by collective bargaining agreement, directly next to Nick's in a jerry-rigged alcove by the lunchroom. If there were "issues" to be addressed, Ashong was not shy about bringing them to Nick's attention. Made Right's colorful history included two full-blown strikes and several slowdowns that threatened to erupt. That said, we had no illusions these days about the power of the union. Gone were the days of industry-wide solidarity and sympathy actions by other labor groups. Any hardball pressure tactics would amount to suicide. Ashong was far too crafty, and practical, to go there.

Ashong liked Nick and he made no effort to hide it, even though his role called for an adversarial pose. Nick was management. True, he might have been hired for questionable reasons (one rumor that held a lot of currency was that Nick did not stumble into Longview, but that Jeremy Jr. had actually contacted the Notre Dame athletic director to see if there were any former gridiron stars who knew manufacturing or were known to be a fast study, and who needed employment). Nick might be just another middle-aged white guy handed an opportunity because that's who always got the breaks. But we were beginning to accept that he could be the real deal. We did not abandon our skepticism, for we had learned never to wholly relinquish that final layer of defense. Inch by inch, we were being persuaded.

Making the rounds, Nick paused by one of the long wooden tables where several women hunched over their whirring Singers and Union Specials, frenetically sliding cut swatches of fabric across the flat metal table, adjusting the thread to keep it free of loops, working the foot pedals like drummers keeping time. Each stitcher had a cardboard shoe box behind her machine to collect the coupons upon which bonuses were calculated (pay based completely on piecework was no longer permitted, a development which in old man Ziglar's mind partially explained our vulnerability to insurgent offshore competition).

Juliet Kladitis occupied the machine on the aisle, a status comparable to first viola in a concert orchestra. Plump, cross-eyed, the hardest worker in the shop, she had a long scar across her right hand, the ugly result of a stitching error she would not make again. She was married with two children of grade school age.

"Juliet," Nick enthused, "you're amazing!"

She did not look up as her fingers busily worked the fabric.

"I've been thinking, Juliet, we should get a camera crew in here. You know, to record exactly how you do it. Then review the film in slow motion. Like those nature shows on public television, where you finally get to see how the hummingbird's wings operate. The human eye is simply not up to the task."

Juliet kept working unwaveringly. She was as likely to engage in conversation as a dental patient would during drilling.

"You know, Juliet, there should be an Olympic competition for real work performed by real people, like yourself. Instead of that dumb stuff you see. Shooting rifles off horseback. Synchronized swimming. Bobsledding. Geez! You'd have yourself a gold medal. No doubt about it."

Now she smiled.

At the conclusion of his regular loop, Nick arrived at the steam presses. These hissing slabs, four in total, were situated beneath the mezzanine overhang where the illumination from the ceiling light was partially blocked. Muted light, billowing steam, the ear splitting squeal of a train yard, equatorial levels of humidity, ninety degrees in summertime even with functioning air conditioning – these elements combined to give Pressing the reputation, and stature, of being a little piece of Hades right here in Longview.

EJ Leonard was a steamer – muscular, pasty-skinned, thirty-something with long blonde hair, wispy goatee, sleeveless shirt and red bandana knotted pirate-style around his scalp. He'd played linebacker for the Bobcats, joined the Marines after graduation, and had seen action in the first Gulf war. EJ claimed his entire platoon had been ordered to shoot at Iraqi Republican Guard who'd already surrendered and were returning home, barefoot and bloodied, to their ruined lives. "Don't call me no hero," was all EJ ever said about his war.

"Nice going on those shipments," Nick congratulated EJ. "Right on the nose."

"It was tight man, real tight." EJ stepped back from his machine to wipe a film of sweat off his pale forehead. "Worked overtime Thursday night, Friday night. Can't keep that pace up."

"I hear you."

"What I don't get," and here EJ stepped away from the press, joining Nick in the aisle, "is they increase orders and lay people off. Tell me: how's that make sense?"

"Offshore competition. That's the game and we got no choice but to play it. And guess what? We're beating 'em back. Thanks to you guys."

"Not so sure." EJ sauntered back to his press, laying a Prussian blue flight attendant coat over the casket-shaped mount. "Hey, that was one great game Saturday."

"I'm only the . . ." Nick chuckled at himself. "Thanks."

Marie was descending the stairs. She wore a knee-length skirt and a beige sweater. Nick took a quick glance back and, sure enough, EJ too was watching. So were a lot of us. Factory days were long and undifferentiated. Financial necessity and the threat of being laid off were not always enough to see us through until shift's end. Sometimes we grabbed for whatever buzz was available, pinched from anywhere it could be found.

Marie carried herself like a ballerina, with a spring to her step that some thought haughty. She held a range of iconoclastic opinions expressly intended to get our goat on subjects from movies ("Julia Roberts isn't all that beautiful") to school curriculum ("Teaching spelling to grade school kids is pointless"). Add to these characteristics the fact that she was the person who had the most frequent contact with and direct access to the Ziglars, and it was no mystery why she stood out.

"Jeremy wants you," she informed Nick. "He's got some international guests up in his office. Koreans. They want a guided tour."

Marie came closer, a bit of a risk knowing what she surely did about the effect any indication of familiarity would have on those watching. "You have dinner plans tonight?"

It had been a long time since Nick had anything that could be truthfully termed "dinner plans," in the sense that he knew who he would dine with, and where, and could look forward to it. No, he indicated with a shake of his head. No plans.

Marie smiled. "My place at seven?"

Junior's office appeared different. The Notre Dame pennants and paraphernalia were still on prominent display. Jeremy would sooner host a meeting in the buff than he would remove those. But by the door was a silk tripartite dressing screen with a simple hand-painted depiction of slender geese winging over an amber hillside. There was a tall ceramic vase by the sofa containing branches of pussy willow. On the coffee table, instead of the half-filled box of glazed donuts, there was a smorgasbord of Chinese takeout delights. Spring rolls, dumplings, deep-fried chunks of pork and beef, wooden skewers with vegetable slices.

A handsome man with jet black hair and the sculpted cheek-bones of a male fashion model was speaking in Korean when Nick entered. He was addressing Jeremy Jr. in a conversational manner while his translator, an equally attractive young woman in a tight wool skirt, stood tight to his side. "Mr. Chong," she stated crisply despite the girlish trill to her voice, "read recent article in Harvard Business. Mr. Chong ask about labor union. Mr. Chong very interested in fixed overhead costs."

"Workers here," Jeremy Jr. proudly explained, "are team players. Every one." His father, seated in an armchair that had been shifted alongside his son, nodded approvingly.

The translator conveyed Junior's remark to Mr. Chong, who gave a puzzled look and said something in return.

"Mr. Chong asks, what is team player?"

"This," Jeremy Jr. declared, rising from his seat and sweeping toward the door like a diva returning for one final bow, "this, my friends, is a team player."

With a hand on Nick's shoulder, Junior introduced him to the South Korea delegation. Besides Chong and the translator, there were two other silver-haired gentlemen in plain navy suits. The entire delegation had arrived last night and were staying at a private antebellum mansion across the river, on the West Virginia side, that Marie had arranged. They had a rented Cadillac and a hired driver for the duration of their stay. The driver was Ross Lilly, himself a laid-off Made Right pattern maker. Later, when we pressed him on what he'd managed to learn concerning the Koreans' true intentions, Ross was useless as a tree stump. He said he couldn't

understand a word they were saying and he couldn't even discern
if the noises they made, which sounded to Ross like karate instructions, amounted to laughter or complaint. We were left as much in
the dark as ever.

This new global economy was a bafflement. The one indisputable fact about this economic shift appeared to be that a few would
emerge as winners while the overwhelming majority could wind up
as satisfied customers, if lucky, disgruntled victims if not.

"Nick is our plant manager and a damn good one," said Junior.
"He's going to give you a little tour. And then we can resume our
discussion."

Jeremy Sr. said something in a phlegmy voice.

"What's that, Dad?"

"Tell them," Jeremy Sr. repeated, "eat some food."

CHAPTER 16

·······································

ick arrived early at Marie's house on East Hunter, having
overestimated how long it would take to drive there from
his hotel. He wore gray Dockers with a pleat, a forest green
polo-style shirt and a pair of brown leather Florsheims
polished to a military shine. He'd shaved again after work. He'd
bought a bouquet of flowers, tulips mostly, at Ramsay's Market.
Labeled freshly cut, they were already beginning to droop. The
checkout clerk at Ramsay's had been a girl he recognized from the
cheerleading squad, and he did not want to make a fuss. She might
ask why he was buying them.

He hesitated on Marie's doorstep before taking the decisive act
of pressing his thumb to the crescent moon doorbell button. There
was a wide picture window to his right but nobody was in there peering out for him. He stepped back and tried to appear nonchalant.

Inside, Marie was finishing preparations for the meal. She'd cut
the chicken cutlet into cubes, chopped the mushrooms and carrot,
diced the onion and garlic, and prepared the sauce in sizzling butter over a back burner while water boiled for the broccoli. She'd set
the table, minus the help from Brian she'd asked for twice. She'd
cleaned the lettuce for the salad, patted the reddish-green leaves
dry with paper toweling, opened two bottles of wine, one a Napa

Merlot, the other German Riesling, not knowing Nick's preference. Hers was Chianti and she was halfway into her second glass.

She too had dressed carefully. She wore a crop cardigan over a dark russet blouse. The pocket skirt might have been a bit matronly in length but was snug at the hips, sending a perfectly mixed message. She was not completely comfortable with the idea of Nick taking pleasure in her appearance. Nor was she uncomfortable with it.

It had been some years for Marie also. To many in town, she seemed excessively proud. Yet that is probably not how she thought of herself, certainly not in the aftermath of her divorce, or separation, or whatever it was. Like a lot of people who get bruised in relationships, Marie had been rudely surprised at how fragile her self-esteem proved to be. She hadn't even loved him, she would tell friends like Maddy. And she did not believe that Rafe ever came close to recognizing, much less appreciating, what was best in her. Yet when he left for good – Arizona, according to the latest reports – Marie was devastated.

Desperate, she'd begun crafting a strategy to win him back. The plan she eventually devised was as eloquent and concise as a one-act play. She would fly to wherever Rafe was living on the pretext of passing through for a plane change stopover. She would phone him from the airport and summon him to meet her at the terminal. A bustling sea of people going about their busy lives was an essential background element for the atmosphere she wished to establish, namely life would go on and she was at peace with that fact. Her alleged flight connection would necessarily limit their time together (fifteen minutes would be what she would inform Rafe, no matter when it was that he showed up). They would find a vacated retail kiosk or an idle gate area where they could be alone. Rafe would be edgy, defensive, wary, but she would quickly disabuse him of the fear that she still had designs. I've changed, she would assure him, and I want only to tell you this: I believe in you still, and always will. She was the sort of woman, she would tell Rafe, who took pride in the lovers she chose and she remained proud for having chosen him. The life he was embarking on would, she hoped, amount to a validation of her affection for him. Live a great life, she would urge him, and remember that I will be cheering you on.

Silence is what her imagined script called for next. She would say nothing, not a word, as Rafe slowly processed this new reality that he was formally, officially absolved of all guilt. He was free as a bird, no strings attached, now and hereafter. He was free to say good-bye to the only woman of character who would ever declare such faith in him.

Abruptly, Marie would check her watch, gasp at the time, and briskly walk away, joining the flow of people scurrying to their purpose-driven lives. The heat of Rafe's stare would singe the back of her neck as she disappeared into the throng. But she would not hesitate, would not turn around. She knew Rafe. She was the goal line and he would soon make a mad dash.

It was a wonderful plan. She felt certain it would work. But in one of the singular epiphanies of her life, it struck her as a shame to waste such a brilliant piece of psychological manipulation on that slug, Rafe Fontune. He just wasn't worth it. The spell she'd been under since high school was broken.

Only lately had Marie been able to catch a gleam of her old self in the mirror. That's what we were seeing around Made Right as she skipped merrily down the iron stairs in outfits that were unnecessarily cute. The idea of meeting a man was no longer repellent to her. But Longview was a settled community, at least socially. There was a party-hard crowd that gathered at biker saloons like the Crossroads, but they tended to be a lot younger than Marie and a lot scruffier. Most of the eligible guys of an eligible age were single for very good reasons.

Married men, however, were interested. Were they ever! You would have thought she'd placed a classified ad in the Gazette with her phone number: helpless horny babe w.o. husband sks mature family guy with wife and family for furtive romantic encounters. Several years back there'd been the little league coach, Richie Beloit, who'd shown what Marie naively construed as surrogate fatherly interest in helping Brian's pitching. He'd call her up at night to discuss training regimens. He'd ask her to bring Brian early to Sunday practice, so he could devote more "special" time to the boy. It was only when he dropped by one evening around ten, on a school night, slightly sloshed, with a Nolan Ryan instructional videotape that she realized something was up. "Is Brian asleep?" he'd asked. "Why don't we watch the tape together? So's I can show you what parts Brian really needs to focus on."

Richie winked, as if Marie was certain to share his thrill at having adroitly maneuvered their relationship to this opportunity. When he moved in for a kiss, she screamed, and that was the end of it.

Sort of. Richie was still someone she saw from time to time. He worked at the agency where she had her auto insurance, and his son played second string in the Bobcats backfield. Only a few weeks ago, she'd encountered him in the parking lot after practice and he mentioned he had a football video, Barry Sanders or someone like that, that could really help Brian out. He'd be happy to lend it to her. Brian's got potential, he added salaciously, with the right instruction.

The doorbell rang as Marie was pouring olive oil into a mixing beaker for the salad dressing.

"Can you get it?"

Brian had just entered the kitchen and was about to set the table, at Marie's direction. Having his coach over for dinner was awkward enough; actually having to go to the door to receive him as a welcome guest seemed beyond the call of duty. He stared coldly.

"Can you?" Marie did not intend this as a question.

Brian trudged through the dining alcove to the hallway, taking his time. When he yanked open the door, Nick was there with a tight smile, holding a bouquet of tulips. There were comic possibilities for how this might play out – Brian could pretend to blush and protest, "Oh, you shouldn't have" – but neither was up to it.

"Evening, Brian."

Brian yelled, "Mom, he's here!"

Lou, who could happily dine on meatloaf every day of the week and favored meatloaf omelets as a breakfast dish, often boasted of his daughter's culinary skills. What impressed him was the various nationalities, French, Mexican, Asian. Marie's flair for atypical cuisine confirmed our sense of her as a woman who was restless.

The recipe she prepared for Nick came from the September 1996 issue of Gourmet magazine that she'd borrowed from Maddy, who shared a subscription with her sister (interestingly, nobody suspected Maddy of being uppity or restless). Marie had prepared this meal once before, when she threw a going-away party for a neighborhood family, the Russells, who'd moved to the Denver area for a promised mechanic's job at the new airport. Brian had remarked that it was the best dinner he'd ever eaten.

Tonight, Brian was persistently sullen. He pushed his food around his plate, hardly eating, never speaking. Nick tried to fill the void by eating and talking enough for several people. He gave an extended account of his visit to the Chamber of Commerce, including commentary on the cuisine ("the chicken was so tough that nobody had time for conversation") and Jeremy's talk ("like a local pol looking to run for statewide office"). He'd hoped his remarks would produce at least a smile from Brian.

When they did not, he tried a less jocular and more informative tack. "Chamber of Commerce, Brian, is something every town's got. Idea is to figure out shared ways to help everyone's business. Kind of a rising-tide-lifts-all-boats approach."

"Just like football."

"Not everything's like football," Nick said, missing Brian's sarcasm, but injecting a bit of his own. "Baseball, for example, is nothing like football."

"A joke," Nick added after a long moment of silence.

Brian stood with his plate and asked to be excused, saying he had a mountain of homework.

"He's sure in a mood," Marie explained after Brian dropped his plate in the sink and disappeared. "Sorry."

"Easy enough to understand."

"It's not like you're the first . . ." Marie hesitated, then accepted the obviousness of where she'd been heading, "not the first man to come for dinner."

Nick had wanted to know more about her. But there was nobody he could ask, at least not without hinting at some of what drove his curiosity. And to ask Marie directly would of course run the risk of eliciting a reciprocal inquiry.

"How long, if you don't mind me asking, since your husband . . . ?"

"Ex-husband. Thirteen years come Christmas. I cried for three solid months. Then he called one day from somewhere, begging. That's when I realized, no, I was better off. I've been fine ever since."

"I got a visit from a guy named Tuna who says . . ."

Marie dropped her fork, which she'd only been using to make patterns in her side dish of baked squash. "He's my ex's brother and he's a true dirt ball. Tell you he's a cop?"

"Is he?"

"He pretends. Part-time security at Made Right and a full-time loser. A very messed up guy."

"He warned me to stay away from you."

"Well, I'm warning you: ignore him."

Clearing the table, they slid past one another sideways like experienced tango partners, shoulder to shoulder, carting plates and platters in outstretched hands. At the sink, Nick rolled up his sleeves and rinsed the dinner plates with a sponge in a gentle pool of lukewarm water, then handed off to Marie who was positioned at the dishwasher.

Her kitchen was largely undecorated, except for the refrigerator door, which was completely covered with scotch-taped photos of Brian in various stages of development – sandbox, on horseback, little league cap nearly covering his eyes, football outfit with oversized shoulder pads. A trio of wooden duck decoys perched atop an antique hutch.

"Where'd you get those?" Nick gestured upward with a tilt of his head since his hands were sunk in rinse water.

"The ducks?" She laughed. "An auction. They cost a dollar each.

Can't beat the price. How do they look?"

He didn't say. "You like auctions?"

"I tell myself it's business." She smiled to let him know it probably was not. And then, seeing his puzzlement, she explained.

A few years ago, Marie had begun a modest antiques business, part-time of course. She scouted for abandoned objects of solid construction and tried to reconfigure or redecorate them to contemporary tastes. She had storage space in a warehouse out by Lou's that was filled with an array of strange, formerly utilitarian items -- dental chairs, stainless steel bank-teller grates, convent prayer benches, industrial foundry patterns framed as wall art. In the spring and summer she would attend regional craft fairs, maybe three or four a season, selling what she could. It didn't amount to much, and she had to be cautious with her overhead. The ducks had been an acquisition that was probably ill-advised. There was really nothing you could do with them, and who would even want them for decoration? Besides her, that is.

The doorbell rang. Before she could straighten up and dry her hands, her father had entered the kitchen.

"Geez, this guy is a heckuva triple threat," Lou enthused, meaning Nick at the sink rinsing the wine glasses.

Lou wore his high school letter jacket, blue woolen torso with worn leather sleeves. He surveyed the dining room table for any leftovers. "I saw Nick's car out front and thought to myself, why don't I just . . ."

"Just come in?"

"Bingo." The table had been cleared, but Lou located the bowl of squash on the counter by the sink. He went to the silverware drawer, extracted a tablespoon.

Lou dug in. Backing up a few steps, he gesticulated with the spoon. "I live just over there," he explained, tilting the spoon in the direction of the front door, the gob of squash clinging precariously. "You know this is the house where Marie here was raised. These days, how often you ever hear of that, someone living in the same damn house they's raised in? Just might be the rarest thing in all the land."

"I'm not proud of it, Daddy."

"You should be. Country's going to hell and it would be a far better place, by a long shot, if more people stayed where they was raised." This was one of Lou's pet rants. Lou held a range of theories for how the world could be a better place. He did this as a hobby, not unlike Marie with her discarded objects. The underappreciated virtues of living your entire life in the same locale was one of them. Others included raising the height of the rim in pro basketball and requiring all high school students to write research papers on the lives of senior citizens who lived in town. Like his praise for Marie's cooking, these theories had been recounted to us more than once.

"A lot of problems," Lou insisted, "a whole of lot problems, are the direct result of people living where they don't really belong."

Marie dropped a wine glass, and angrily cursed, effectively ending the discussion. She ordered Lou to fetch the dustpan and motioned for Nick to move away.

The two men leaned against the kitchenette partition, idly watching as Marie bent nimbly at the waist, finishing the job. The classical music station was still playing. Lou handed the dustpan to Marie. "I haven't even told you what I came here for."

Marie frowned. Her father dropping by casually was complication enough; as a man with a mission, he could be dangerous.

With no encouragement, Lou launched another of his long-winded preambles. These could sometimes consume a full five minutes before even a remote guess could be ventured as to where it was heading, or why. This one had to do with his nephew up in Cleveland. The boy was his brother's son, Marie's first cousin, although they were more than twenty-five years apart and had nothing in common.

"It'd mean the world to him to meet Nick," said Lou, coming to what appeared to be the point.

Marie stood holding her dustpan of glistening shards. "Daddy, please."

Lou ignored her plea. "The boy's name – get this – is Nick. His dad's a huge football fan. Huge. Named each of his three sons that way. There's Vince, after Lombardi, of course. There's Nicky, after you and Buoniconti, who played for the Dolphins. The oldest, I'm sorry to say, was originally named Oscar Jerome, OJ for short. Now they just call him Buddy."

Nick lifted his wrist to check the time. His one material indulgence was a titanium Casio watch that shone like a tiara on his thick wrist. He valued time, that was clear.

"I'm thinking maybe pizza after a game, something like that. They've been wanting to come down to see Brian play. See, the boy's having trouble in school. Dropped off the team, getting sorry grades. Meeting you'd give him some motivation. That's what I'm thinking."

Nick snorted, "What do you think I am, a faith healer?"

Lou was tone deaf, reacting as if all Nick needed was further persuasion. "Thing is, the kid's heard all the stories about your career. Knows all that there is. When he was younger, he'd go to the library – with his dad – and research the old newspaper clippings on . . . what do they call it?"

"Microfilm," Marie guessed.

"That's it. The kid's like a scholar on the subject of Notre Dame. At least he was. Christ, if he paid half that kind of attention in school . . ."

Nick went for his leather coat, which hung on a coat rack fashioned from a wooden surveyor's tripod, another of Marie's prized items. "I had a wonderful evening," Nick said. "No need to see me out."

She followed him anyway. In the darkened vestibule, with Lou in the kitchen whistling annoyingly, she squeezed his hand. "Thanks for coming."

Her hand was still slopped with soapy water. He did not quickly let it go.

CHAPTER

....

During lunch break at Made Right on mild days like this –
upper 60's, sun beaming down the valley, breeze streaming
from the southwest – a festive atmosphere took over the patch
of lawn on the bluff overlooking the river. At the wooden picnic tables, workers eating out of their paper sacks and lunch pails
slapped down dominos, briskly cut a deck of cards, all the while
talking, laughing, lounging in the unseasonably warm air. Someone
had brought a soccer ball and several guys formed a circle, passing
it around, showing off for the ladies who paid no attention.

Two autumns back, Flora McNulty, pear-shaped, gray-haired,
third-generation Made Right, for reasons that were utterly whimsi-
cal, had brought a plastic bottle of soap solution and a plastic wand
for blowing gigantic bubbles. You would have thought it was a birthday party of preschoolers, the way we dropped everything we were
doing to gawk at the improbably lazy ascent of enormous translu-
cent shapes, fat as beach balls. Above the tables, above the lawn,
above the valley, higher, higher . . . And when the billowed bubbles
finally popped, it seemed as likely to be from the sheer excitement
of the journey as any structural deficiency or obsolescence.

Over time, Flora's bubbles became an unofficial Made Right
tradition. Not every day and not even every fair-weather day. Just

128

every day that Flora felt the time was right. The rest of us were free, of course, to bring our own bubble wands and soapy solutions. But no one ever did. It was Flora who'd introduced it as a lunchtime pastime and there was an unstated acknowledgement that the stunt belonged to her, to implement or not, as she so chose.

The decision-making mechanism by which Flora came to "officially" declare a "bubble day," was a topic of much conjecture. Nice weather was one of her inscrutable preconditions, but not the only one. An upbeat mood on the factory floor seemed to be a criterion, but that was hardly a clear-cut circumstance and could not be measured. Sometimes we'd ask her point-blank, even beg her, is today a bubble day? But she clarified no more about her inner processes than a jazz musician might. "When I know it," she said. "I know it."

At lunchtime, particularly when the weather was fair, Flora would saunter outside, find a seat at one of the picnic tables, unwrap her ham-and-cheese. We'd follow her movements and await her judgment. Some days all she did was eat and chat, usually with Gretchen Fixx and the skinny kid named Sid from maintenance and repair. Our eyes would be trained on her, awaiting her signal which had over time become highly ritualized. Ceremoniously, her index finger would lift overhead to test the breeze. She'd reach into her handbag and fumble around a moment. And then, if conditions were right, out would come her bubble apparatus. We'd slap five – yes, wagers were sometimes placed – and get ready for the launch.

Nick did not typically take a lunch break. His habit was to eat on the move as he roved the floor, usually a cold ham or turkey sandwich on a roll tough as cardboard purchased at Ramsay's the night before. Today, however, he'd popped outside just as Flora was getting started. A moment later, Marie emerged, blinking in the sunlight. Nick feigned surprise at seeing her. We knew better.

There was still nothing overt about their relationship. We knew they liked each other. We knew he'd gone to her house for dinner. We knew that she was single and so was he. There was no need for them to be furtive, since it was inevitable that we would learn whatever there was to be learned. It was mildly amusing to watch them slink from the plant a few minutes apart and meet, ostensibly by coincidence, in the parking lot at 12:15. As they converged at Marie's station wagon, parked in the executive section alongside Jeremy Jr.'s silver BMW, one of Flora's giant bubbles wobbled directly overhead, obese and shimmering, effortlessly gliding in defiance of the laws of physics.

With childlike awe, we watched the plump bubble drift up Arrowhead like an apparition, veering lazily eastward toward town hall square. It rose no higher, nor did it sink. Buoyed by an unseen current, the bubble seemed to be coddled, nurtured, protected, encouraged. When it burst – if it ever burst – it had strayed well out of sight.

Marie drove out Rosholt Road past the Legion Hall to where it joined East Bluff. The road followed a branch of the Norfolk Southern track for a quarter-mile, then swerved around a small lake. When it rejoined the track, the crossing gate was down and the first cars of a freight train were rumbling past. They had to wait.

She had been prodding Nick to get an apartment. To be fair, others had mentioned this to him also. A few weeks in a hotel (it had been over a month now) was fine for a temporary worker or, had the Ohio been classier, a high-spending exec who couldn't be bothered to make his own bed. Whether he would have taken the initiative to actually get out and do it without Marie escorting him every step of the way was subject to debate.

The apartment Marie had found for him was just on the other side of the tracks. You could spot the third-story windows of the plain brick building – it was actually a row of small attached buildings – above the rattling railroad cars.

Nick stared, almost longingly, it seemed to Marie, at the dust-caked freight clanging past, faded paint and rusted iron, cattle cars, flatcars, tank cars, gondolas, each bearing the name of a place – Sioux City, Kankakee, Hays, Joplin, Rockford, Hastings – that was a synonym for "out there." Usually Marie avoided the subject, knowing how he disliked discussing it after hours and especially with parents. Here was her chance to ask him.

"That field goal by Timmy? End of the Upham game? Everyone says you had time for another play. Why chance it?"

She was startled when he actually answered. "Something pure about one last play," he said. "One last final chance, you've got no choice but to take your best shot. Why pretend you got a bunch of second chances if the best shot you'll get is staring right at you?" Nick turned intently to her. "That make sense?"

It did to him, and for now that was good enough. "These long freights," she sighed, "sure do stop you in your tracks."

He said, "I don't mind."

The apartment building was on a street directly facing the tracks. There were several similar buildings, three-story brick cubes that would not have looked out of place in areas of Cleveland or Detroit where low-rent housing had been hastily constructed for an influx of workers with steady jobs. Except for the buildings, the landscape was pure Midwest prairie. One could almost visualize Indians paddling a birchbark canoe down this tree-lined stretch of river valley back to their encampment.

Rocky Brendek, the landlord, met them downstairs per appointment. He was erratically shaven with unruly gray hair and a lazy eye. Marie thought he might be one of her father's Legion buddies.

"Third floor's the best," he said, leading the way up the narrow stairwell that was painted a dreary flax color. "You'll see. The views."

Rocky slowed on the stair so Nick could keep up. On the second floor landing, they had to step around a tricycle and a few other playthings.

"Kids?" asked Marie.

"They'll get this cleaned up," Rocky assured them.

"How many?"

"A few. Very well-behaved. They read a lot."

Marie had to suppress a laugh. It was like her father on the subject of a used auto's previous owner: always an elderly woman with minimal intown needs.

"We'll get along fine," said Nick. "I like to read."

That was Marie's first indication that Nick was going to take the place. He was going to sign his name to a lease and plunk down a security deposit. Living in an apartment was different from living in a hotel. It was the difference between moving in and passing through.

Rocky fiddled with the lock, grumbled in frustration. He went back to his trouser pocket for a few more keys and found one that worked. The haphazard way he went about it made Marie think there might have been more than one key that could do the trick. The door swung open. Rocky stood at the threshold ceremonially beckoning them in, like a maitre d' greeting a party of V.I.P.'s.

There was not much to the place, two bedrooms, a living room, a kitchen and dining alcove. No furniture, cleanly swept for the most part. The view was what Rocky hoped they would admire, the view out the back across a vacant patch of sandy brown prairie grass, toward the ridge of trees and the river valley beyond. The apartment was no palace. Yet there were palaces that lacked such a view.

"I bet this is something at sunset," Nick said.

"Sunrise too," Rocky added.

....

Friday night, October 22. Guthrie High School field. Temperature at game time: 47 degrees. Wind: imperceptible. Sky: perfectly clear. Moon: waxing crescent.

Night games were an exhilarating holiday for our players. Bobcat boosters looked forward to them like they were Christmas eve, not so much in expectation of presents but for that cozy warm glow of gathering together for a shared interlude of enjoyment. Or frustration, as was so often the case. Either way, we were together, clapping our hands and rooting for our guys.

Longview was not one of those fabled Friday night lights football hotbeds. We took the sport seriously but we liked to think we did so with a sense of balanced priorities, unlike the nut cases we'd read about in Texas and Oklahoma where the coach got paid more than the Governor and star players enjoyed the equivalent of caddies handing them fresh towels when they came off the field and refilling their Gatorade cups for them. High schools in our region had not invested exorbitant sums in lavish athletic complexes that featured outdoor lighting suitable for interscholastic nighttime contests. But there was one such school in our conference. Guthrie possessed a state-of-the-art athletic complex paid for by a class-of-1962 alum who'd made a fortune importing Toyotas before most Americans even knew an automotive industry existed outside of the United States and Germany. There you had it, a classic global economy trade-off: a few thousand jobs lost to overseas competition in exchange for a new stadium with towering poles hoisting 1000-watt Halide lamps that lit the night to a high noon brightness.

A night game was special. The lights giddily magnified every twist and turn on the field. From kickoff to the final whistle, it was the same game of football under same old rules. And by the contest's end, bruised and drained, the players might feel no different than they would on a dreary Saturday afternoon in the drizzle. But at the start, with adrenalin peaking, it was electric. The yard markers imprinted with crisp white lime, almost iridescent under the mega-watt illumination. The joy we felt to be in the cool fresh air. The players so acutely aware that every move they made, every twist and lunge, every spin and dash, every slap on the helmet, swig of water, thrust of the fist and flexing of the arm, every stray bit of ribbing and poking with a teammate on the bench, was being watched. It was as though the Bobcats were actors onstage. In the bleachers, we felt it also, the hyped-up buzz of lights blazing down, trained on center ring. School was out. Office closed. Factory shut. Let the show begin!

Marie parked her car in the gravel lot that also serviced the neighboring indoor skating rink. The team had arrived by yellow school bus. Guthrie was a fifteen-mile drive. Marie had intended to drive with Maddy, but circumstances – the need to deposit her paycheck before the batch of bills she mailed out midweek pushed her account into the red zone, squeezing in a grocery shop so she'd have time to attend an auction tomorrow – had her running late and she was forced to make the trip alone.

When Brian was a toddler and her free time was spent at the swings and sandboxes and climbing structures of Riverside Park, Marie had been a devout member of that vast club called motherhood.

Now the pudgy toddlers with pudgy knees poking from cute shorts had all morphed into teenagers wearing gladiator helmets with shoulder pads that made them appear as monsters. And when the season was done, when these seasons of their lives had turned, they would graduate to the bleachers and join us in exhorting the next generation to give it all they had, to play hard and hope for the best.

It was so much fun, and it was all so sad. Those two sensations were jumbled together more often than anybody liked. Of course it was just a game, a fun game that would be over too soon.

Guthrie High's visiting team bleachers, one-third the seating capacity of the home team's, were packed when Marie arrived. Maddy spotted her and stood waving her arms like airport ground crew directing a 727 to its gate. Their friendship, casual through elementary school, had been solidified as teenagers when they each landed bit parts in a youth theater production of "The Music Man." They played Pickalittle ladies and assorted townspeople.

As the teams lined up, Timmy carefully set the ball in the kick-off tee. Guthrie was spread in formation to receive. Maddy patted the space of the seat she'd saved. Marie plunked down, delighted to have arrived in time.

"How's it going?"

"Fine."

"I mean, how's it going with the coach?"

There was a cost to overreacting, even with Maddy. "He's a very nice man."

"Careful."

Marie eyed her coldly. "Being careful, as you very well know, isn't usually my problem."

The Guthrie community access cable station, Channel 63, video-taped the game, and many of us who didn't make the drive were able to pick it up as part of our local package. The opportunity to view a Bobcat game at home in real time was another rare occurrence. Channel 63 employed one lone camera perched on a wobbly tripod atop the home team grandstand, twelve rows up. The voiceover narration was done by an ambitious student named Guy Hoard who went on to a professional position as a news producer in Akron. Guy's skills were in a decidedly nascent stage at this time. On some plays, he nailed it like a pro with a crisp declaration of who'd carried the ball, the yard line where the runner had been stopped, what down was next and how many yards to go. Other times, he seemed to lose his sense of purpose and slipped into aimless chitchat with high school chums who dropped by for the express purpose of insinuating their own voices into the broadcast, like audio graffiti.

"Second and nine," Guy reported, straining to sound older, and more profound.

"You sure about that?" another voice chided.

"Maybe I should go onto the field, you know, for one of those injury reports."

"Nobody's been injured."

"Make something up."

"You mean blabber like the real guys do?"

The Guthrie squad in their orange and black uniforms hauled in the opening kickoff and carried it back across midfield. Two plays later, the QB faked a hand-off and threw a long pass that was caught for a touchdown. The TD precipitated a pig-pile of Guthrie players.

We did little in our first possession. A Bobcat running play went nowhere. The identical play was called next with more or less identical results. On the Channel 63 video, Guy momentarily stepped outside his play-by-play obligations to try his hand at color commentary.

"They need to mix it up," Guy opined. "This Guthrie defense is just too tough when you run straight at 'em."

Longview punted, but not very far. Guthrie's next sequence could have been an instructional film. Each off-tackle running play was like a textbook demonstration, achieving a steady 10-12 yard gain until, perhaps out of boredom, they launched a pass.

"Touchdown Guthrie!" Guy again declared.

There was grumbling in our section of the grandstand. "Back to their old habits," Ernie Luppert said disgustedly, and he was far from a pessimist.

"Their head's not in it," Brad Zelk agreed.

Marie wheeled on them. "They're trying their best."

Brad stood his ground. "At this level, that is not enough."

Eyes wide, Marie feigned an exaggerated flash of enlightenment. "Oh, I see," she asserted with a giddy trill, her tone thick with sarcasm. Even Marie might have been succumbing to pressure.

The night before, she'd confided to Maddy that Nick had called her at home to discuss a conversation he'd had with Sherman. It wasn't Nick's style to reveal much about the team, certainly not behind-the-scenes details.

Sherman, it seemed, had finally issued a direct plea: he'd begged Nick to take over. He wanted Nick to be solely, explicitly, officially in charge. The kids were aware that Sherman didn't know beans about the intricacies of the game while Nick, his nominal assistant, was reputed to be expert. The situation was awkward and embarrassing and left Sherman the butt of much joking, not all of it sophomoric. When the team won, Sherman would receive robust congratulations in the faculty lounge or in the aisle at K-mart, and he knew – he knew – there was a healthy dose of ridicule behind the ostensible praise. And it was spilling over to realms where he did actually know what he was doing.

At a teacher conference recently with a mother who wanted to know why her daughter wasn't in Advanced Placement math, Sherman simply stated that the girl, a sophomore, needed to first master basic long division (he was tempted to throw in subtraction). "If you're such a smarty," the mom retorted, "how come you're just a teacher?"

That type of scorn, Sherman feared, was a direct outgrowth of his recent reputation as an imposter. In teaching, authority was everything. Tarnish that and you might as well surrender. In pleading with Nick to take the reins, Sherman hoped to preserve his own sinking credibility – for the sake of the students in his classes – and legitimately bolster the Bobcats. It was a classic twofer.

The players, Sherman had insisted to Nick, were genuinely curious and there was a cost to avoiding it. "They want to know about you. Geez, you got old guys around town who blocked a punt thirty years ago and they're bragging about it still, and here you don't say boo about your exploits. It's downright weird."

"And so?" Marie had asked.

"Said I'd think about it."

At half time, Guthrie led 13-0, yet the score did not accurately reflect the large gap between the teams. We had only one first down, and that was the result of an off sides penalty. Penalties also played a fortunate role in suppressing Guthrie's point total, for they had twice marched to first-and-goal situations that came to naught due to major infractions (twin fifteen-yard unnecessary roughness calls on one drive).

Each team was assigned a sovereign patch of end zone during half-time where they could sit, relax, re-tape, strategize. Coach Pruitt would often use this time to offer a few pointers. Depending on the responsiveness of the kids – they were all functionally afflicted by attention deficit disorder at this point of a game – he'd offer a short inspirational pitch. Pruitt was good at this, and many folks felt that he might have missed his calling as a preacher. "Easier winning a ball game than getting 'em into heaven," he was known to respond whenever this suggestion arose.

The Bobcats flopped wearily onto the cold turf. Sherman carried two large plastic jugs of water with a stack of paper cups tucked under one arm. Nick caught up to him, offering to help. Sherman wheeled on him.

"If you really want to help, you can talk some damn life into them."

They were like some bedraggled Confederate army brigade, the 4th Volunteers of Tennessee in one of those haunting Antietam interludes, young faces masked by the grit of fatigue and looming defeat.

They sipped water, massaged cold hands, too tired even to complain.

Sherman moved to the middle of the group. The Guthrie high band was attempting a medley of motion picture soundtracks, starting with Star Wars. Da da da da daa.

"We need," Sherman announced with a professor's matter-of-factness, "to raise our level of concentration. We need to play smart, to rely more on our strengths."

"Come on. Get real."

Sherman spun to see who'd said it. They all hung their heads, conspiring anonymously.

"We need to upgrade our focus out there, guys." Sherman's nasal whine was almost a parody of the ineffectual professor. "We need to get our heads more into it. We need to . . . "

"That's bull!" Brian defiantly lifted his head so anyone who was curious would know who'd said it. "That ain't our problem."

Nick shoved forward. "Brian? Why don't you tell everyone exactly what you think is our problem?"

Brian shrugged insolently. "Uh, they might just be better than us?"

It took a moment for the clucking to subside. Nick stomped directly to where Brian sat and stood commandingly above him. "So?" he asked, almost sweetly.

Nick asked again, "So? You think the best team always wins? You're a smart kid, Brian. Is that what you've observed? Best team always wins? Or is that just something you read about in Sunday school?"

Nick had gravitated incrementally, even involuntarily, to the center of the group. Sherman eagerly gave way. Nick had the floor, and he had their attention. "Who here thinks the best always win and there's not a darn thing anyone can do about it?"

Nobody stirred.

"Heck, maybe what we should just do is just give some damn ability test. You know, like the SATs. You guys've heard of the SATs, right? Let's just award the game to which ever team's got the most ability. That would save a lot of hassle, wouldn't it?" Nick began to circle the group as he spoke, like a workshop leader prowling among trainees. "Who here thinks that's a good idea, just determine which side's got the most ability and settle the game just like that?"

Judging from their silence, none of the Bobcats seemed to think it was such a great idea.

"Let me tell you something. Just cause someone's better doesn't mean crap. It certainly doesn't mean they'll win. This isn't an IQ test or the fifty-yard dash. It's a game, a pretty complicated one. You can play smarter. You can want it more. You can be tricky. You can be daring. I've seen plenty of games where the so-called best team came up short. And you know what? Nobody thought they were the best anymore."

Nick backed off, saying nothing. At the edge of the circle, he turned to smile, maybe the first smile we'd seen on his face.

"Let's go, Bobcats!" he shouted.

Brian snagged the second half kickoff and sprinted to the flank behind a couple of determined linemen. An opening emerged. A tackler managed to grab Brian at the waist and for a moment he looked to be stopped. But after a momentary tussle that looked like a police pat-down for firearms, Brian was suddenly, inexplicably liberated. It was all very confusing.

Guy Hoard's Channel 63 color commentary did little to clarify the action. "Zanay cuts right behind a wall of blockers. He's at the thirty-five, the forty . . . geez, what? . . . looks like, hmmm . . . Looks like Racklin has the ball now. He's at the forty, the thirty . . ."

It was a classic reverse play, executed with far more subtlety and stealth than Guthrie could handle. We had not seen one of these for quite some time. Pruitt was not big on reverses. On kick-offs and punts he thought they sacrificed precious ground when old-fashioned speed and blocking (as if we possessed those assets) should suffice. On plays from the line of scrimmage, he felt reverses signaled that the offense was insecure about its abilities to grind it out the gutsy way.

Eventually Will was caught from behind on the sixteen yard line. Three running plays later, the Bobcats scored. And made the extra point. Guthrie 13, Longview 7.

The score stayed that way through the third quarter. The Guthrie offense, which in the first half had looked capable of ripping off a first down nearly every time they ran the football, now bogged down. Or were thwarted, depending on one's analytical bias. Guy Hoard unhesitatingly attributed it all to the "gritty determination" of the Longview defense who were, "giving it all one hundred ten percent, maybe more. Reminds me of the famous steel curtain up in Pittsburgh."

Even if Maddy had not pointed it out, jabbing her in the rib and shoving the binoculars on her for purposes of verification, Marie would have noticed. Everyone noticed. Nick had assumed command. He was active, involved, assertive, demonstrative. When players trotted off the field, they came to him. When possession of the ball turned over, the players about to enter the game (approximately half the Longview players went both ways, offense and defense) clustered briefly around Nick, as though receiving benediction. Sherman was still present but seemed primarily concerned with keeping his ears warm, tugging at his blue wool cap, and blowing on his ungloved hands.

With two minutes remaining and the score unchanged, Longview had the ball in the floodlit middle of the field. True fans knew this to be the vaunted crunch time in which the steely-eyed head coach with his air traffic control headset rushes forward to signal the QB that he's devised a special play that he urgently needs to explain to him. It's possible that Sherman had seen sagacious coaches on TV do just that, for he suddenly stepped to the chalk mark on the sideline nearest to where the Bobcats were huddling, waved his arms wildly, and cupped his hands to his mouth to amplify what he wanted to say. He never got a word out.

Nick stormed over, shoving Sherman aside. Sherman looked more pleased than distressed.

"Time!" Nick hollered, lifting his hands above his head to form a perpendicular "T" configuration. "Time out!"

The entire offense hustled to the sideline for a quick conference. Nick instructed them to run the fourteen play, a quarterback roll-out option. It was a play we had run several times already in this game, and it had yet to gain more than three yards. It was precisely the sort of unimaginative, prosaic, doomed-to-failure suggestion we'd expect from Sherman. And Nick received the same skeptical look that Sherman had received so many times.

"When you get tackled," Nick continued, "I want . . ."

"Excuse me?" Brian wondered with incredulity. "When we what?"

"When you get tackled," Nick continued, "I want you to line up immediately. I mean immediately! Pronto! No huddle. Then go with the dual right 20 trap. Okay? Before they get set. Got it? Brian?"

Brian had loosened his helmet strap. Each of his cheeks bore a big bright red dot from exertion. We watched as Nick placed a hand firmly on Brian's shoulder pad. It was one those Kodak snapshot moments, iconic in its way, that make you think life really is a passing of the baton, generation to generation.

"Brian, now remember what I told you?"

Brian flashed that dull, blank, back-row gaze of an ill-prepared student unexpectedly called upon by the teacher.

"Ah . . . no, coach. I don't."

"Please, Brian, try your best not to get tackled."

The fourteen option play went pretty much like all the others before it. Will scrambled to his right behind the flawed blocking of Mickey Herman and the undersized Sean Eck. Guthrie sent a phalanx of tacklers at him, smothering him before he could pitch out or pass. A loss of two yards.

Up in the stands, of course, we were blissfully ignorant of any scheme on the Bobcats' part. The Bobcats were known for hard-nosed, schemeless football. And for losing a lot of games. Our old resignation, never far from the surface, was rearing up again.

"Playing like girls," complained Rip Royston, a legionnaire who knew his football, at least the televised variety.

"Pretty ones, though," chortled Jimbo Kluge. "Other kind's been known to play tough."

"Got a point there."

The Guthrie tacklers who'd smothered Will, all six of them, were preoccupied in congratulating themselves, NFL-style, with wagging forefingers gesticulating skyward to the gridiron gods. The Bobcats, in blue and gold, instantly lined up in formation. Those of us not already sunk too deep in self-pity saw it unfolding, a trick maneuver of the sort long derided by Pruitt as sissified and unworthy of our gritty tradition. We saw it and were gleeful. We were afraid even to exchange comments, not a word, for fear of jinxing it. Frozen by superstition, we held each others' hands and awaited the outcome like political supporters watching the newscast for the final tally from the last deciding precinct. Those few Guthrie players who were even aware a play from scrimmage was about to begin had no clue as to the whereabouts of the ball and no means of getting the attention of their teammates.

Will took the snap. A fake hand-off to the fullback momentarily sent Guthrie's few alert defenders in the wrong direction. Brian, clutching the ball, had only one tackler in his vicinity, and three blockers to escort him downfield. The tackler tripped before there was any solid contact.

It was like a dream, a sweet and satisfying dream where all those snarling scurvy tormentors fall away like dominoes toppled by an unseen hand, and the carefree child suddenly finds himself safe on the hard, moist sand of a sunny beach at low tide.

As Timmy jogged onto the field to attempt the extra point, there seemed to be no doubt about the destiny of this game, and maybe the destiny of this team, and who knew what else. Sports can do that. We try to resist (unlike those fanatics in Texas), knowing it's only a game, a diversionary recreational pastime. Yet sports can also manufacture the kind of wild onrush of unanticipated joy that gives rise to an otherwise insupportable belief that, damn it, our fortunes, yes our very fortunes, just might be improving.

The bus was parked just outside Guthrie field. As the Bobcats came clattering over the asphalt, dirt-smudged and jabbering, still wearing their helmets, we formed a reception line. We were happy, possibly joyous. Is that too strong a reaction to a relatively inconsequential football contest? So be it. Deep down, we probably realized that the thrill would fade, as it always does. Deep down, we also realized that you take what you can get, every bit of it, when it's offered. Anything less amounted to a kind of sacrilege.

The coaching brain trust, Sherman and Nick, stood by the bus door, welcoming the players on board.

"Great game."

"Thanks, coach."

"Way to go, Petey."

"Thanks."

The reception line narrowed as we pressed closer, slapping those giant shoulder pads, calling out instructions when to be home, where to be picked up. Marie stood on her tiptoes for a better view like a star-struck fan at the backstage exit hoping for an encounter. She'd actually done something like that once, driving up to Columbus with three friends to see a show by John Cougar at the

Ohio State University basketball arena. When the rocker finally did appear, there was a mad rush by dozens of girls trying to see him, touch him, get noticed by him. Marie and her friends, all juniors at the time at Longview High, never got close.

Tonight was different. Marie broke rank and went straight up to Nick. It was not like her to take a chance on drawing attention. She must have known that we were already prowling for signals concerning her relationship to Nick. Her boldness, if you want to call it that, showed that she'd come to that fateful juncture when the greater risk lay in holding back. There would not be another night like this.

"I'm driving back," she said to Nick, softly yet in easy earshot of us. "If you'd like to take the scenic route."

There actually was a scenic route home from Guthrie, although how much scenery could actually be enjoyed in the darkness at 40 mph was debatable. Marie took Guthrie Road southeast, across Stone Mill Run, past Lake Copeland. This was not a route she knew well, yet the topography was predictable. As the road cut past a long stretch of woodland, you could almost feel the closeness of the trees. Nick made no move to turn on the radio.

For the first miles, they did not exchange a word. Marie was aware of Nick studying her features in the aqua glow of the dashboard lights, yet she resisted the urge to fill the void with chatter. Eventually there would be plenty to say.

It was a full five minutes before Nick broke the silence. "Sure happy about Brian."

"The whole team, I would think."

"Especially Brian. How often does a kid make just the right move just when it counts?"

"Or any of us."

The whirring of the tires across the open night were lulling. "Or any of us," he agreed.

"He's not another Nick Nocero," Marie gently chided.

Marie toed the brake and swung the car onto a rutted and narrow dirt road. Her headlights swept a line of birch trees with paper-smooth trunks.

"A little detour," she explained.

It was no explanation at all, but Nick let her drive on. They crossed a narrow wooden bridge, bouncing over the uneven planks. Soon they came to what looked to be the road's end. Overhanging tree limbs lit from below by the car's high beams appeared like beckoning arms. Marie switched off the engine, opened her door.

There was a worn footpath through the tall prairie grass. She took his hand, and he followed. He could not see a thing. It was like that game where you're supposed to cultivate trust by allowing your body to helplessly topple backward, against all instincts, trusting that your companion will be there to intercede. Trust was a good thing to have. And a hardship to lose.

In a minute, they came to a clearing where there were no trees, only the vast star-speckled night. Soon they were high on a hillside with the wide valley stretched before them, vast and starlit.

"Those lights," Marie pointed, "way over there."

Nick gazed at the galaxy of stars in the infinite night.

"That's us. Way over there. That's Longview."

Now he saw it, lower in the sky, the tight cluster of tiny lights like a constellation that had lost its way. When she kissed him, it came as a shock. She would insist later that he kissed her first, and Nick came to see the wisdom in letting her maintain that fiction. But he knew better. And so did she.

It was Marie who pulled away, instinct mostly, a throwback to the feigned shyness of adolescence, when it was the girl's role to set limits, to fend off the boy's hurried insistence. She took his hand again and Nick would have followed her blindfolded over a cliff if that was the destination she had selected for them. They walked downhill over loose stones the size of chestnuts. The air was thicker here, and humid. He could hear the rushing water of a nearby

stream, muffled by the surrounding thicket. The breeze was men-
tholated by tiny droplets of spray.

They came to another clearing beneath a beguiling swatch of
glittering stars. Marie folded down. Nick bent his knees, creakily,
and did the same. She leaned her head against his shoulder for
support and they eased back, theater-goers in no particular hurry
for the program to begin.

Nick asked if she needed to get home any special time. For Brian.

That wasn't what was on her mind. She said, "I don't really
know you, Nick. Do I?"

Until now, they'd avoided this discussion, perhaps assuming in
the giddiness of courtship that sheer momentum might propel them
beyond the need for it. He plucked a long blade of grass, and used its
waxy tip to tickle her throat. "You know all the stuff that matters."

She inched back. "And that is?"

Nick chose his words carefully. "I am who I am. I am what
you see."

"Gosh, that sounds dull as dishwater."

"I am . . . what I do. What I'm able to do."

"There's more than that. There's more to everyone."

"More facts? Sure, there's more facts."

There was a bristling in his voice, a hardness. We'd figured it
was in there somewhere, and she must have also. A former athlete
who never quite made it to the pinnacle was bound to harbor bitterness, was bound to have some bruised spots prickly to the touch.

"More facts'll do," she said. "They'll do just fine."

He rattled them off rapid-fire, one after another, like a court
stenographer obliged to recite a transcript back to the judge. Born
in Iowa, a town not unlike Longview. Happy boyhood, fishing in
streams, playing ball behind the church yard. Father up and disappeared when he was thirteen. Sure, that was upsetting, but nothing
that time couldn't heal. Moved to California as a teen and grew into
an all-American jerk (his words), hot-tempered and selfish. School
didn't matter. Nothing beyond sports seemed to matter. Worked

one summer in a factory that made men's shirts. Most of the workers were Mexicans. Good people. He liked them a lot.

Marie complained, "I already know this."

After football, after college, the roar inside him (his words again) persisted. Took a stab at audio equipment sales. Then back to clothing. First in California, then elsewhere. Kept head above water. Eyes peeled for just the right chance. Different jobs. Lots of lateral motion, treading water. Zig left, zag right. Some hard times, yes. Drinking played a role, a symptom not a cause. Married briefly, sweet lady addicted to little white pills. No children. No scars. Lots of arguments. Wish her well, wherever she may be.

"You want me to keep going?" Nick was worked up now, and maybe resentful. "I could. I could go on all night, if that's really what you want. I've got lots of facts, Marie. Tons. A man like me's got a whole damn suitcase full of facts."

"Then why don't you tell me the big one, Nick? Why you've come all this way to a place where nobody knows you?"

"You know me. You know everything that counts. Those facts, that mountain of facts, they're just so much confusion."

"I can live with confusion."

Nick shifted uneasily. Not so far away that she couldn't still touch him, but far enough to force her to adjust her balance, now that she couldn't lean on his shoulder. The breeze was like a purring, nuzzling their ears, humming against the leaves.

"I lost some good years, Marie. And that is the one single fact that counts. You mean more to me, this life in Longview means more to me, than everything I've ever done all put together. I may not have amounted to much, but that's not because I don't have a dream. I do. What I've wanted is to matter. To pitch in and help out and belong. How do you sign up for that? Where do you train for that? You can't. You can only keep moving, keep hoping. That's the only faith I've ever had, that some day I'd find a situation where I was needed for who I am and what I have to offer. That sound nuts? So be it. But it's the truth. I've been a very long time getting here,

Marie. I would have arrived sooner if I'd known the way. I lost some good years, what most people would call a man's prime years. That should not happen to a person, but it did. It happened to me and I am trying, trying with every fiber of my being, to earn it back the only way I know how. The hard way, the right way. Now. Right now. Here. Right here. With you."

Marie had no reply, no further questions, except to kiss him tenderly on the mouth and hold him close. And he said no more.

The drive home floated by in a dazed dream-state. They were too contented and too dizzy to speak or think. The roads were empty and Marie navigated the Taurus as if by autopilot, as if in a trance. She remembered telling Nick, as she would Brian, to fasten his seat belt. Then suddenly they were entering Longview. She had a boyfriend now. A complicated man, yes, but a good one. She was sure of that.

In town, there was little traffic. Waiting for the light to turn green at the intersection of Bluff and Main, Marie figured it would be best to let Nick get out here. (He was still staying at the Ohio; his apartment lease didn't begin until next Tuesday, first of the month.) Now that they were a couple, it might be wise to take extra measures to conceal it. Then she thought: I've lived here all my life, I'm a grown woman, I'm not playing games. Screw it!

"Screw what?" Nick asked.

Marie was not aware that she'd even spoken aloud. "Oh, nothing."

The stoplight had turned green, and Marie rolled to the curb, in front of Atlas Travel with its giant posters of Disneyworld and Paris and Caribbean beaches few townsfolk would ever see.

"See you," he said.

One last quick kiss. "See you," she trilled, and drove off.

Approaching the Riverview Tavern, he hesitated. If the bar wasn't too crowded, he might just climb onto a stool, near to the juke, and savor a shot of Old Grand Dad. A sallow light leaked from the Riverview. Tuna was lumbering out. He wore his blue-gray

Made Right security uniform, at least the shirt portion of it.

Nick abruptly changed course. There was no percentage in mixing it up with Tuna, no percentage tangling with a big townie oaf who had nothing to lose and nothing but time.

Tuna taunted, "You don't listen too good, Mister . . . ah . . ."

Nick might have kept his distance. But this had been a magical night and he was halfway drunk on all that had happened, and all that was yet to come. He strode back to where Tuna still leaned in the Riverview's doorway with studied insolence.

"Nocero," Nick snarled. "Got that? Nocero." And with a fey doffing of his imaginary top hat, he jauntily entered the bar.

CHAPTER 20

．．．．．．．．．．．．．．．．．．．．．．．．．．．．．．．．．．．

He'd arrived in Longview less than two months ago with no more connection to us than a swaddled infant anonymously abandoned on a cold concrete doorstep. Now he had a job, a girlfriend, a life. And us? We had an effective plant manager, a skilled coach, and a neighbor we were proud to call a friend, plus the added subliminal boost of enjoying his evident pleasure in our humble community. He'd come to us with wide eyes and the fresh perspective of a tourist. To the extent he saw us through rose-colored glasses, that is not a bad way to be seen. It felt pretty good to momentarily place ourselves in his shoes and try on that brightened outlook. Rose-colored glasses, after all, were not demonstrably less accurate than no glasses whatsoever.

Something was happening, something real and positive and promising. But stroking our chins and making a leisurely assessment of how the tide might be turning was not our style. We were preoccupied with treading water, doing our darndest to stay afloat.

Which isn't to say there was no discussion. There certainly was. Snippets of conversation, idle chat around the picnic tables outside Made Right or in the line at the post office or the grandstand between quarters, just chewing it over, tasty morsels we preferred to savor rather than gulp right down. Nick interested us. The few details we knew were ample for conversational purposes. We were like impassioned callers to those amped-up radio talk shows where the fact that nobody knows what the heck they're talking about presents no impediment whatsoever. Mostly, we were curious how a man with so much evident capability could be so content in our modest corner of the country. We wondered how a man who'd known such glories, the adulation as well as the unmentionable perks, could not be bitter at having to serve time so far from any place where the limelight would ever shine. Tuna had his own set of conjectures. His continuing research had failed to produce a bombshell, yet he claimed there was a good reason Nick's former Notre Dame teammates wanted nothing to do with him and the evidence was being covered up by powerful alumni.

Just let us know when you've got the goods, was our response. Humoring Tuna was the best way to deal with him. It was a method that had worked for twenty years.

In the meantime, it gave us a boost to place ourselves in Nick's shoes. Not surprisingly, we found that, yes, it made a rough kind of sense. Why not seek a place of solace after a stretch of turbulence and disappointment? Why not return to the basics? Starting anew in a struggling yet honorable town like ours? Why the hell not? It seemed entirely appropriate that a man of his complicated background could be content, even thankful, to participate in our community, to have this job, this privilege, this honor to chew the fat with Gus in the lobby, to hunker over a cheese steak sub at the O-P, to nod affable hellos while ambling our downtown walks, to exchange pleasantries with Brenda and Hilda and Juliet as they methodically worked a curved swatch of slate-gray fabric through their Singers.

"What you think, Nick? About our chances."

"Chances?"

"Beating Prescott. Last year . . . I don't even want to talk about it."

"Kids keep improving, who knows?" He'd moved beyond that annoying "I'm just the assistant" disclaimer. There was no keeping the parts of his life separate now.

"Realistically, you think we got a shot?"

"Realistically . . . Why not?"

"You know Timmy?"

"Sure. Our kicker."

"My sister's husband's nephew."

"Great kid."

"He thinks you're great too."

Nick continued down the center aisle, cheery and light of foot. Ashong sprang from behind a tall pile of navy sleeves. "We got to talk."

"Now?"

"Now."

We'd been unionized since the 1940's. Initially it was pretty contentious, with skirmishes in the parking lot and bomb threats. But since then, a kind of truce had taken hold and, though we didn't know all the Ziglars' stratagems, labor-management relations had been fairly painless as these things went. By the terms of the collective bargaining agreement, the union rep was entitled to spend up to 5.25 hours per week on union-related affairs, paid for by the company, and was given private office space on the premises. A guy like Ashong, who was a mediator by nature and training, contributed to this semblance of harmony.

Ashong led Nick at a brisk pace down to a shabby wooden door with a combination lock. Ashong's office was no-frills. A vinyl-covered card table, three folding chairs that might have been pinched from a grammar school, a drab office-green, four-drawer metal file cabinet, and a Valley Insurance wall calendar with a Norman Rockwell drawing of a family gathered around a baked turkey on a platter, the very picture of November.

"A grievance?" Nick asked.

"Not yet."

Ashong took a seat behind his desk. He was a divorced father of two boys, co-leader of a Boy Scout troop, co-head of the middle school fund-raising committee. A second generation American by way of Jamaica, he was high-spirited, determined, and bright. You might assume that race, or racism, might be factor in his situation since Longview had few black families. But other than a few drunken slurs Ashong had the misfortune to be exposed to, and which he dismissed, appropriately, as little more than hothead rants, he was just another neighbor busting his ass to get by. He had our respect, and he had Nick's.

"We got another rush job. Ladies' coats."

"So?"

"Every other order they're now calling 'rush'. They're messing with the definition and that's . . ."

"Rush means fast. Nothing confusing about that. Pronto. Fast as we can."

"You seen the order. That's more coats in less time than we could pull off before the layoffs."

Nick wasn't buying it. That was where his job knocked directly against Ashong's. "You know the score. You know what we're up against. By 'we' I mean you, your people, me, my people. And yes, the Ziglars too. I'll spell it out again. Made Right agrees to the designated date, you can call it rush or call it just doing business, we agree and we get that order. We don't, we don't."

"Understood. But check the contract, man. Check the language. Rush can be fast but it can't be no damn miracle."

"Listen, Isaac. I know all about the contract. But there's something else I know, and you know it too, damn it. We got one option: go all out all the time. We're in a battle. Not too long ago you might have called it a losing battle. But we just snagged an airline re-order that was bound for overseas, and now this lady coat rush job. And I'm thinking just maybe . . ."

"Still," Ashong spread his arms like an evangelical preacher beseeching the heavens, "can't ask for no damn miracle."

Nick saw this for the concession it was. "You're wrong, Isaac," he grinned. "Can't demand miracles. But we can ask."

That afternoon, Nick showed up at the high school the same time as usual, just as classes were letting out. He parked the Grand Prix in the corner of the lot far from the kids and teachers bustling toward their cars. The day was cold and overcast, with gray heavy clouds hanging low. If precipitation fell, there could be a few snowflakes mixed in. The line of trees beyond the lot still held a few brittle leaves, a smattering of ambers and reddish-browns. One mighty gust and they too would be gone.

Nick, as was the case with Sherman and Pruitt before him, wanted the kids on the field, loosening up, no later than 3:15. Some excuses for tardiness were acceptable, but goofing off, hanging with friends, and that consummate, all-purpose teenage explanation – "I forgot" – were not among them. Nick wanted his squad working in concert. Stragglers detracted.

The Bobcats needed two more wins to qualify for the big game that was referred to as the "Superbowl." In actuality, it was nothing so glorified. For the past forty-plus years, the leading football team from two rival conferences –Valley East and Central Valley – had a tradition of meeting on Thanksgiving Day morning at 11 a.m. In the early 60's, we had a streak of making it to the big game six out of eight years, but it had been slim pickings since then. In the grand scheme of things, it didn't mean much. But it gave us something to talk about, to care about, to aim for. Making the Superbowl made life a little bit better. Not making it meant everything pretty much remained the way it was. Or got worse.

The Prescott game would be crucial, and Nick was keen on devoting practice time to a range of fine-tuning drills and dress rehearsals. Only a few weeks ago, the idea of tweaking and fine-tuning auxiliary facets of their game would have seemed absurd, even to the Bobcat players. It was the kind of notion that high school coaches are deluded into embracing not because it necessarily paid off but because they'd watched too many NFL telecasts with experts opining about the game plans. Yet, astonishingly, we had become sufficiently adept, or so it seemed in recent games, at fundamental aspects of play, blocking downfield, eleven-man team defense, etc., that stepping up to the "next level", another concept beloved by football announcers, wasn't mere fantasy.

So the time had come to shore up the special teams. Specialization had been a sore spot around the Bobcats for years. Quite simply, Pruitt did not believe in the concept. He was old school all the way. Good athletes, he would often state, are all he sought because a good athlete can adapt to any position and carry out any game plan. Nobody wanted to speak ill of Coach Pruitt in his infirm and hospitalized state, but his absence did open the door to a heretofore suppressed criticism of his approach. Yes, Pruitt's methods could be valid if the squad had an abundance of talented all-around athletes. There was a belief, now surfacing, that Pruitt, for all his legitimately admirable traits, was seriously behind the times. Even by our standards.

Improving the special teams, kickoffs and punts, was one way to gain an edge while also providing playing time for kids who were not part of the regular offensive and defensive units. Special teams were a way to knit it all together, uniting the glamour chores with behind-the-scenes tasks, synching up sales with production. While Sherman graded a stack of midterm math papers spread across the bench, Nick gave the team a quick rundown on the importance of special teams. He patiently explained how games, particularly tight ones, can be decided by a few extra yards achieved on ball transition situations, kicking off, and punting. Nobody is going to blow us out, he told them, and it's not too likely we'll blow anyone out. The right chance or the wrong mistake can easily be what it comes down to. They'd heard it all before, from Pruitt and Pop Warner coaches before that. Yet now they appeared to be listening. Nick held a clipboard as he spoke, which he now consulted in order to read off the list of names.

"Terry Clayton. Chris DiNuncio. James Walsh . . ."

There was muttering among the Bobcats. Nick kept reading.

"Joe Turlock. Dennis O'Keefe, Marty Richfield." These were second-stringers, third-stringers, no stringers. Yet these were also kids who'd come to every practice and worked hard. These were not the ones to run for touchdowns, or make the timely tackle. These were, however, exactly the kids we needed to reward; there were a lot more of them than there were the others.

"Any questions?"

The question many had was: why, just when we're putting together a winning streak, why are we now experimenting with kids who, frankly, were not the fastest, strongest, biggest we had?

James Mulanovitz, for example, was a big-eared, rotund senior who'd been called Tubby so often he actually answered to the nickname. He took nearly eight full seconds to run the fifty-yard dash, and by the time he got there, wherever there was, he was too exhausted to do more than catch his breath. Having a player like James on the team had its positives. He was outgoing and fun, and if you needed someone to pick on, as groups of boys often did, better it be someone like James whose essential good nature kept the taunting from turning cruel and who, amazingly, kept coming back for more. But inserting him in the lineup, even if it was just the special teams? How come? What for? Why now?

Perfectly valid questions. And the reason nobody dared come forward to ask them was another measure of Nick's impact: these second-stringers were their teammates, and the Bobcats were a team.

The drizzle held off until nearly the end of practice. The sky was a thickening quilt of dark gray clouds. There was a dank chill in the air; snow would almost be a relief. Nick blew his whistle. Call it a day. The players, muddied and puffing hard, trotted off to change.

Sherman shut his leather satchel and joined Nick on the walk to the lot. Rounding the corner of the bleachers, they were intercepted (accosted would be a better description) by Earl Muntch. Muntch's left eye displayed a nasty black and purple shiner, and there was prominent bruise lower on the cheekbone.

"Hope the other guy looks worse," Sherman said.

"Domestic dispute."

"Thought you were single."

"For good reason."

Muntch tagged along, keeping pace. "Bobcats looking pretty good," he said. "My sources tell me you're running some old Notre Dame plays."

Sherman scowled. "Sources? Geez, Earl, you've been watching too much TV."

They arrived at the parking lot. Nick's car was nearest. The drizzle finally started, cold plump droplets that couldn't wait any longer to fall.

"I want to interview you," said Muntch.

"Nick's not much on bragging," interceded Sherman. "If that's what you're after."

"All I'm after is an interview. People're curious as heck. Anyway, humble and shy makes a darn good story. In capable hands."

Nick opened his car door and lowered himself into the seat. "Tell you what. After the championship game. It'll be a better story then."

Earl Muntch was an odd duck. Like a lot of guys steeped in a sports culture that shamelessly extols boldness on the field while encouraging couch-potato passivity at home, Earl was both hardened skeptic and eager believer, nonconformist as well as sycophant. Originally from Toledo, he was forever trying to extricate himself from Longview, sending a regular flurry of resumes to every promising opening posted in Editor & Publisher. Yet he also fit right in. We'd even taken to teasing him that he was starting to display early warning signs of being a Longview lifer. It was an enjoyable joke, even if the joke was on us.

"You really think the Bobcats'll get to the Superbowl?"

"I do. And the players do too."

"Can I quote you?"

"Just say: your sources."

Pulling out, Nick swung by the turnaround in front of the school. Clusters of students who'd stayed late for drama club, computer lab, or makeup exams, lingered beneath the concrete overhang, keeping dry until their rides arrived. Nick switched on the defrost and, when the windshield cleared, there was Brian crossing the road, blithely unaware of an oncoming vehicle.

Nick braked, tapped the horn, zipped down the window. "Give you a lift?"

Brian loped around to the passenger side and climbed in.

Nick tailed the line of other departing cars along Flint Road. Brian stared out the window, tapping his fingers on the armrest as though keeping time to rock and roll.

They stopped at the red light at Vernon.

"Where to?" Nick asked.

"Bowling alley."

"No homework?"

"Drop me here if it rubs you the wrong way."

They were suddenly blasted by the raw metallic roar of an unmuffled eight-cylinder engine pulled tight beside them at the stoplight. It was the black Buick with the jagged bolts of flame spray-painted on its sides, slipped into neutral with the motor gunning, an icon of automotive menace.

The driver of the car was familiar to Nick from the their exchange at the O-P. Fritz Bolton's long straight hair was pushed back with a headband. He leaned his head out the window and made a surly puckering gesture toward Brian. The light turned green, and the Buick thundered away.

"That," Nick said, pointing to the Buick, "is why your mom wants you to go to college." They drove in silence, past the Department of Natural Resources Water Inspection facility and Tolson Brothers' lumberyard.

"Alley's up there," said Brian. "Just behind Phil's."

"You're smart enough. Smart enough to know it'd be damn stupid not to."

Nick steered the Grand Prix onto the dirt access road by Phil's Auto Body. A giant neon bowling pin, yellow, blue, and white, marked the parking lot entrance. The windowless building looked like a warehouse. Outside, several teenagers were smoking cigarettes. Nick pulled up short of the group.

Brian grabbed his backpack off the floor of the car. "Thanks, coach. For all the wise counseling."

It could have been a caustic remark. As Brian opened the passenger door, Nick thrust his arm sideways across Brian's torso, pinning him backward like a steel safety bar on an amusement park thrill ride.

Nick stared hard to make sure Brian was listening. "My dad was a sonofabitch. I was angrier than you'll ever be. Want to know what I learned?"

Brian's smooth cheeks reflected the pulsating colors of the neon bowling pin. He said nothing.

"Bastard wasn't worth it. That's what I learned. Wasn't worth the anger, wasn't worth all the dumb things I did to prove I didn't give a shit."

Brian considered this a moment. "Why you telling me?"

Nick retracted his arm. "Because I'm not your dad."

As Nick pulled away, Brian turned up his collar and loped over to the group of kids, his homies. From a pale girl with red earmuffs, he accepted a cigarette and leaned forward with cupped hands to protect the proffered match from the wind. He took a drag, then sauntered back in the direction of Phil's.

It was cold, heading down to freezing according to the forecasts. Brian lingered beneath the neon bowling pin. He blew a smoke ring. Remarkably, it lifted in the frigid air without losing its shape. When it finally dispersed, high over Phil's, Brian sucked deeply and exhaled another perfectly formed halo.

Leaving the alley lot, Nick noticed some papers on the floorboard that must have spilled from Brian's backpack. Thinking it might be important, he pulled to the gravel shoulder. But it wasn't home-work. It was about a dozen pages, stapled together, with writing and graphics, almost spastically laid out. Best as he could tell, it was a mock-up – or perhaps the real thing – of some kind of literary magazine. "LoNGNG #3" was written on the cover page.

Poems, short stories, sketches, crudely reproduced photo-graphs. The authors wrote under pen names drawn from a culture Nick knew nothing of. SwampGrl, BackRim, Venom44XX. Nick thumbed through it, transfixed.

"Peel the pale skin off my chest. Make sure your hands are clean. Probe with your wild bloodshot eyes the tender muck of who I am. And please, please, please act like you care. I, my pet, would do the same for you."

Nick had to squint to read it. "I am a perfectly gorgeous blend of color and light and sound and spirit and meaning possessing great political significance that will soothe this rotten world and if you disagree, if you dare question this obvious fact, then you my friend have but one choice and you must act on it without hesitation: strip off my clothes and strip off yours and come my way. I am one gor-geous artform. I am an artform and do not give one fuck what the critics say."

What would become of kids like this who felt life so intensely?

Sadly, we all knew the answer. They'd have to grow out of it.

CHAPTER 21

....

S econd week in November, and the word filtered out that Made
Right was holding its own. Pre-Christmas orders of our lightweight women's suit coats were unexpectedly high, and overall orders were running six percent above the year before. It
was a figure that might not astound Wall Street analysts, if they
could be bothered, and was hardly cause for celebration even by
Jeremy Jr., who knew, although he held his cards close, that it would
take more output than that to stabilize our precarious situation.

Nonetheless, it was a number that mattered.

It mattered to shopkeepers and merchants and tradesmen
and professionals who dearly wanted to believe what they'd heard
about the vaunted ripple effect of consumer confidence. It mattered
to civic leaders and clergy and realtors and medical practitioners
who knew more than they could officially admit concerning our
near total dependence on the health and viability of Made Right.
It mattered to those of us working at the plant who, lacking a data-
driven prospectus to forecast our prospects or illuminate our futil-
ity, needed a number, any number, to latch onto. And it mattered to
Nick, who strove to instill in every man and woman on the floor a
recognition that six percent was a whole lot better than no percent,
and could well be an upward trend. "Shoulder to the boulder", he'd

exclaim in a voice that was equal parts work gang foreman and car-nival barker. "Six percent and rising. We're moving the sucker up the hill!"

We'd just completed another successful on-time shipment to our current biggest account, Valley Air, and the mood was almost celebratory. As EJ Leonard put it, "Difference between the Titanic and a cruise ship, in terms of spirit."

We were reality-based in our outlook and took a bullheaded pride in being that way. Our default position was to assume, perhaps defen-sively, a reality that was more likely to disappoint than not. We enjoyed diversion as much as anyone, all those Hollywood blockbusters (yes, like *Rudy*) with handsome actors dramatizing the impossible uphill triumphs of good-hearted underdog souls. But we could never forgot that they were fiction. We never suspended our disbelief. We weren't dreamers except deep in slumber when we couldn't help it.

Pep talks, even those delivered by Coach Pruitt, no slouch when it came to stirring oratory, were water off the proverbial duck's back to us. We'd heard it all, or versions of it, and were effectively numb. A few years ago, Junior had convened a rare mandatory-attendance meeting for all employees to discuss how the company was doing (poorly), and why (offshore competition), and what might be done to improve the downward spiral (work harder, faster).

The fact that this meeting was held during working factory hours made a very loud statement about the importance Junior placed on it. At the end of the session, which was conducted on the main floor with chairs and benches arranged for a town meeting type of effect, Jeremy had everyone watch a video. It was projected on a huge monitor he'd rented for the occasion, situated beneath the overhang by the vending machines. The video was of a speech by Lou Holtz, the head football coach of Notre Dame. The camera showed a close-up of Holtz's lean and boyish face as he recounted how his squad, against the odds, came back from a 17-point defi-cit in the fourth to beat favored USC. As the game clock wound down, as the score tightened, as Holtz's players increasingly began to believe that, yes, they could do it, the video would cut away to the audience attending the speech. But the cutaway shots to the Holtz audience only underscored all the ways that our problems at Made Right were in a whole different league, and a lot harder to fix. The crowd viewed on the video was dressed in smart suits, white-collar professional all the way. They looked as different as Martians from us in our sweatshirts and jeans and Dacron blouses. The subtext, which Jeremy might have been too self-absorbed to notice, was brutally obvious: the valuable truths expressed by Holtz did not apply to people sunk in a predicament as dire as ours.

Afterward, Jeremy wanted to know what we thought the message was, what were the video's take-away points. Ashong's hand shot up. "Shouldn't bet against Notre Dame," he said. "That's what I got out of it."

Words were insufficient. Nick knew that. What was needed, and here he was in agreement with Coach Holtz, was an all-out, unconditional effort by all able bodies all the time. Nick arrived at work earlier now, as early as 5 a.m. He stayed later, returning most afternoons after football practice and remaining until nine in the evening or beyond. He made a point of having direct personal conversation with every worker at least once a week to check how we were doing, to ask what we might need, to let us know we were being watched, but in a good way, not surveillance. He was in the trenches, more deeply entrenched than most if we stopped to think about it. When we were shorthanded at shipping or the serge machines needed another pair of hands or a logjam flared up between stations, he'd hustle over soon as he was notified, like an Army inductee reporting for duty.

"What's the problem?" he'd asked Larry Ricks, a vaguely Polynesian-looking man with short legs and tattooed arms.

"The usual. Too much work, too few hands."

"What can I do?"

It took Larry a moment to understand that the question was not some boss man's mockery. Larry pointed to an empty dolly of the last bundles delivered to him and before he knew it Nick had whisked it away. A few minutes later, he returned carting a new stack of linings.

Larry turned to EJ. "Gotta be some catch."

"Catch is," replied EJ, "Dude wants to win."

Second week in November, the Chamber of Commerce held another of its monthly luncheons. Usually scheduled the third week of every month, this one was moved up due to multiple conflicts (Arch's youngest daughter was getting married that weekend in Louisville and many would be driving down early to attend) and the following week was complicated by Thanksgiving and conceivably – fingers crossed – the Superbowl.

The site for this gathering was Spaghetti's, the Italian restaurant out Arrowhead owned by an actual Italian couple. There were no guest speakers. Just updates and schmooze. Todd Whelton gave a brief report on relevant economic "data" from the Ohio Bureau of Economic Development.

"The good news," he enthused, "is that there really isn't any bad news. No business closings in the past six months and – knock wood – this year could be the first in almost a decade without any. Of course there aren't that many of us left," Todd added, eliciting an edgy chuckle. "But those of us still in business? Hey, we're hanging tough."

He cited a survey, this from the U.S. Chamber of Commerce, stating that most businesses that fail tend to do so within their first year and that businesses of more than four years duration were, like cancer survivors, less vulnerable to failure with each passing year. It was an unfortunate analogy and Todd probably should not have said it. It was just one of those formulations that came to him on the spur of the moment. He'd attended a regional Toastmasters conference last spring, down in Wheeling, where the focus had been on improvisation as a technique to counterbalance the stiffness and anxiety that can result from adhering to a prepared text. Todd, for all of his good intentions, was an exceedingly drab platform speaker – he had the bad habit of peering downward as though he were reading notes even when he wasn't – and this litany of economic data from government reports, even when heartening, was hardly the stuff to make an audience want to stand up and cheer.

"Question," shouted out Bo Renaldo, the owner of Spaghetti's. "Any news about the tree lighting? I mean, we still hoping to get a celebrity or something?"

Todd looked for elucidation to Arch Robinson, who had nothing to offer, then he glanced at Jeremy Jr., seated a few feet away at the head table.

"Working on it," Jeremy responded as he twirled several strands of spaghetti on his upraised fork. "It remains a contingency." This was met by a chorus of grumbling. "By contingency," Jeremy hastily clarified, "I mean a long shot. I hope I don't need to remind you that we businesspeople cannot afford to rely on long shots."

Todd saw where this was going and sought to rescue the moment. "No closings in six months, you have to admit, was a long shot. And guess what? We made it!"

Second week in November, and the Bobcats were 6-1. Marie, reluctant to acknowledge football as a factor, had to admit that the household was happier. Brian was pitching in more with the small domestic chores that made her life easier, emptying the dishwasher, changing the water filter, hauling the garbage out to the street for Tuesday pickup. More importantly, he was buckling down to his studies. One evening, she overheard him mumbling aloud in his room and it turned out he was practicing an oral presentation for Spanish class. A trend? She hoped so. On school mornings, he'd arise without any of the obligatory nagging and arrive at the breakfast table with a book. Speaking of books, she'd recently spotted a few, hardbacks with Dewey decimal codes stenciled on their spines.

When she'd asked, instead of his typically minimalist response, Brian told her he was writing a paper on the Scopes trial. He disclosed not just the fact that he was writing this paper, but what the paper was actually about! Did she know that Scopes, the poor rural science teacher, had actually lost his case? No, she was thrilled to admit, tell me about it. And so he did, enthusiastically.

Monday morning, second week in November, the Veteran's Day holiday. Lou dropped by unannounced. Unannounced but not a complete surprise, as Marie had spotted him from the living room window while watching for Nick to drive up. It was a school holiday and one of the nine official paid calendar holidays conceded by Made Right. They'd planned a day trip to a country estate auction.

Beer was on Lou's breath. "How's my tailback?" he bellowed.

Brian emerged from his room, zipping his letter jacket, and Lou made a show of hunching over as though bracing for a tackle. "Big game Saturday, kid."

"We're high school kids, Gramps. Get a life."

Indignant, Lou threw up his arms in disgust. "Who teaches these kids?" Then, facing Brian, "I have a wonderful life, thank you. It becomes a little more wonderful when the Bobcats are on a winning streak. Tell me what's wrong with that."

Brian did not deign to answer. "I'm going to Will's to study," he said, hoisting his school backpack.

A month ago, Marie would have understood that to be the lamest of cover stories; covering for what, she hadn't the foggiest. Now she beamed with pride.

"Attaboy," Lou loudly saluted. "Football's not everything."

Brian grunted and left.

"Just nerves," said Lou.

"You're a lot of help."

"What time's he picking you up?"

"Any minute."

"Bet Nick's the sort who's on time."

Marie nodded.

"Ask you a favor?"

Marie rolled her eyes to put him on warning that it better be reasonable.

Lou plopped onto the sofa. He struggled to appear grave but the beer was undermining his performance. He slumped backward, then jerked upright, overcompensating. "Fellows at the Legion Hall been on me about this. They really would like to meet Nick. In person. I told 'em he's one of these no-nonsense, all business types. And kind of on the shy side."

"Nick's not shy. He just doesn't make a fetish of reliving the past."

"What makes you think . . . ?"

"That your Legion buddies would want to talk to Nick about his glory days playing football at Notre Dame? Did I leap to a wrong conclusion?"

"You did."

"Correct me."

"The fellows at the hall are multi . . . what's the term? . . . multi . . ."

"Dimensional?"

"Bingo!"

"Sure they are, Daddy. They can talk about the weather, sports. Hmm. Let's see. Did I omit anything?"

"World history, for one."

"Like the wars they were in? Or almost in?" She was not sure why she was giving him such a hard time. Her dad was only being who he'd always been, and he was only asking for what anyone in his situation would ask for: just a little something special, some special acknowledgement, no matter how silly, no matter how superficial, to invigorate the monotony of life.

"It's Veteran's Day," Lou protested. "Give me a break. What I'm thinking is if Nick could pop by, just pop by and say hello. Guys made me promise to ask."

Outside, Nick's car horn sounded and Marie pranced away. "I'll ask," she consented, and grabbed her red jacket with the fake fur collar and scooted out the door.

There was an estate auction over in Ferris that started at 2 p.m. Marie had learned of it from a nurse practitioner acquaintance who dabbled in fair weather flea markets. A homestead that had been continuously occupied by members of the same family since the late nineteenth century was changing hands. An estate's biography was always a clue to what you might expect to find. According to the nurse practitioner, who had it on good account from a partner in the Haynesville law firm that was handling the property sale and administering the auction, the Hunt family were railroad people (always a good sign) who'd come to the region in the 1870's from Philadelphia (another promising sign) and prospered between the world wars. There'd been spinster sisters (also promising) and a talented if peculiar grandson who became an inventor responsible for several patents that were acquired by Proctor and Gamble. He passed away in July, and it was his son and daughter, now located in California, who were liquidating.

Marie was not the only woman in Longview who was into antiques, but she had typically taken it to another level, one that suited her personal interests and distinguished her from pedestrian dealers and collectors. In our opinion, the stuff she acquired and ostensibly improved was pretentious, a waste of money even at the rock-bottom prices only an idiot would pay. That said, the items were interesting in an offbeat way.

She did not have a specific checklist of items she was seeking. To her mind, expectations were blinders. Even when she came away empty-handed she found that her time had been spiced with pleasant surprises. How many situations could deliver that? What she sought were neglected objects she could refashion and resell. How she went about it was to wander and drift. She was fond of the saying – we'd all heard her quote it some time or another – that when you do not know precisely where you're going, any road will get you there. Sounded to us like a lame excuse for not getting what you wanted, and a pretty good excuse at that. We made mental note to use it ourselves if occasion arose.

Nick drove the back roads carving west, then traced the river along a ridge that offered a panoramic view of golden fields of empty corn stalks in the sun.

"You're kind of quiet," Nick said.

Marie had not been aware of it. "Sorry."

The next thing she said, a good ten minutes later, was, "Up at that church, turn right."

"You sure?"

"No, I'm not sure. So long as we have gas in the tank . . ."

He squinted at the dashboard. "Oh my god!" But he was joking.

The church was in the middle of nowhere. It was an old white wooden structure with a steeple, the kind of erect and virtuous design that presides over manicured village greens in New England hamlets that attract leaf-peepers in the fall. Nick turned right at Marie's direction onto what turned out to be a long private drive-way through a magnificent grove of birches. Golden leaves still fluttered from many of the branches. The papery bark of the trunks was the shiny white of fresh paint.

They came into a clearing. The Hunt home was a three-story Victorian structure with a wraparound porch and a pair of second-floor dormers. Near the barn was a billowing white tent, open at the sides.

Nick followed another car through an old cattle gate and across a rutted field that was already filled with vans and pickup trucks. Getting out, they heard an announcement cackling over a PA system. Marie grabbed his hand to hurry him along. Her eagerness was palpable and it took Nick a moment to figure out what this reminded him of, this gathering expectation, this sense of impending action. It was like the scene outside a football stadium, with streaming fans hastened by the thrill of what was to come. "You can run ahead," he told her.

She tightened her grip on his hand and slowed her pace.

As they came beneath the tent, an auctioneer with a nasal twang was midstream in an announcement. It was a sunny day and there was a sudden coolness as they came into the shade. The ground was moist with trampled grass and black earth. The tent layout resembled that of a gothic church, with a raised platform at the far end for the auctioneer and his assistant, surrounded by a mass of vases, mirrors, armchairs, dining tables, all tagged with auction numbers. Rows of folding chairs filled the center of the tent.

The seats were about half full. Marie grabbed a bidder number and a program of stapled pages and settled near the front. Nick had no way to assess the prices of items, or whether they were worth what the people were bidding. Was $125 for a set of delicate china teacups and matching porcelain tray a bargain or abuse? He guessed the latter, and then a young man in a charcoal fleece offered $150 without blinking.

Marie had her eye on several thick glass railway signal lenses. The bidding on these was not scheduled until later in the auction. Nick asked how high she was willing to go for them. They seemed like items that would be routinely trashed.

"Whatever it takes."

"You're kidding. Will anyone else even be interested?"

"I'm hoping no. A shrewd eye for the unwanted. That's my strength. That's my game plan."

"What if they're unwanted for good reason?"

Marie had no patience with such dubious reasoning. The items of obvious value were beyond her budget. And besides, what was the challenge in pursuing what everyone else was drawn to?

The auctioneer was a man about Lou's age who wore a grandiose stovepipe hat and red suspenders, and sported a deftly twirled handlebar moustache that added to his aura. He signaled to an assistant for help and the pair hoisted the carved wooden headboard of a bed onto the auction platform. Marie checked her program.

"A genuine Shaker four poster," declared the auctioneer. "Number 16. Let's start at an even number. One hundred dollars.

CHAPTER TWENTY-ONE

One hundred dollars for this . . ."

"You're going to need a bed," Marie said.

"Have I told you I'm a mattress-on-the-floor kind of guy?"

"Have I told you I'm a four-poster type of girl?"

"One hundred!" he heard himself shout.

Nick got the bed, not at that price, but eventually. Marie bought a Douglas fir hallway door with an inset mirror (why? Nick knew better than to ask) but passed on the signal lenses. Astonishingly, there were other bidders. Some items, it turned out, were not unwanted enough.

The bed and the mirrored door would be transported, Marie assured him, by one of Lou's legion buddies who was more or less in the moving business.

"Which reminds me . . . My dad? It would mean a lot to him if you could stop by the Legion Hall tonight. Just to say hello to the guys."

Nick cringed, "It's not my thing."

"As a favor to him? Some things are easiest, Nick, and a lot less painful, if you get them over with sooner. You're just like Brian."

"Meaning?"

"Meaning you wish people would just leave you alone sometime. Nothing wrong with that . . . except it ain't gonna happen."

On the drive back from the auction, they stopped at a log cabin road-house tucked in the woods. It was one of those rural gems, lit by neon beer signs, known only to people who'd been there before. There were but a half-dozen people in the joint. Joey's Lounge, it was called.

Waiting for supper – burgers and beer – Marie fed quarters into a glowing juke box that played actual 45's. They leaned over the glass hood, warmed by its interior lights, and watched the mechanical arm fetch the black vinyl platter from the back shelf and slip it precisely onto the twirling turntable.

Marie jingled a quarter in her palm. "You want to choose?"

"Anything's fine," he said. "So long as I've heard it before."

She found the Hank Williams tune, *So Lonesome I Could Cry*. Their song. They had become a bona fide couple with a history that was growing every day. On the warped floorboards beside their booth, they swayed to the languid steel guitar. Their waitress waited politely as they danced. She had a cigarette tucked above her ear. Her hair was a bright cartoon orange. When the music stopped, she said that they made such a nice couple, the next round would be on the house. Anticipating their protest, she shrugged and nodded to the bar tender, a big old smiling bear of a man with a plaid shirt and eye patch. The offer, she implied, came straight from upper management.

"That there's Joey," she said, as she brought over two more drafts. "People think he's my old man but he ain't. And he ain't gonna be."

CHAPTER **22**

The Longview American Legion hall contained the basic features of a private gentleman's club – comfortable sofas, card tables and a ready deck, cable TV and a bar with private stock. Yet it would never be confused with one of those sleek martini lounges tucked in the shadows of urban financial districts where revved-up professionals water-hole after a frenetic day of insider trading. Business at the hall pretty much meant no business whatsoever. Nobody came here to further their career or for self-improvement. The hall was a cave, a retreat, an isolation tank. It embraced the aimlessness and languor of a remote tropical outpost. All it lacked was ocean, sand, sun, and bodies that would be halfway presentable in a swimsuit.

It was not, however, without its comforts and refinements. We had carpeting. The cushioned armchairs were upholstered in a thick leathery material and there was a tropical fish tank that cast an eerie turquoise shimmer across the pool table and cue rack. Old Glory was spread across the wall behind the bar alongside a black flag with gold lettering that warned not to forget our MIAs. The bar itself was a convincing facsimile of polished walnut, and long enough for eight stools. The sign on the bathroom door read, "Please Don't Eat the Urinal Cakes." If you didn't find this funny you'd be better off somewhere else.

There'd been a significant drop in American Legion membership nationally but ours was holding steady with regular participation by a couple of dozen guys, including some younger fellows who'd served in recent campaigns in Panama, Grenada, and the Persian Gulf. About the only time the hall was vacant was Christmas morning; by suppertime on December 25, attendance was generally back to normal.

Nick chose to park a block away on North Sycamore. The windowless cobalt door gave the place an off-limits speakeasy quality and Nick opened it as gingerly as a cat burglar.

Lou accosted him before he had time to let go of the doorknob. "Boys are in a mellow mood," he informed Nick. Gesturing to the TV perched high atop a sort of jerry-rigged duck blind above the bar, he added, "Georgia Tech and LSU don't exactly get our juices flowing."

"Not like the Fightin' Irish!" A hollow-cheeked fellow with greasy gray hair hanging from a Cincinnati Reds cap rose unsteadily from his armchair, beer in hand, to let Nick know who'd said it.

"Nick," said Lou. "Meet Rip Royston."

Soon Nick was surrounded like a pinup blonde at a bachelor party. Guys scurried over to shake his hand and exchange scraps of small talk. Compliment him on the job he was doing at Made Right and suggest lineup adjustments for the Bobcats. Drop the name of a guy they'd known in Nam who'd played with him, or so they thought. Although some pretended to be above it, we were as inclined as anyone to be smitten by fame, and our geographical isolation may have made us more susceptible, not less. In the late 1950's, the TV cowboy Gene Autry came through town for reasons nobody could recall. Even though the gunslinging crooner stayed but two hours to grab a full meal at the Ohio (yes, the Ohio back then was perfectly suitable), it was still talked about by the few of us who claimed to have seen him. It was like some trickle-down form of religious faith, this belief that out there somewhere was a world of consequence and to touch it, even momentarily, could lift a body to a better place.

"Fifteen minutes," Nick warned Lou as he was being escorted to the lounge area. "Then I gotta split."

"The Purdue game," nudged Rip, putting down his beer to show respect. "Fourth quarter. What? Two minutes left? Boilermakers get one more first down and you guys are toast. What was it like for you then?"

"I was offense."

"On the sideline. I mean. You need possession to have a shot and there they go, marchin' down the field, eatin' up the clock."

"Hey, that was a long time ago, fellas."

Some guys figured Nick was simply toying with them, ratcheting up the suspense a bit before launching into a dramatic retelling. Isn't that what storytellers did, especially sports guys, slowly build the tension before spinning out a gripping yarn?

"How about that first half you had against the Spartans?" urged Herm Rhinehaus, who everyone called Rhino. Tall, square-shouldered, with the same buzz cut he'd favored in high school (although now gray, not blonde), Herm had served during the Korean War, but mostly in Europe. "You had what, something like 134 yards in 14 carries? One of the best performances in a single half ever?"

We tilted toward Nick, awaiting his response. He folded and unfolded his hands, like a wary suspect interrogated by an array of law enforcement agencies. Finally, he muttered, "Big holes in that line. Anybody could've."

We exchanged knowing smirks, privately pleased. It only heightened our admiration to learn that Nick was big-time humble, like all the great ones should be. Still, we would have liked to have more from the horse's mouth.

Rhino put it into words for everyone. "Not like those hot dogs today, playing with their dicks every time they do one dang thing right."

We had a good yuck over that, slapping five all around (Nick declined) and hoisting a toast to football as it was played like it was meant to be played and all the vanishing virtues that the game, and Nick as its living symbol, represented.

Nick stood to leave.

"Whoa there!" yelped Lou, bouncing up faster than we thought he could in order to block Nick's path. Nick wheeled on him, but swiftly checked himself. It was no mystery that Nick and Marie were having a fling – as if Lou was about to keep that one a secret! There was bound to be simmering tension between them.

"It's late guys," Nick said. "I'm a working man."

"Come on," Lou encouraged. "How about Penn State? Where your knee got busted and you gutted it out. Gaining what, another sixty-three yards? On a bum knee."

Lou followed Nick outside. The night was clear and nippy, approaching frost conditions. Folks were talking about an early winter.

"There now," said Lou with a patronizing edge. "That wasn't so bad."

"Says who?"

Nick kept walking up the block towards his car. Lou kept pace. They arrived at the Grand Prix.

"This weekend," Lou said, "my nephew from Cleveland?"

"What?"

"My nephew's boy, remember? The one named after you, sort of? He's having such troubles in school and . . . "

"Are you crazy?"

"They're driving down Saturday. A few words from you . . . "

Nick grabbed Lou's shoulders. "Enough! Geez! Enough already!" He quickly relinquished Lou but he was furious.

"The kid, he idolizes you."

"He doesn't even know me, you old fool."

"Damn good thing he doesn't," Lou sputtered. Before Nick could disappear completely into his car, Lou added, "Maybe Tuna's right about you after all."

Nick froze, the car door still open. "About what?"

"Stuff."

"Like what exactly?"

"Says he knows why you were fired in California."

CHAPTER TWENTY-TWO

"The plant shut down."

"Back at Notre Dame. Police report concerning a cheerleader?"

Nick slammed the car door and gunned the engine. He careened into the Made Right lot on two screaming wheels, pulled to the curb, and bolted out. It was all instinct now, responding to the oncoming pressure without necessarily seeing it.

The Made Right guard booth was a glass-windowed hutch that threw a long rectangle of light into the surrounding darkness. Nobody ever came around on holiday evenings and the only reason Made Right bothered with an on-duty guard had to do with insurance stipulations. Tuna was deep into his girlie magazines, which he boasted of never buying for the articles. On that, we believed him.

He slid open the booth window, and peered down at Nick. "Help you?"

"Don't fuck with me, Tuna."

The smug dude holding all the cards was another role Tuna had essentially memorized from cop shows. He arched his eyebrows with feigned naiveté. "Scuse me?"

"This job, this life – don't fuck it up for me, Tuna." Nick threw his shoulder against the booth's vinyl side, rocking the entire structure. "You hear me?"

....

A voluptuous firecracker, vivacious in spirit and appearance, Brenda tended to dress in tight clothes of fabrics that shimmered even in the subdued light of the factory floor where she'd worked since graduating Longview High nearly twelve years ago. Guys went out of their way, way out of their way, to pass by her work station, and she knew it. Had she not been such a motivated, reliable, productive, exemplary worker, continually meeting or exceeding her output benchmarks, there might have been some attempt by management to suppress her flamboyance. Instead, she was treasured as a local quirk, like the soap bubbles, that humanized our hard-driving production schedules and relieved, if only for the duration of a quick peek at her bust line, the drudgery of the work.

Nick had to watch himself around her. She'd chewed him out early on, right to his face with others watching, for a perceived infraction. Something to do with him getting one of the stitching gals (these were all women) to relocate temporarily from collars to sleeves. Brenda felt that Nick made it sound less like a request and more like a command. She had no reluctance to step forward and give Nick, or anyone, an earful. Plus, the energy she threw off as she bobbed rhythmically at her machine was so palpably sexual that Nick was afraid to even glance her way for fear of accusations. This morning after Veteran's Day, he only noticed her because she was angrily barking a complaint. At Ashong, as it turned out.

"No, no, no, no no!" she shouted.

Nick was not eager to intervene but obligated to at least investigate.

"You ain't hearing me!" Brenda insisted, her hand jerking emphatically at her ear for emphasis.

Ashong seemed every bit as defensive as Nick would be. "I looked up the repair history. We'll get you a replacement. We've asked the machinist to come in tonight. S'all I can do."

"All I can do. All I can do," she repeated mockingly, playing to our growing gallery of onlookers. "Might as well hang a dang sign round your neck: All I can do."

Nick's presence gave Ashong an excuse to break away.

"What's up?" Nick asked.

"Give that girl an education, she'd be running the world. And it probably would be a better world," he added.

Ashong escorted Nick back to his cubbyhole office. Rumor had it that a deal with the Koreans was going down, and lately the rumor had been coming on with heightened intensity and a shortening lag time between updates, like labor pains. A news item in the Gazette last Friday, quoting sources at Made Right, made mention of a "strategic partnership" being developed with "international" interests. We understood that the source could only be one of the Ziglars since anyone else on the inside – if there was anyone else on the inside – would be summarily fired for leaking such information. "Strategic partnership" was one of those nebulous phrases that was probably popular in the business sector precisely for its lack of specific meaning. To us, it could have been a concept culled from astrology. The Gazette's source went on to reassure that the beauty (their word) of this new arrangement was that it would be, quote, a win-win situation.

We knew the score. In due time we would discover the details concerning how this new strategic partnership with a multinational manufacturing enterprise located in a country famous for preposterously low wages and impossibly high productivity might affect our individual circumstances. It would then be our burden to try and make the best of it. There was a name for that kind of situation, but it wasn't win-win. It was more like awaiting the results of a biopsy.

Ashong pulled a newspaper from the top drawer of his desk and handed it to Nick, pointing to an article on the folded underside of page one.

"Meeting of the Ohio Manufacturing Council last weekend," Ashong added, in case Nick needed to know the context.

Nick took a minute to peruse the article. "So?"

"Paper quotes Jeremy using the word 'dinosaur'. In reference to guess who. Nick, you mind if I use a football analogy?"

"It's not necessary."

"He says if dinosaurs could've known what was coming down, they'd have changed their habits. Now I'm no biologist . . . "

"Paleontologist."

"Whatever. Point is, you got players busting their butts on the field and here he goes . . . Listen, it would only be Junior shooting his mouth off except for the Korean thing. We know something's going down. We know it's going to have an impact. We worry that whatever it is, it ain't gonna be good. Least not for everyone. We're not animals in a zoo, and we sure ain't dinosaurs."

"You're getting way ahead of yourself, Isaac. Way ahead."

"Then tell me, what do you know?"

"I don't."

Ashong rolled his eyes, unconvinced. "You're in the dark, like us? That's what you're telling me?"

"I only know what you know, and what we've all always known."

"And that is?"

"That is . . . "

A loud popping noise, like a slightly muffled firecracker, burst above the machine clatter, followed quickly by a piercing shriek. Nick sprang up, Ashong tight on his heels. Beneath the mezzanine,

back by the steam presses, Ray Long, Robby Harris, and Brenda
were hunkered by the steam tunnel. That this was not Brenda's
work area was a clue that whatever was happening had something
to do with her. That, and the identity of the gunman.

A young man we all knew, all except Nick that is, held a small
silver pistol in his outstretched hand. The grease-stained barn
jacket he wore appeared several sizes too large. He seemed to be
waving the gun more to display it menacingly than aim it at anyone in particular. A shot had been fired; there did not immediately
appear to be anyone wounded. At least nobody was huddled on the
floor. Or bleeding. In fact, it was very, very quiet.

"Drake." Ashong spoke the man's name as calmly as he could.
"What's up, fella?"

Harlan Drake had been laid off a few months back, just before
Nick started at Made Right. A lunchtime going-away party had
been held for him on one of those sweltering late August afternoons. Except Drake never really went away. We would occasionally
spot him in the parking lot after the day shift, joshing with some of
the guys, shooting the breeze, possibly waiting to pick someone up.
Possibly Brenda? We hadn't paid much attention. There was something about him that discouraged curiosity. Why ask questions
when you'd rather not know the answers? He hadn't seemed like a
bad guy, just worn down and edgy. He had a broad face that verged
on handsome except his eyes were like tiny black BBs and too close
together. He was of middling height, maybe 5'7", and muscle-bound,
a body builder. At the going-away affair there'd been talk, silver lining kind of stuff, about how he'd now have more time to devote to
the sport. If you wanted to call it a sport.

Drake eyed Ashong nervously, then Nick. Quickly, he retrained
his focus on Brenda. Robby and Ray slipped rapidly away. Drake
ignored them. Brenda tried the same.

"Don't," Drake snapped. "Don't try."

Brenda did not look flamboyant now. She look terrified, and
maybe that was the point.

It was weird. Many of us had known Drake much of his life. We didn't know him well, but knew him well enough. None of us believed he was capable of doing something as violent and dumb and basically suicidal as shooting someone in plain sight with witnesses everywhere. Yet isn't that what people always say about the deranged gunman afterward?

Brenda backpedaled, not taking her eyes off Drake, who stood five yards away. It was a showdown except only one party was armed. Then Nick made a forward move. Drake aimed the gun his way. Nick kept coming.

"Give it to me," Nick said, struggling to sound calm. It was a gambit from countless TV dramas, always in situations where the outcome was roughly foretold by the tenor of the background music. Even on those rare occasions when the good guy bit the dust, it was only entertainment.

No music playing now. There remained a chance this would unfold as a horribly stupid yet essentially victimless act committed by a fundamentally reasonable guy having an especially rotten day. No harm, no foul. Not yet. What Nick was attempting seemed needlessly provocative, and reckless, and wrong.

The factory floor was by now vacant. All machines had stopped. The place was quieter than Made Right ever got during working hours. Those hiding in the far recesses, peering stealthily over thick bundles of fabric, were in no hurry to know what happened next. We wanted "next" to be a long, long time from now.

"Please give me the gun," Nick repeated. "Let it go now, and life can start again. Hopefully for the better."

Drake's face was a mask. His narrow eyes appeared more wistful than incensed. If rage is what had prompted him, it had seemingly vanished. Yet he still held the Kimber Compact and he was still aiming it. He did not have to be enraged or ragingly insane to activate a few minor muscles in his forefinger. A hiccup could do it.

Nick came another step. He reached out his hand.

"No cops?" Drake asked.

Nick moved closer still. "Not if I can help it." Christ! we thought. Tell Drake whatever the hell he wants to hear. This was no time to quibble.

Drake sheepishly handed over the handgun. And then he began to cry.

Nick took the pistol. Ashong poked out from behind the steam tunnel. Nick passed Ashong the weapon. Then, he put his arm around Drake, who stayed tucked against Nick's chest, whimpering like a child.

Perspiration gushed off Nick's forehead. His eyes dropped shut, like a monk in solemn prayer, even as he held Drake tight. Only then did we realize that what he'd done was far from second nature for him. He was drained, same as any of us would be. He wasn't Superman.

A couple of the guys who knew him best, Brewster and Rainey, escorted Drake outside, propping him up like he was an injured teammate being helped off the field. The threat effectively defused, we slowly began filtering back to the floor, cautiously emerging from behind a bank of giant fans that were being stored in the corner until warm weather returned. Ashong was the first to say anything and his tone caught us by surprise.

"That was one reckless dumb-ass move, man," he scolded Nick. "Real dumb."

Our guess was that Ashong was also still in a state of shock. Irritation at Nick was not what we felt. We surged forward to surround him, pat him on the back and show our thanks. Mostly, we wanted to hear Nick's version. Why'd he do it? What was he thinking? Did he detect some softening or indecision in Drake? How did he assess the risk? When did he know to make his move? That sort of thing. We knew that he was not big on rehashing his gridiron exploits, but this was different. It wasn't a game and it wasn't in the distant past. It had just occurred before our trembling gaze. We saw it, we felt it, we'd been in the heat of harm's way. The whiff of gunpowder lingered. The sharp pop of Drake's pistol still echoed in our ears. Our nerves still jangled. This was not some TV movie. This was no ESPN replay.

Why, we asked him?

What if?

Weren't you afraid?

What we wanted to know was: what if Drake with his finger on the trigger had done what, in a blink and a twitch, he might so easily have done? What about us?

Nick looked around at Ashong and Flora and EJ and the rest, blinking his eyes hard as if adjusting to a different light. A long dry sigh seeped from his chest and he finally said, "I don't know. I didn't think." His voiced faltered. When he spoke again, it was so soft we had to bunch even closer to hear him. "I didn't think. That's all."

Ashong was still upset. "Man, you could have got yourself shot."

We waited for a more detailed post event analysis from Nick, waited for his retrospective play-by-play of how he came to make the bold choice that champs always do. Or, how it was no big deal, how he simply acted the way anyone would. That would be certifiably untrue, yet we might, as passive observers, let it go at that.

Within an hour, Made Right was functioning normally. Workers who'd fled outside now stamped out their cigarettes and returned from the parking lot. The machines were soon humming again. Brenda was given the rest of the day off and advised to go someplace safe. Drake was told to go home.

The police were notified (this was not the sort of incident that could remain in-house). Charges would need to be brought and probably that was a good thing. Two officers were dispatched, just in case, to the walk-up apartment Drake shared with two others, over on lower Hackney Road, not too far from Nick's. Lieutenants Donahue and Estes knocked on the door. When there was no answer, they entered.

They found Drake seated in his living room with the TV tuned to a fishing program. They ordered him to stand but he didn't move. Cautiously circling the sofa, they saw blood covering what remained of his face.

CHAPTER TWENTY-THREE

"Self-inflicted" was how the wound was described in the official report.

The Gazette account told of Drake's "typical" childhood, his participation in the Boy Scouts, Little League, and Presbyterian church youth programs, his offensive line play with the Bobcats in the early 80's, his two year service in the Army, mostly at Fort Benning, Georgia, and the playful affection he was known to have lavished on his adored nieces and nephews. Jeremy Jr. was quoted as terming the incident "tragic and unfortunate," adding that the county offered an excellent retraining program for laid-off workers that Drake, for reasons known only to himself, had chosen to decline.

CHAPTER 24

··

ou, Salvy, and Salvy's son Nicky arrived at Made Right field a full twenty minutes before game time to secure prime seats as near as possible to the fifty-yard line. The temperature had peaked in the low 40's. The clammy metal bleachers amplified the chill. Lou and Salvy wore winter parkas and woolen caps. Nicky wore only a hooded black sweatshirt inscribed with silver lettering: SKRU U.

"What's that?" Lou had asked.

"The college I'm thinking of going to," Nicky answered smartly. It was about the first thing he'd said since arriving in Longview. Certainly the first thing he'd said without mumbling.

Lou was pleased to finally have a shot at engaging the sullen teen. "Tell me, what's the S-K-R-U stand for?"

Nicky poked his pale face from the cave of his dark hood. "You're shittin' me."

Salvy yanked his son admonishingly by the lip of his hood. "Thinks he knows everything," he apologized to Lou.

"Stage we all go through."

"Some never grow out of it. It happens."

Nicky tugged the hood further over his head and sat tapping his feet to his own private music.

"Meeting Nick'll do him a world of good," said Salvy.

"We'll play it by ear," said Lou.

Salvy Zanay was the oldest son of Lou's younger brother, Jack, a former Bobcat first stringer, offense and defense, who'd died young from a motorcycle accident. Salvy was Marie's first cousin. They had very little in common, a fact that was evident only on those rare occasions like weddings and funerals when the extended family was awkwardly mashed together and compelled to act fraternal and jolly. Even when they were kids, they had nothing in common. The fact that Salvy looked so much like Lou – same wide mouth, same kindly eyes, same broad forehead – was for Marie a bit uncomfortable. But family could be like that. Salvy worked in one of the building trades, though she could never remember which.

The night before, Salvy had driven down from Cleveland with Nicky, whose academic floundering was the ostensible reason for the trip. Nicky was Brian's age, although a year behind him in school. A year behind and falling rapidly farther. His father had tried everything to instill in Nicky a passion for football, which taught, Salvy was convinced, core lessons about perseverance and teamwork that not only assisted kids in their schoolwork but would benefit them throughout adulthood. His two older sons, Vince and Buddy, had played right through high school. Some of the most satisfying experiences of Salvy's life – more satisfying than the Browns' three-point victory over the Steelers in '86 – had been in the bleachers at his sons' games. Even when the boys played poorly or barely played at all, which happened periodically since neither was a star and their assigned slots, offensive line, were hardly glamour positions, Salvy still found himself more engaged, more absorbed, more into it, than with nearly anything else he'd ever been part of, including some unmentionables. And didn't Vince and Buddy both graduate high school and land good jobs afterward, one at Goodyear, the other on the ground crew at Jacobs Field?

Young Nicky, ironically, actually had athletic talent. Or so it once had seemed. From fourth grade through eighth, he'd been a Pop

Warner running back. It was a thrill for Salvy to finally watch his kid carry the ball and hear the voices of other parents shouting, as he himself had so often shouted, for his own son to go, go, go! The Kennedy High coach was a notorious hard-ass and had an old-style, three-yards-and-a-cloud-of-dust approach to offensive play. Freshmen year, Nicky was pegged for special teams. This didn't set well and Salvy had to have a talk with him. Everything about football, he told his son, even the disappointments, especially the disappointments, are a test. Life, Salvy had pointed out, is one long brutal test. One long football game, actually, when you get right down to it. Perform the role you are assigned and make sure that you do your best. "If you got what it takes," he promised his son, "you'll get your shot."

Salvy believed that. He didn't have a lot of evidence, but he did believe it.

Sophomore year, Nicky stuck it out. Due to an injury in the starting backfield, he got the chance to play the last two games of the season at blocking back. He never carried the ball, but he was getting closer.

This year, his junior season, after a summer of working with weights and running stairs while attending summer school math and English to maintain his academic eligibility, he hurt his shoulder during a late August practice. They took him to three ortho specialists, including an Iranian doctor who had some affiliation with the Cleveland Browns. They couldn't find a thing wrong with Nicky's shoulder and told him to just rest it. Which, it turned out, Nicky was quite happy to do.

Initially, even with the injury, he'd suited up and diligently gone to practices at Salvy's urging so he could remain part of the team in anticipation of a speedy return. The shoulder still hurt, Nicky insisted, and the discomfort was spreading down his arm and upper back. He had an MRI with contrast, a bone scan, intensive physical therapy using an assortment of gizmos and electrical stimulation (all paid for by medical insurance), and finally a cortisone injection with a needle so long it might have been used on cattle. No improvement in Nicky's discomfort or range of motion. Salvy grew angry with the doctors who continued to be frustrated in their efforts to pinpoint a cause. Rest was all they suggested. And more rest. By the end of September, Nicky figured there were better places to rest than the sideline of a football practice. His buddy Wilson's house, for example. The dude had video games galore, and access to beer. And zero parental supervision.

All the while, Salvy was under the impression that Nicky was still attending football practice, keeping up with the team. It was a call from the police that alerted him otherwise. Nothing horrible, nothing that would make the news. Nicky and Wilson had been nabbed in a part of East Cleveland where they had no business being and the two young ladies they were caught with had police records for prostitution.

Salvy called Uncle Lou for his advice. It was something he'd been doing since his father had died. The Zanay clan had, if not a tradition of demonstrable male wisdom, a long-standing tribal custom of seeking counsel from the eldest surviving male. Uncle Lou said why not bring the kid down here to meet his namesake, Coach Nocero. It might make a difference. Look at all he's done for Brian and the Bobcats.

What Lou had in mind was for young Nicky to spend a bit of time with big Nick over a slice of pizza or something. A few words of wisdom, a nudge to work hard at school and on the field (big Nick didn't necessarily need to know that the kid had quit the team), a reminder that the game of life is what he's preparing for and how there's no shortcuts to success. Coming from Coach Nocero, it could be just the thing to turn the kid around. It had been known to happen. Look at the Bobcats.

The Longview band had filed into their section near the twenty and were warming up. Their initial bleats and honks were so discordant it required an act of faith even for us to imagine music resulting. But faith is what we had.

Salvy raised his voice to make sure his son could hear. "Sometimes I think to myself, what if I'd had better coaching? Don't get me wrong. Roof work's a great field. But I coulda done better."

Marie, climbing the ramp to the bleachers, caught Lou's attention and he flapped his arms like a crazed orchestra conductor to flag her down. She had no choice but to veer toward them.

"Man, she looks great," grinned Salvy.

"Watch it. She's your cousin."

"I don't get it. She looks better than ever."

"Genes," Lou said proudly.

"Coaching," countered a mumbled voice.

Salvy and Lou turned to the hooded figure beside them. Yep, it was Nicky who'd said it. The kid had a dry wit.

Two black Lincoln Town Cars pulled up to the curb outside the entrance to the field. A frail Jeremy Sr., recovering from the flu, took his time climbing out. He was followed by two Korean businessmen, familiar faces, in black overcoats and trailed by their translator in a beige camels hair. From the other car, Junior emerged along with Arch Robinson and Todd Whelton. Perhaps it was the polished black auto or their stiff bearing, but it was hard not to be reminded of a funeral – ours.

We'd heard the Koreans were back. Deliberations, we understood, were under way. Backroom discussions were taking place that wouldn't involve us except insofar as, like defendants in a courtroom, the fate being decided was ours. Nonetheless, it was jarring to witness such a public display. Typically, the Koreans did not make a show of their presence beyond touring the Made Right plant and conferring privately in the executive suites. Attending a Bobcat home game accompanied by the Ziglars and the Chamber of Commerce inner circle felt to us a bit like a victory parade, the kind of smug post touchdown end zone taunt that was frowned upon by traditionalists, and mightily resented by the losing team.

Of course nothing had yet been officially announced, and until the verdict was formally and finally handed down we were oddly content to accept the benign "strategic partnership" explanation. We'd had other scares. A year earlier there'd been an "informational exchange" that, among other things, was supposed to explain Junior's extended trip to Asia. We'd asked Marie to shed further light, since she had access to conversations and documents and other bits of peripheral evidence, but she insisted the cover story was the only story she was privy to. Although she did use the term "cover story." The Korean visit of a few weeks back had been described to us as an exploration of common areas of overlapping interests. Which could mean just about anything, including getting outsourced, bought out, merged, or turned into a theme park commemorating nineteenth- and twentieth-century American economic productivity.

Both teams had taken the field and were stretching out, the Bobcats in their blue and gold, the Prescott Shamrocks in bright green and white. The band's first official tune started as if it were "Taps" but proved to be a Sousa march. From the bleachers, we watched the Koreans take their seats near the fifty, the Ziglars on one side of them and Whelton and Arch on the other side. We responded the way we might to a toothache. Eventually we'd need to see a dentist, but not this day, not football Saturday, not as long as the Bobcats had a game to play. We would not let our mood get tarnished by unsubstantiated rumors even if in all probability they were true. We were pig headed that way.

Salvy stood to give Marie a big hug. "Looking great, Marie."

"You too, Salvy. And this fine young man?" She nodded toward the hooded lump tapping his foot.

"My youngest son, Nicky. Named partly after your very own Mr. Nocero. What are the odds, a coincidence like this?"

The marching band grew louder as they began the familiar Bobcat fight song. "Remind me again," said Marie, "what coincidence?"

Prescott kicked off. The ball was a pop-up, high but short. Brian caught it on a full run at the thirty, made one cut after avoiding the first tacklers, and suddenly there was nobody in front of him.

A Prescott lineman, number 71, faster than suggested by his girth, nearly caught Brian from behind. Five more yards and he might have nabbed him. Touchdown.

We leaned across rows to clap Marie on the shoulder. Salvy checked on Nicky. See, he implied, see the kind of genes we got on this side of the family. But Nicky was leering at the cheerleaders. Salvy thought: at least the kid's paying attention to something besides the inscrutable rhythm section in his head.

Nick gathered the Bobcats for a sideline huddle.

"He's telling 'em not to get cocky," Lou explained without, of course, possessing any such knowledge.

"Always play like you're two touchdowns behind," Salvy agreed.

"Or more."

"Right. Or more."

Earl Muntch was at the huddle's edge, prowling for telling details. In his account of the Prescott game that would appear in the Gazette, Earl quoted Nick as imploring the kids to "show 'em what we're made of." It was one of those quotes that even while reading it we didn't truly believe he'd said it. It sounded too scripted, like dialogue in a TV show.

On second down from their own thirty-four, Prescott's tailback fumbled after getting whacked from behind. We recovered.

"Momentum is real, if inexact", was another of Muntch's purported quotes from Nick. "Seize it when you feel it." First play from scrimmage, Will dropped back and lofted a long pass that Petey Finch, who'd not caught one all season, grabbed on the ten and glided in.

And so it went. Prescott could do nothing right, offense or defense. Trying for a quick strike on their next possession, their strong-armed QB, who was said to have the attention of Division II college scouts, hurled a gorgeous spiral perfectly timed for the speeding flanker who misjudged it and lunged too far. The pass ticked the flanker's face mask and bounded upward, where it was easily intercepted by the our defensive back, who until that moment had been hopelessly beaten. Five running plays later, each executed with production line efficiency, and we had another touchdown. 20-0 with seven minutes left in the second quarter.

Marie turned to Lou, her checks bright from the brisk air. "I'm starting to feel bad for Prescott."

"Sure. Go ahead." To Salvy, he quipped, "You and Nicky're good luck. Should come more often."

At the half, it was 26-0. Young Nicky said he wanted to roam around and maybe get a hot dog and coke. Sure, said Salvy, go ahead.

"Money?" Nicky held out his hand.

Salvy found his wallet and came up with a five.

"Guess I spoil him," he allowed once Nicky had shuffled away.

In the third quarter, following another Longview score off a keystone cops-like broken field goal attempt, Nick sent in an entire squad of substitutes with clean uniforms. The Ziglars stood along with their Korean guests, like family relatives excusing themselves from a sprawling wedding party, and began to make their way toward the ramp.

"Back to Korea," boomed a gruff catcall.

"Game ain't over," shouted another.

"Guess you guys wouldn't know that. Football's American."

"Hey, ask Junior. He knows the rules."

"Hell, he makes the rules."

"Back to Korea!"

We craned our necks to identify who'd done the heckling. A few guys in the top row kept vigorously glancing about, scanning for the culprits like school kids flagrantly dodging the blame. Jimbo Kluge and some fellows from the Legion Hall were behind most of it. When we did manage to identify them, they just gave those big, shit-eating, whas-up shrugs, a confession of sorts. The cat was inching out of the bag. We remained in the bleachers but our rumbling was no longer fully repressed. Nor, however, did it amount to anything more than noise.

The lopsided score didn't produce anything like the happy delirium we'd experienced, say, at the Guthrie game. But it was a novelty and it left us proud and happy for the kids. They always say that sports are a great teaching tool, and so they are. But they are also a test and an assessment. They test what you are capable of and assess your capacity to get there. The Bobcats were going to the Superbowl!

When the game was finally over, we clamored onto the field to congratulate the kids. Lou and Salvy were scrambling to catch up with Marie, who was heading briskly toward the bench. Young Nicky followed at his own lagging pace.

"He's expecting us?" Salvy nudged. "Right, Uncle Lou?"

Lou caught Marie by the elbow. "Could you . . . "

She jerked away. "This is your thing. Leave me out of it."

There was an explosion of whooping from the swarm by the Bobcat bench, like the synchronized burst at a surprise birthday party when the guest of honor enters the room. Players, laughing uproariously, leapt aside so they wouldn't get splashed. The remains of several gallon jugs of orange Gatorade were being dumped on Nick. Brian and Will were the instigators, but the whole squad quickly gathered around to share the blame. Nick pretended to be displeased, stomping his feet and shaking moisture from his hair. But he sure looked happy.

Seeing this unfold, Earl Muntch directed his photographer, a pretty young woman in a pink ski jacket, to get a close-up shot of Nick, drenched and victorious, surrounded by enthusiastic Bobcats. It turned out to be the photo, in color, that illustrated Monday's front page article (the Gazette did not have a Sunday edition) with the headline, "Superbowl Here We Come!"

Lou approached as Nick was toweling off. His graying hair was soaked and flattened across his scalp. His cheeks were rosy. He had the joyful look of a swimmer up from a refreshing dip.

"Great game," said Lou, clapping a hand on Nick's shoulder.

"Thanks."

"You've heard me mention my nephew, Salvy?"

Salvy came forward, shoving the shuffling, recalcitrant Nicky ahead of him.

"And this here's his boy Nicky. They've come down from Cleveland. I'm thinking pizza at the O-P . . . "

Nick's smile vanished as if he'd been slapped. "Not today, fellas." He turned his back, and started down the shortcut beneath the bleachers.

Salvy was miffed. "What the . . . "

"Nerves, I guess," Lou said, groping for an explanation.

Young Nicky squirmed from his father's grasp. In the same sullen undertone mumble he'd employed throughout the day, he said, "It ain't him."

We were rowdy and festive and delighted by the sight of Nick, drenched in Gatorade, pretending to be irritated when we knew how supremely proud he felt. Even if the boy had made a clear and concise statement, properly enunciated, we would have paid no heed.

"Football's only one small part of his life," Lou continued. "Guy's plate is full, very full. He's got big-time pressures at Made Right."

"Telling you, it ain't him."

Later, Salvy would say that should have been a warning. His son Nicky never, ever deigned to repeat a statement twice unless it was a request for money. The kid was sharp in his own way, even if he was a screw-up. He noticed things, always had. The high school guidance counselor had termed Nicky a "visual learner." There were, or so the counselor maintained, various forms of intelligence. Visual sense was just as valid as the ability to read and do math. It just didn't get you anywhere, from what Salvy could tell. But his kid definitely had it.

Earl Muntch knew nothing about this laconic teen in the black hooded sweatshirt. But he was intrigued at the way the kid kept repeating the same darn thing, over and over, like he was autistic or OCD or something.

Lou maintained a stream of diversionary banter to distract

Salvy from his mounting disappointment. "Nick's got Made Right going like gangbusters, all out, all the time. He glanced around for Marie, hoping to enlist her, but she'd disappeared, probably chasing after Nick. "Lot a wear and tear at the plant," he kept on yapping. "Unbelievable pressure. This globalization's no joke. Takes its toll. Definitely takes a toll."

"Dude just ain't tall enough," young Nicky again insisted, and this time he said it loud enough and clear enough that Lou and Salvy and a few others who were hovering nearby had no choice but to hear it.

CHAPTER 25

....

Marie accompanied Nick back to his apartment that evening. We'd seen this coming, even if they had not, and were happy for them. In Longview, there are not that many midlife match-ups that can, so to speak, withstand the light of day. People get it on in dark corners at odd hours in impromptu intoxi-cated flings or after years of indecisive dallying. Yet unless the tryst involves wounded pride or an ugly custody battle, we don't tend to begrudge anyone whatever small pleasures can be grabbed. Nor, generally, do we even find it worth mentioning. People do what they have to do to get by, and that can involve matters of sex and love as often as shelter and employment. At church weddings, we mer-rily toss rice at the bride and weep fat salt tears at the launching of young lives down that tricky timeworn river. Love in the middle years, if that's what you want to call it, is different. Don't ask, don't tell comes close to summarizing our policy. Privately, we were root-ing for something to happen between Nick and Marie.

Marie brought two sizeable nutmeg-scented candles to his apartment, sensing that candlelight was finally what they were ready for. A romantic dinner atmosphere is what she had in mind; Nick's place was bare bulb, 75-watt GE all the way. He was the one to suggest that they first sample what candlelight might do to enhance the bedroom. It was, in hindsight, the direction they'd been heading in since that initial encounter on the factory floor the September day he arrived.

Until now, Nick had been mostly reactive, the awkward male ballroom partner coaxed every step. It was Marie who'd invited him to dinner, who'd helped find an apartment, who'd led him by the hand through the darkness of the enchanted woods to the clearing overlooking the valley where they first kissed. She'd even coaxed him, however subtly, during the job interview with Junior. It was his turn now to take the lead.

He drew her close. He grazed her lips with his lips. With his forefinger, he traced the meandering pathway from her earlobe to her collarbone to the dip in her neckline. Candles flickering, eyes closed, kisses moist, fingers cool, fingers trembling, first a taste, just a sip, fingertips warming to heated skin. She would have thought the dizzying thrill of being undressed by a man, button by incremental button, clasp by loosened buckle, would have dimmed by this stage in her life. It had not.

She leaned back on his bed, pulling her legs up, and he was right there with her, never losing touch. She held him momentarily at bay with open palm extended, needing room to wiggle, but only inches. Her hand slid from his hip. He would not have thought the mere touch of tender fingers could still spill him headlong into a swoon. It could.

Afterward, he told her, "I am truly the luckiest guy alive."

"No argument from me."

"You haven't done too shabby yourself, Ms. Zanay."

"You'll stay for a while?" Marie asked coyly, a girlish parody of the sort of gal she never had been.

Nick took her seriously. "For the rest of time."

Eventually, they made it to the kitchen for dinner. Along with the candles, Marie had brought a roasted chicken and the makings of a spinach salad. Neither of them, however, had any appetite for chicken. Cold meat, no matter how expertly cooked, had lost its appeal, lost in transition. But the salad, sprinkled with goat cheese and dried cranberries and cherry tomatoes, went down smoothly with wine. They brought the candles from the bedroom to eat their meal in a soft warm glow, and after dinner they carried the candles back.

Marie did not awaken until dawn. When she did, she was up in a panic and out the apartment door in a flash, hastily buttoning her blouse as she skipped down the hallway stairs. She wanted to be home before Brian awoke. She left Nick sleeping, or pretending to.

Entering her house, Marie was surprised to find Brian stretched on the sofa in his underwear. Eight o'clock on a Sunday morning was generally not a time to find him out of bed. He was watching a cartoon show. A muscular superhero in silver spandex was – pow! pow! – teaching a lesson to a vaguely Arabic-looking bad guy.

She tried to sound her perky morning self. "Hey, up already?"

Brian never shifted his eyes from the TV set. "Don't tell me you were out shopping."

Marie dropped with a sigh onto the arm of the sofa, blocking Brian's line of vision to the TV. "I wasn't out shopping."

"Duh."

"I spent the night at . . . at Mr. Nocero's. There comes a time . . ."

"Spare me."

"We are two mature adults and . . . "

"You get horny, you do it. Same as everyone else."

"That is not what this is about!"

"He was an all-star at Notre Dame. Big deal."

"Nick is a fine man. What he's done for Made Right, for your team, for all of us . . . "

"Hope you got his autograph." With that, Brian hopped up and fled to his room. Marie was angry. The accusation was cheap and unfair. Brian was wrong about Nick and absolutely wrong about her. But one of the little lessons she'd learned about being a mom, and maybe a human being, was how little it sometimes meant to be right. The way Brian saw the world was not necessarily correct, nor objective, nor fair.

He saw it the way he needed to see it. And there was no room in his world, at least not now, for his mom falling in love.

Marie flopped onto the sofa, stung by confusion, staring vacantly at the vengeful square-jawed superhero, aggressively righting a world of wrongs.

Pow, pow!

CHAPTER 26

....

We were not exactly superstitious, yet we'd been conditioned over generations to be wary of anything going too well. It was a hard-earned psychological adaptation to a long history of letdowns, false promises, and plain old failure. The repeat visit from the Koreans should have been an omen, and subconsciously it probably was. But for whatever reasons, be it the stabilization at Made Right, the relative absence of business closings, the surprise of the Bobcats being on the march, or the onset of the holiday season, we had let our guard slip. We'd fallen into the trap of believing the best was yet to come.

Afterward, when the initial shock had somewhat subsided, we could clearly recognize that the turning point had been precisely timed with the occasion of Nick's greatest fulfillment, and ours, as if all our apprehensions were a finely calibrated GPS charting our course to nowhere.

If it came as a surprise to Nick, we had no way of knowing. He was in his apartment busily rearranging his living room to create a homier feel. Marie had recommended that he acquire some window treatments, shades or curtains or something. The living room was too exposed to the front lawn where the downstairs families often congregated. So that's what Nick was doing when the phone rang, assessing the shortcomings of his apartment's interior décor, squinting at the bare walls and bare windows with the cocked eye of a Parisian portrait painter. Like some fancy Dan.

Earl Muntch was calling. His tape recording of the conversation remains a permanent record of what transpired. Earl was not normally a practitioner of such fastidious (and surreptitious) journalism, but he sensed that this story might take him to a new depth, one that required enhanced professional methods. He was vaguely aware that there could be some legal prohibition against taping a phone call without the consent of the other party. But that was a bridge he'd cross later.

One ring, two rings. Nick's voice picking up was initially chirpy. "Hi, babe," he said, expecting Marie.

"Nick? Earl Muntch here." A pause, then Earl continued. "My sources – I'll be straight with you – my sources at Notre Dame clarified some things. Stuff you're gonna want to answer for."

For Nick it was like that discombobulating instant when a movie projector overheats and the film suddenly jerks to a halt, dissolving into a goulash of liquefied blotches. Except Nick was not a casual viewer relaxing in a darkened theater. He was the leading man.

"Can I come over?" Earl asked. "I'm on a deadline."

They agreed on 6 p.m. that night.

Earl, we learned, had made some phone calls to Notre Dame. It was the sort of initiative he did not normally display and we took it to mean that he really was desperate to move on to another newspaper job. What Earl termed his "sources" was essentially Aurelia Wu, assistant to the director of sports information, whose job it was to cheerfully track down the answers for any journalist making a request. Earl had merely asked Aurelia if she knew the current whereabouts of the great tailback from the 1970's, Nick Nocero. Aurelia asked when he needed the information; this was late on Saturday afternoon after the Prescott game. Earl said soon as possible. An hour later, she phoned back. The answer was right there in a computer file the university athletic department maintained on all former players. Nick Nocero, she reported, was a partner in a real estate sales and development outfit based in Newport Beach, California.

"You sure?" Earl had asked.

"What it says."

"Do you have a phone number for him?"

And that's how Early came to place a telephone call, long distance, to the real Nick Nocero. Earl imagined the former star taking the call while sunbathing on his patio, cocktail in hand, gazing on the emerald expanse of the Pacific.

Earl tape-recorded this conversation also.

"So, you are not the plant manager for Made Right Industries? You are not, just to make this perfectly clear, coaching the high school football team down here in Longview, Ohio?"

"That's Buckeye territory," Nocero had joked. "Not me, pal."

"Well, thanks for your time."

Once we learned the truth, we too visualized the former tailback in what we had to admit with a little embarrassment was a far more likely circumstance, tanned and relaxed, just a few pounds over his old playing weight of 205 lbs., drawing a sip of an iced Daiquiri while shielding his eyes from the brightness above.

"Did people back there in, ah . . . whatever the town's called, actually think I'd be doing something like that?"

Damn straight we did!

After Nick hung up with Muntch, he stared a long while out his apartment window. The dark outline of another dusty freight was clattering westward. Probably he wished he was on board. When the freight had finally rumbled on, he phoned Marie. He needed to speak with her before others got to her first.

"Right now?"

"Yes. Right now."

He suggested Riverside Park. It was far from ideal weather for strolling about and probably that's what prompted his wish to be outdoors. This would be brief, harsh, inclement.

"Nick, is there something wrong?"

"Just meet me. We need to talk."

It was almost dark when Marie arrived. Nick hovered, shivering, just inside the elm tree archway. He wore the dark wool pea coat she'd helped him pick out, the collar turned against the wind, like a lonesome sailor in an unfriendly port. His hands were deep in his pockets. The hard ground retained some of the frozenness from the night before when the temperature had dipped below freezing.

She hurried to him but he backpedaled, keeping a few yards' margin between them.

She feared what he was about to disclose. "Cancer?"

He shook his head. There was a look on his face that sent a chill through her.

"A crime. You're wanted for . . . "

"I am not . . . " Nick faltered.

Marie could hardly stand it. This was going way too slow. "For godsake, tell me!"

He scuffed the frozen earth, then looked up, sad and lost. "I am not . . . I am not Nick Nocero. That's not my real name. I am not a former football star."

The sound that burst from her was less a shriek than a sputter, and not a horrified one.

"I did not go to Notre Dame."

Marie was smiling now. She reached to hug him.

"I did not play in the Cotton Bowl. I did not . . . "

"You're not dying?" She was growing giddy. "You're not . . . married?"

"Marie, I . . . "

"You're not a criminal? You're not wanted by the FBI?" Her tension was pouring into her feet, where she was doing an anxious sort of tap dance. "You're not gay?"

206

He grabbed her by the shoulders to slow her down, to end this cascade of lesser charges he was not guilty of. "Marie, I am not who people think. Listen to me."

"You listen to me, Nick! I don't need a football star. And you, my wonderful man, don't need to be one."

"But others? Jeremy? The workers? Brian? The team?"

"So?"

"The story is going to come out in the Gazette."

"Let it."

She was laughing now. Her shoulders shook and her eyes crinkled from the force of her joy, and her feet did a giddy little soft-shoe on the hard dirt.

This response struck Nick as deranged. "You're not," he wanted to know, "angry?"

Her laughing abruptly halted and out of nowhere a righteous fury took its place. "If I get angry, whatever your name is, it won't because you are not the famous Nick Nocero. It will be because you asked me to trust you. You asked me to trust the person I can see and touch and talk to. Well, damn it, I did! Now you've got to trust that person too!"

With that, Marie stomped away. Nick might have scampered after her, except he was certain she was mistaken. She lacked exposure to the harsh reality of people's unwillingness to forgive. She had lived in one town, in one house, her entire life. The fact that he found her to be attractive and wise did not mask how little real experience Marie had with the hard knock world outside Longview. And it would be those values and that vindictiveness that would take over from here.

CHAPTER

....

Uncharacteristically, Earl had taken extensive notes during his interview with Nick, sensing he was onto a good piece. He sought not just to document Nick's answers – the Sony recorder sufficed for that – but to gather atmospheric observations, the kind of scene-specific details that could enrich a column or a longer feature exploration. Nick's apartment, Earl noted, was "spare," "spit shine clean," "smelled of scented candles that put you in a holiday mood." Nick's face looked like it "could use a shave and a month of naps." Nick's voice "sounded like a nursing home codger." None of these made it past the copy editor at the Gazette but they did find their way into the 1000-word magazine proposal Earl drew up but never submitted.

Earl sat in the synthetic suede armchair. Nick chose to stay by the window, pacing.

From a transcript of the interview Earl Muntch conducted on the evening of Nov. 26 at Nick's apartment:

Nick: So you spoke to him?

Muntch: I did.

Nick: How'd he react?

Muntch: How do you think? The guy's sitting home in southern California and gets a call asking if he's coaching high school football in Ohio.

Nick: I guess I should apologize to him.

Munch: I told him the factory part, he laughed. He's in real estate.

Nick: When will this appear?

Munch: Day after tomorrow, probably.

Nick: Before the game?

Munch: 'Fraid so.

Nick: So what else you need from me?

Munch: Basically, why?

Nick: I needed the job. I needed a break. When you've spent half your life watching others make good, waiting, hoping . . . you see an opening, you take it.

Munch: A football analogy? {pause; no reply} Were you qualified to do the job?

Nick: Ask the people who work for me.

Munch: So you really are sort of the right guy. Funny when you think about it. Answer me this. You ever actually play football?

Nick: High school. Junior year we won the county.

Munch: I'll need to verify that.

Nick: You do that, Mr. Munch. Now please get out.

Even before the November 26 edition of the Gazette hit the streets, we were compulsively discussing – processing would be the clinical term – the disclosures. Each presumed tidbit was a bitter pill to swallow but we had no choice: Nick never played for Notre Dame. He was nobody's all-American, second team or any team. His resume was a work of fiction that showed but a pedestrian imagination and a sorry disregard for style. His experience in factories – we assumed he'd had some; how else to account for his familiarity with processes and jargon? – was suspect. Whatever he happened to know about being a plant manager he must have picked up through native shrewdness. He was not a coach or an athlete or an expert in any realm except chicanery and identify theft. He was not a heroic turnaround artist. He was not a leader. He was not the mysterious stranger whom every-one at some point hopes will arrive in their life. Other than the gall he demonstrated in conjuring and then perpetuating a con job, Nick was as ordinary and unexciting in his aspirations as anyone else.

At the Post Office, at Walgreen's check-out counter, at the gas station self-service kiosks, at Ramsay's and Phil's Auto Body, at the Riverview and the Carnegie Library, in the offices of Town Hall and at school bus stops, on the benches outside Made Right and our long wooden work tables, at just about any place where two or more of us gathered, there was disappointment but mostly there was anger. The news was a punch to the groin. We'd been hit there before; the sensa-tion was not unfamiliar. We knew its progression and knew that if we could grit it out, the pain would subside. Surviving the hurt would require a kind of mind-body discipline. Without taking any special pride in this capability, we'd become fairly adept at the practice.

There would be no retreating from the now indisputable facts, no repairing that wound or masking the crimson scar. It would be part of our lore and even if nobody ever mentioned it again, an utter impossibility, it had already been permanently inscribed on our identity, like the Manley house saga. You did not have to be a Bobcat booster or high school parent or Made Right worker or downtown shopkeeper to recognize that our choices were the ones that losers are always left with: claim it really didn't matter (it did); claim it could have happened to anyone (it probably could not); move on.

The Gazette did not mince words. "THE GREAT IMPOSTER" was their huge banner headline on page one. The account was illus-trated with a file photo that depicted Nick with the coach's whistle dangling from a string around his neck, his right hand clenched in an upraised fist. The photo had been taken on the sideline of a recent game. The steely determination on his face and the vehe-ment defiance suggested by his clenched fist reinforced an iconic image familiar to media consumers everywhere: the guilty suspect

(Mafia defendant, deposed dictator, corrupt politician), newly convicted, lashing out at his accuser.

"High School Coach, Made Right Manager Confesses to Fraud" was the subhead. It was of course an overstatement. There might even have been something like actionable liable in the Gazette's use of the word "fraud" with its direct implication of criminal behavior. Another person in Nick's predicament, a person with resources and a firmer foothold, might consider using this journalistic transgression as an opportunity to mount some counter-spin. Staying and defending himself might have made sense for a person with deeper roots and a broader base. After all, he'd committed no crime. But our hunch was that Nick could see the way it would likely unfold: a campaign of self-defense would only inflame the situation. Quietly into the night was probably the best way to go.

He'd come close. Actually, he'd come more than close. He'd hit pay dirt. It simply did not last very long.

The Gazette article even trumped what would otherwise be the news highlight of the season, preview coverage of the Bobcats' upcoming Thanksgiving Day Superbowl clash. On the editorial page, the lead opinion piece was titled, "What A Tangled Web We Weave." The gist of the piece was that life is fraught with temptations to falsify and deceive and that, in the short run, it can be easy to succumb. "Nick Whoever" – that's how the editorial referred to him – "has left his mark on Longview and that mark looks an awful lot like a black eye."

The Gazette's reporting had a rather astonishing ripple effect on the regional broadcast media. For reasons we found baffling, they found the story fascinating. By late morning, the Made Right parking lot was aswarm with TV mobile vans from Youngstown, Wheeling, Akron, and Columbus. Assignment editors at these outlets (WFMJ-Youngstown, WTRF-Wheeling, WTOV-Upham), sensing some elusive "human interest," ordered their camera crews and reporters to stake out the Arrowhead gate like it was the front steps of the Supreme Court on the day a critical decision is handed down.

Some combination of elements – the manipulative con job, the banality of our gullibility, the grand tradition of fighting Irish football, an exceedingly slow news cycle – had made our situation the aren't-you-glad-this-didn't-happen-to-you diversionary news nugget du jour. The Associated Press dispatched a stringer from their state capital bureau with instructions to file both an afternoon and late night report. Soon, the AP found that its dispatches were being run in daily newspapers throughout the country, and used as filler riffs by wise-cracking talk radio deejays and news pundits. The story somehow had "legs," and we could only hope they would be short ones.

To us, this coverage felt like an act of sadism, a sucker punch thrown by a dilettante who couldn't care less. It seemed vengeful to have our minor ignominy inflated into prurient amusement for news consumers who'd never set foot in Longview and never would. There was, of course, no referee to blow a shrill whistle and call a halt to this unnecessary piling on.

Nicolle Maillet, a local reporter for WTOV (you can see her these days as the weather person on KSAS-Wichita), drove down that morning accompanied by her cameraman. Her assignment was to grab some interviews with Made Right colleagues and kids on the football team. Two years out of Ohio University journalism school, Nicolle had silver-blonde hair permed in tight fiddlehead ringlets. Her real name was Barbara, we were amused to later discover. She and her cameraman went straight to the factory. It was morning break. Despite the chilly air, quite a few were outdoors sipping coffee on benches overlooking the gray valley. EJ was the first to be approached. He'd never been interviewed before, not even for a job. But he'd watched enough TV, especially sports, to know the drill. They ask you a question, then extend the microphone toward your face, and you're supposed to reply without hesitation or too much thought.

Nicolle treated EJ like he was a prime minister. "We're speaking about the revelations concerning your plant manager. Do you feel cheated?"

"Yep. Every goddamn day."

Eventually she landed one local resident willing to go on record with the type of incensed condemnation that was closer to what she was hoping for. On the news segment that night, Nicolle was careful to introduce Tuna as "a security official who stressed he was speaking only for himself," not the company.

Tuna wore a hybrid uniform, half Made Right, half Longview police. "Makes you sick to your stomach," he asserted. "Nothing lower than cheatin' and lyin' and taking advantage of good folks."

....

Ashong was mediating a dispute in sleeves at the moment Nick entered. We'd not expected to see him again. He'd kept out of sight since the revelation, which at least showed that he was in touch with reality. Supposedly, not even Marie had seen him, though it was known that she'd tried.

Earlier, she'd gone to the depot, a logical place to look, and Wally Pfaff informed her that Nick had purchased a ticket for tomorrow's 6:58 a.m. westbound. It saddened Wally the way all this had developed, and he didn't mind saying so. Other than Marie, he was probably the only person in town to express sympathy. To him, it seemed like only yesterday that the sturdy fellow with the limp had tumbled off the train, rumpled and tired, squinting into the fog. Wally even remembered their brief exchange. "Everyone needs the right man," Nick had said, or something to that effect. An attitude like that made Wally want to root for him.

As Nick came through the Plexiglas divider separating the factory floor from the vestibule, all heads, all eyes, all attention turned. The strain of trying to appear calm was taking a toll, as the labored hitch in his gait appeared more severe than usual. Or perhaps we were at long last ready to dispense with those rose-colored glasses, and focus clearly on the weaknesses, and with them the flaws, we'd been so willing to overlook.

There was an eerie walk-the-plank stoicism about Nick as he made his way silently past the design cubicles, the fabric rollers, past bundling and toward the staircase. Ashong signaled to get his attention, but Nick did not veer.

Slowly, he mounted the winding iron stairs.

Marie was in Jeremy Jr.'s office, displaying for his consideration a stack of documents that required his signature where indicated by the red arrow stickers. Jeremy stiffened at sight of him, and with an emphatic nod indicated for Marie to vacate.

Passing Nick, Marie pleaded under her breath, "Call me tonight?"

Jeremy Jr. shut the door behind her. He was in his shirtsleeves, his tie rakishly loosened at the neck.

Nick had not come to appeal for a stay of execution. "I'll make it easy," he said. "I quit."

A chill rain was sweeping into the valley. A good day to stay indoors. Junior held Nick's final paycheck in a company envelope but made no effort to offer it across the expanse of his desk. It was as if he were waiting for Nick in his desperation to grab at it. "You've embarrassed me and Made Right and the entire town," Jeremy spat. "My workers are upset and I can't even imagine what's in the hearts of those poor kids on the team. Christ, I should've seen it. All that drifting, all those jobs scattered across the country. This is your pattern, isn't it?"

Nick bristled, "Not this time. This is where . . . where the pattern changed. This is where I gave it the best I had. I don't expect you to say thanks, under the circumstances. But I do want you to know: I left it all on the field, for Made Right and for this town."

Junior, unmoved, finally handed over the paycheck. "If you say so."

"I'd like the chance to speak to everyone, to say good-bye. A few minutes. That's all I ask. I want to apologize. I owe them that much."

Junior reacted with indignation. "Absolutely not! Permission denied! Do you know how much you've cost me? This impacts Made Right in multiple ways, which I don't think I need to spell out for you."

"The Koreans?"

Junior did not deign to answer. "You have a lot of hate in you, Nick. I hope you get help. Now go."

We'd been huddled in the center of the shop floor, waiting to see what might happen upstairs. Now we watched his painful descent down the spiral stairs. Not really knowing what to say, we said nothing as he solemnly filed past us and out the main door.

Too bad. We could have benefited from Nick coming before us to give a straightforward accounting. His tone of voice, his body language, the look in his eyes as he looked in ours, all might have helped fill in those troublesome gaps. It really was a missed opportunity. You never know what a person will come up with when all is lost. Sometimes it can turn out to be the truth.

The truth, we subsequently learned, made a kind of sense. His real name was Nick Remke, as stated on his original Made Right resume. He'd spent his formative years in Dubuque, Iowa, where his father worked as a traveling salesman, mostly appliances. He had a younger sister Norma with whom he'd walk to school, just the two of them kicking clumps of leaves along the way. Summers they would visit relatives in Illinois and he would return with stories of wading through ponds teeming with leeches, catching snakes in the forest, nabbing monarch butterflies in meadows, as though central Illinois was equatorial Africa. There had been a dramatic fishing expedition from which his dad never returned. Only several years later, too late to matter, was he informed that the old man had merely left to start a new life, and a drab one at that. Another wife, another sales rep job, another son.

His Aunt Kate lived in California and the summer following seventh grade, instead of going to the wilds of Illinois, they moved to Long Beach. Jobs were plentiful in the booming defense industry, and Nick's mom landed a contract administrator position with a division of Hughes Aircraft. Nick did play football in high school and was considered talented. He was a fast runner and a fearless tackler. We know this because Earl Muntch kept at it, conducting additional phone interviews with former classmates and friends of Nick's sister. He even enlisted a research assistant in California to dig up local newspaper records. Nowadays, with Google, it would be a snap.

Nick made varsity his junior year and the team swept the conference. Senior year, he was named cocaptain. After two games, he quit. The speculation as to why ranged from home problems to girl problems to disagreements with Coach Bennett about the playbook. The team went 5-5. The remainder of his senior year flew by in a blur. At the age of eighteen, he set forth with a high school diploma, and little ambition beyond the short-term thrills of girls and cars and being cool. In this sense, Nick was indeed All-American. He had a misshapen sense of what the world owed him and how it would come due, the classic rebel without a cause. What he really wanted was a grand and exciting life. The specific components of this dream were always vague, as were his means of achieving them. It wasn't much of a game plan.

After graduation, he took a clerk's job at a stereo and electronics store. Then he got a part-time job in the Long Beach plant where he'd worked previously. Nick's first assignment was as a bundle boy, carting torsos from one stage in the process to the next. The plant was dingy and airless, like the high school weight room during the off-season. The regular paycheck, the companionship of fellow workers, the hard physical labor, the grit of the factory floor, the noise and bustle, all these suited him just fine. And the great heave of satisfaction in being able to shower it all off at the end of the day, the dried sweat and the grit in his thick hair, was an added bonus. The weekends started Friday night without a care and extended until dawn on Monday. A good gig, as far as it went.

He mastered the cutting and sewing machines, learned some design and rudimentary mechanical repair. Way led to way. At almost any time over the ensuing decades, if a better option had come along, a job that was legal and stable and halfway interesting, he would have been open to it. If one of his old high school running mates had popped up with a hot suggestion, like heading to Central America to set up an import scam or fishing for salmon off Kodiak Island, who knows? But it never happened. It might have, but didn't.

In the cities and towns where he worked, he made a habit of scouring the small print Help Wanteds in the local newspaper, the Herald, the *Post Dispatch*, the *Sun-Times*, the *Courier Journal*. Occasional listings caught his eye – Wilson sporting goods sales rep, insurance investigator requiring extensive travel in the tri-state area, produce inspector for the Department of Agriculture – but his deficits were obvious; no college degree, limited work experience, lack of anything that could be called a career trajectory. So he tweaked the resume, adding, for example, a BA degree from Notre Dame. It seemed harmless enough; it wasn't as bald-faced as Harvard or Yale.

There was a marriage that he never discussed except to say he could have been nicer to her if he knew himself better, and liked himself more. She was a pretty girl from Michigan who had a weight problem she controlled through pills that made her crazy. No kids, for which he was very thankful. He'd heard she remarried and had a son, and he was thankful for that also, assuming the information was true.

Other fellows he worked with were content to save their paltry sixteen dollars per week, and make strategic plans for a calculated future that was but a minor improvement on the present. The key to such success, from what Nick could tell, was to work hard, demonstrate maximum reliability, and gradually, so gradually that it was hardly noticeable, downgrade your hopes and dreams. That was the magic formula. It interested him not at all.

That vast gray sea of small type in the Help Wanteds, page after page on Sunday, became his crystal ball. Aramco was looking for men to work rigs in the Persian Gulf. A town in western Minnesota sought a director of parks and recreation. An opening level sports reporter job at a chain of weeklies outside Atlanta. Each time he sent off his cover letter he felt like he'd entered a sweepstake contest. He never did find out who was the winner. His roommate in Chicago, an emergency medical technician named Gavin – they shared a two-bedroom place on West Belmont during his two year

stint at the suit coat manufacturer, Hart, Schaffner and Marx –
once mentioned to Nick that he might fare better if he used someone else's resume. It was a joke.

"Like who?"

"How about an astronaut?" Gavin had quipped. "Everyone loves
those guys. You look a little like the one they sent to the moon . . .
what's his name?"

Could that throwaway suggestion, however buried in his sub-
conscious, have triggered it all? Nick doubted it. He acknowledged
there would be a great clamor, once the demonizing subsided, to
psychoanalyze him. It was the tabloid tradition. The moral impli-
cations of his saga would comprise irresistible fodder for the long
winter of Monday morning quarterbacking we had ahead of us.
There was nothing he could do to stop it. By now we were seeking a
hot smoking gun, a bloody set of fingerprints, a paper trail of prior
deviousness, a high voltage cause, a dire explanation equal to the
enormity of the hurt we'd suffered. The ordinary truth, so ordinary
it might apply to many of us, was not likely to prove acceptable.

Yet the truth as Nick knew it was almost ludicrously simple.
He'd needed a job. The pedestrian need to land an ordinary job was
what it had all come down to. Nothing more. At the precise moment
in Jeremy Jr.'s office when he'd learned he'd been thwarted after the
long journey getting here, Nick had done what any halfway sentient gamer would do. He'd thrown a Hail Mary. He did not secretly
yearn to be someone else. All he'd wanted was a chance to be his full
and complete self, the man he had always known, albeit without
much confirming evidence, that he could be.

Nothing he could do would stop us from referring to his deed,
now and forever, in the unequivocal terminologies we needed to
employ: his error, his fumble, his lie, his subterfuge, his deception,
his sin. Whatever we chose to call it, Nick thought of it in only one
way: his big break.

He had finally done what he had longed to do. He'd made for
himself a life. He'd come so very close.

CHAPTER 29

L ife goes on. That phrase, neither artful nor inventive nor especially wise, was the one you heard more than any other around Longview, uttered by parents to children, neighbor to neighbor, clerks to customers, colleague to colleague. You don't live in Longview if glory is what you're seeking, and in Longview you don't sink into self-pity if glory is denied. Hopes are soap bubbles. They emerge and take shape, they ascend and catch the breeze. They hover and dance. Then they burst. Life goes on.

Jeremy Jr. issued an official written statement that was circulated to the news media and posted throughout the factory. "We failed in our obligation to exercise the appropriate background checks. We have offered an apology to the real Mr. Nocero and ask his forgiveness. New hiring procedures have been put into place. This will not happen again."

Chief of Police Magnuson stated that his investigation was ongoing but there was no preliminary evidence that a crime, felony or otherwise, had been committed. That said, he made it known that he was personally repulsed by what Nick had done and he pointed out that the responsibility of the police in a community like Longview did not begin and end with criminal behavior. There was the matter of morality and character. "As a police officer, there may prove to be nothing I can do about this," Magnuson explained in a statement that also ran as a letter-to-the-editor in the Gazette. "But as a parent of school age children and a concerned citizen, I pledge to do all that I can to restore our commitment to integrity."

Superintendent of Schools Schmitz announced that Nick would have no further involvement with the high school football team and that an internal committee would be established to review the threshold qualifications for coaching all the sports teams, not just football. After Thanksgiving break, counseling services would be made available to players and to all other students who felt, in the Superintendent's words, "damaged by these unfortunate events."

On the Wednesday before Thanksgiving, the town council sub-committee on schools had its regular monthly meeting. By design, the subcommittee consisted of the three council members who truly knew how to get things done and were motivated to do so – Arch, Mayor Luppert, and Heidi Heinz, a round-shouldered, platinum-haired dental assistant who used her time working with stainless steel gizmos on the gaping mouths of captive patients to proselytize for a range of civic improvements.

The subcommittee's main agenda item was the proposed budget allocation for promoting the Benjamin Manley House as a classroom field trip destination for school districts throughout the region. The proposal had been pending for months. A deci-sion had been tabled since late summer and Heidi, who'd come up with the idea, could be put off no longer. Heidi had done her home-work. Supplemental state and federal funds were indeed available if Longview could clearly demonstrate that acquainting students with the Civil War- era events surrounding the free slave Joseph Charles enhanced their performance on standardized tests being developed by the Ohio Board of Education.

Teachers unions, Heidi had learned, were vigorously lobbying to have the social studies section of the state proficiency exams go beyond the typically rote questions about name, date, and place, and instead focus on broader ethical and social values. The trick was to squeeze these concepts into a multiple-choice format. The Manley House incident, if properly framed, just might fill the bill. What should townspeople have done during that confrontation in 1859 when a lawful slave owner from Kentucky showed up on a riverboat to reclaim his rightful property in the person of poor Joseph Charles? A) Leave matters to the proper authorities; B) Petition their elected representatives to amend the laws; C) Take matters into their own hands; D) None of the above.

Heidi was recommending that the town allot as much as $750 for an upgrade of the current pamphlet, adding color graphics and some footnotes referencing esteemed texts, and printing several hundred glossy copies to send to curriculum directors throughout neighboring counties as well as board of ed officials in Columbus. "Your classic win-win," was how she had characterized the proposal to numerous supine dental patients powerless to do more than grunt their assent.

When Arch arrived ten minutes late to the board meeting, Heidi and Ernie Luppert were seated at the oval table. The high-ceilinged conference room had tall windows that looked out on the square, and they were watching a man in a hooded sweatshirt attempt to loop a string of Christmas lights across an elevated branch of one of the thick elms that went back to frontier days.

Mayor Luppert cautioned, "We need to call the meeting to order. State law." After pausing an appropriate beat, he declared, "Meeting called to order."

Heidi's pumpkin face and enormous cheek dimples made it nearly impossible not to reflexively smile back at her. It was thought she had designs on becoming mayor, and there was little doubt she could succeed if she decided to make the run. "All in favor?" she asked.

"Believe me," Arch said, "Longview is not a place the state of Ohio is eager to advertise. Not after what happened this week. I'm even thinking we should change our name . . . just kidding."

"Ha, ha," said Mayor Luppert joylessly.

"Sure, it's only a few hundred dollars. But this'll be tantamount to throwing it away. A week ago, I'd have thought differently."

Mayor Luppert said, by way of agreeing, "Calling attention to Longview's quote-unquote historic past, at least right now, is just going to lead to bad jokes. At our expense. The lower our profile the better."

Heidi stared glumly, or as glumly as was possible given her effusive nature.

"What we should do," Arch offered, "is issue a public statement. Condemn what Nick's done and draw the lessons for all to see. Heck, we could write a draft right now. Get the full council to ratify it later."

"Put it on the record," echoed Luppert. "No ifs, ands, or buts."

"Exactly. Show that we stand firmly on the side of . . . of . . . "

"Truth. For starters."

Arch abruptly began to pace the room so the idea he was hatching, and the physicality of the thought process so vital to developing it, would not be constrained. "Absolutely. All this unwanted, and unwarranted if you ask me, media attention, we can turn it to our advantage. This could be a golden chance. Our teachable moment. We've got everyone's attention. We've suffered a shock. So what lessons do we choose to impart?"

Arch eagerly answered his own question. "This is a setback only if it sets us back. This is our shot to show everyone what good people do in the face of subterfuge and deception."

"Which is . . . "

"Which is, we go back to the fundamentals. Honesty. Hard work. Loyalty. Free enterprise. Honesty."

"You said that one already," Ernie pointed out.

"Well, it bears repeating. Honesty."

Heidi, who had been silent, came back to the point, "Regarding my proposal?"

"We probably have a few more pressing matters," Arch allowed, "than re-fighting the Civil War."

The TV crews had been told to stay off the field and stay away from the kids until practice concluded. Professional players might be able to tune out the media attention. Not the Longview Bobcats. As the reporters warmed themselves in their idling minivans and cameramen set up in the end zone, establishing background shots, the Bobcats proceeded to act like second graders, mugging and shoving, and in one case, which did not make the evening news, mooning a bare white ass.

Disgusted, Sherman tried to assert control. "Anybody seen my whistle?" he barked with atypical frustration.

Will, who'd been reclining on his back, tilted up to say, "Last I seen, our Great Imposter had it."

"Probably swiped it," Brian added, "as a souvenir."

"That's enough, guys," Sherman snapped. "That's enough."

It wasn't nearly enough for Will. "Did you see what the real Notre Dame dude had to say on the news? 'People really think I'd be working in a factory?'"

"No, no," Brian quickly corrected. "Dude said, 'Did those people think? You know, *those* idiots. *Those* suckers. *Those* dumb assholes."

With that, Brian ripped off his helmet and stomped away. Will followed. From the end zone, a cameraman tracked their exit.

Valerie Kelly, one of the two Bobcat cheerleaders with some gymnastic ability, was in the parking lot waiting for her mother to pick her up and take her to the doctor for a strep test. Valerie was a sophomore and hardly knew Will and Brian, except as number 14 and number 23. She would have liked knowing them better.

"No practice today, guys?"

"Not for us there ain't."

"You're gonna win tomorrow."

"Spoken like a true cheerleader."

"Are you bummed," Valerie asked sweetly, thinking a touch of empathy might help, "on account of Coach Nick?"

"Hell no," Brian snorted. "We're thankful. It's just a stupid game."

These days, practice was generally over by 5:15 p.m. since it was getting dark so early. Players made their way home by varied means. Late-shift school bus service had been discontinued fifteen years earlier due to budget cuts that were supposed to have been temporary. A few of the Bobcats had cars, or access to them, but most relied on parents or relatives or friends.

Probably no group in town was more distressed about the Nick debacle than the football parents. Teenagers were notoriously fragile, and there was widespread worry that any minor setback, not to mention big disruptions like this, could permanently derail even the most achievement-oriented young men. After this last practice before the big game, more parents than usual showed up after practice, lured in part by a desire to commiserate and share their fears. In the parking lot, they bunched together like church elders before the start of a funeral, facing their responsibilities but hardly overjoyed at the prospect.

Rita Talbot, a full-figured mother of four bundled in a puffy white ski jacket, was among the more outspoken. "Josh is really hurtin'," she complained, her mascara-lined eyes barely visible in a beam of light from the school foyer. "Says he felt like he was kicked smack in the nuts."

"He talks that way with you?" Maddy wondered.

"When he's upset he does." And added proudly, "Hey, at least he talks to me."

If forced to pretend the predicament contained a silver lining, that was probably it: at least the boys were talking. High school jocks are not a group known for freely expressing their thoughts, but this topic was certainly stimulating high-octane conversation. It dominated dinner table discussion and in many instances pre-empted popular TV shows. We're pretty good at ignoring national and world events – war in the Balkans, scandals in Congress – but this one hit home. Why'd he do it? What is the proper penalty? And of course the big one, why us?

We were curious about Maddy's reaction, given her closeness to Marie. But her views were the same as ours, pissed off and confused where to go from here.

"What troubles me is," said Maddy, stepping back as the head-lights of an approaching auto swept by, "is what're the lessons?"

"I'll tell you the lessons," offered Brett Rustich, a kitchen match wagging from the corner of his mouth. A balding man with an off-center nose, Brett had been a middle linebacker under Coach Pruitt and felt this gave him special authority in the matter. "Don't lie," he stridently declared, "cause you're bound to get caught."

Marie's Taurus came flying into the lot and pulled to the curb without bothering to find a space. Parents silenced as she came over, as though she was the object of salacious gossip that had to be quickly curtailed.

"He's leaving," Marie announced with alarm, as though this was an unexpected development. "Tomorrow."

Her tone had the desperation of a union organizer imploring the labor force to recognize its own self-interest. Whatever it was she had in mind, we sure didn't see it.

"Bottom line," said Brett, "guy's a fraud."

"Nick made a mistake," Marie allowed. Her tone was not defensive.

"I'd say so," agreed Rita caustically. "Big-time."

Maddy cut in. "It hurts me to say this, Marie, because I know it hurts you. But he's a sack of crap, just like Rafe, and the sooner you . . . "

"You're wrong!"

"Am I? Everyone knows you're getting it on with him, Marie. That's completely your business. But when you try to defend him . . . "

"I'm not defending him. But I do insist on the truth."

"Which is?"

"He never said: Hey, I'm a big shot. Bow down and kiss my feet."

"Nobody," Brett complained indignantly, "done that."

"Oh, yeah? Don't kid yourself." Marie looked them over, one by one, as if they were the objects of cross-examination. "All Nick said was he'd give it his best shot. All he said was he'd do his best. And guess what? He made good on that promise. I look at you, talking up a storm, and I've got to wonder: Are you angry because Made Right is hanging in there? Are you angry because your sons are proud of what they've accomplished this season? Are you angry because lately you've been thinking to yourself, hey, maybe I can turn it around too? Because if that's what you're thinking, it's just another way of saying he's the real deal. He just isn't Nick Nocero, the former Notre Dame great."

Marie probably had not intended a speech, and she now backed away, a bit stunned that she'd just delivered one.

Brett wasn't buying it. "Well he didn't need to goddam lie."

"Tell me, Brett. You think he would have been given a shot if he was a nobody? A nobody who just happens to be good at what he does? You think he'd get a fair shake if that's who he was? Rita? Maddy? All of you? You think the world works that way?"

"Well," Brett stammered. "Well . . . it sure ought to."

CHAPTER 30

With the temperature outside dipping, there was a cozy heated-cabin feel to the Legion hall. Guys were huddled around the bar watching a dramatic fourth quarter drive by the Green Bay Packers, led by the legendary Bart Starr. Each time the camera cut away to Coach Lombardi stalking the sideline, vapor pumping from his nostrils like a snorting bull, exhorting his team to accomplish the impossible, guys clinked their beer bottles and swigged. It was a mock ritual of ours, toasting long ago heroics as enthusiastically as if they'd just occurred. That was the beauty of reruns; they were invariably nail-biting dramas and we managed to enjoy them as though every play was fresh, the outcome hanging by a thread.

Lou was trying hard to get our butts over to the tree lighting. With the exception of the hitch he served in the Army around the time of the Korean conflict (his tour was all Stateside), Lou had not missed a tree lighting ceremony since his own childhood. Truthfully, once you've heard one grammar school choir's rendition of "Deck the Halls" you might as well have heard them all. But Lou felt it was something akin to a civic duty to attend, especially in light of the sorry turnout we'd been experiencing. Two years ago it was pouring rain, which might have explained it. But last year was clear and fifty degrees and we still only had fifty or so people, and a good chunk of those were doting parents or close relatives of the singers. You would have thought our sense of tradition had been outsourced.

"Come on," Lou urged. "Fifteen minutes till tree lighting."

"After this drive," protested one of the guys, eyes glued to the screen. A forty-yard touchdown pass was coming soon. Jimbo Kluge tapped Lou's shoulder. "See that black guy back there playing pool?"

Lou turned. A few of the young guys were fairly new, and they only came irregularly. Probably had jobs or girlfriends or some obligation they couldn't shirk. One had served in the Gulf War. Another said he'd been stationed in Central America but wasn't allowed to talk about it.

"Yeah, I see him," Lou replied. "So what?"

"That there's Michael Jordan," said Kluge. "Case your daughter's back in the market."

Guys erupted in laughter. Lou wheeled on them. "Screw all of you. Don't tell me nobody here never claimed they done something they never done. Jimbo? How 'bout that Silver Star you used to wear on your hunting jacket?"

Nobody was laughing now.

Town Hall Square was the oldest part of Longview center and the least changed over the years. The town hall itself was a formidable limestone structure with airy, high-ceilinged rooms and tall windows. It contained the mayor's office, council chambers, clerk and zoning and assessor's offices, and more. The courthouse and police station, both built in the 1880's, were nearly identical structures – same architect, same building materials, same seriousness of purpose. Sandwiched between the buildings was a swath of lawn rimmed with park benches. In the coldest months, January and February, the town flooded a portion of this space for use as a skating rink. Several ancient oaks endured from the town's earliest settlement, and these were the trees we always draped with the colored lights that would be ceremonially switched on in the annual Celebration of Lights.

The Harding School choir, all twenty-four of them, wore stocking hats and thick coats and were cute as buttons beneath the fat snow-flakes floating down like tiny feathers through the halo of streetlights. Even to Lou, a certifiable optimist, the turnout was a disappointment: half a dozen Chamber of Commerce members, one or two councilors, a couple of cops on duty, the three-person Fire Department honor guard, several children who were siblings of choir members, a dozen parents. We weren't far from a day when the whole thing might be scrapped and we could just show a video of past ceremonies on the local cable access channel, like classic sports, for anyone who cared.

Adding insult, the Bolton kid's spray-painted Buick roared into the square, with boombox blaring. Mrs. Sampson, the choir director (she taught music at each of the town's elementary schools), did her best with vigorous hand gestures to keep the children on task. They were a distractible bunch. She turned to angrily glare, hoping her school marm's disapproval would scare the Buick away. Fat chance.

In time, the Buick moved on, its roar fading but not fast enough. When peace returned, and the fa-la-la-las reached their semiharmo-nized conclusion, Arch Robinson stepped forward. He wore a tai-lored black overcoat, red scarf, and red earmuffs. He had the deep, sonorous speaking voice of an NBC broadcaster. We could imagine him looking perfectly at home performing a similar function under klieg lights in Rockefeller Center amidst the gleaming skyscrapers.

"Thank you all for coming," Arch said. "This marks the fifty-third . . . "

A white stretch limousine with Pennsylvania plates glided into the square from the north. Initially, we did a good job of ignoring it, trying to show allegiance to the ceremony at hand. We assumed it was lost. Like a raccoon prowling for grub, the limo took a halt-ing exploratory lap of the square, then came to a dead stop near to where Arch stood.

" . . the fifty- third consecutive year that . . . "

The driver's door opened. A compact man in black suit and matching livery driver's cap got out. He came the long way around the front of the limo, and opened a rear door.

Arch was saying some encouraging words about the spirit of the upcoming holiday season and, most importantly, the benefits in shopping locally.

A tall, handsome man with broad shoulders climbed stiffly from the limo. He was dressed in a bright turquoise ski sweater. There was a hint of a suntan on the smooth skin of his pleasant face. His dark hair glistened, as though pomaded. He stretched his arms overhead and yawned. He had the kind of easy confidence we're used to admiring in supporting actors.

Dan Marino, the legendary quarterback, clapped his leather gloves against the frigid air and announced, "Sorry I'm late, guys."

You could have knocked us over with a feather.

With a practiced eye, Marino made a swift glance downfield to assess our modest conclave, then stepped briskly forward to shake Arch's hand. "Where do you want me?"

Arch would later contend, in response to gentle ribbing, that he did not blush like a female fanclub autograph seeker. It was the cold air playing havoc with his complexion. Nor was his momentary pause in replying to Marino's question about where he should situate himself the awestruck schoolgirl speechlessness everyone later accused him of. Rather, Arch maintained, he wanted to give the quarterback a minute after the long drive to take in the splendor of the town square before getting down to the business at hand. Nobody believed him.

Lou was as shocked as anyone, and it made him wish some of those smug jerks from the Legion were here to get a load of this. On the other hand, he felt it served them right to miss it.

Eventually, Arch guided Marino to the thick orange power cable wrapped around the base of the big maple directly behind them. "Right over here," he instructed the all-star QB in what he hoped was a tone of casual authority, not obsequiousness.

During its lap of the square, Marino's limo had rolled directly past the spray-painted Buick, which had blessedly cut its engine and was parked in front of Wrenshaw's Appliance on the far side of the square. Brian and Will and Josh Talbot were in the back seat, sipping Rolling Rocks and pretending to enjoy the taste, even commenting on the smooth woodsy flavor. The limo had caught Fritz Bolton's eye (even the teachers who'd flunked him believed he had an artistic sensibility, and not simply because he'd done so poorly in math and history) and Fritz rolled down his window to stare in amazement. "Looks like those dudes sure got lost," he remarked to his companions, coughing from the strain of holding in the smoke. "Instead of taking a left turn to L.A., they took the right fork to nowhere. Big mistake."

"Forks in the road, man," Brian agreed. "Got to watch 'em close."

The quartet sat in the car, sipping and smoking, and had watched with mounting bemusement as the limo eventually parked across the square and the fancy dude with the big shoulders and thick sweater went straight to the tree lighting gathering as if that was his intention all along.

Brian smacked Fritz on the skull from behind. "Hey, that's . . . I mean, isn't that . . . "

"No way."

"It's him! That's him all right."

"No fuckin' way."

"Yeah? Check the gloves. Definitely him."

"In Longview? Ha! Get real."

"It's real. It's him." With that, Brian shoved open the Buick's back door. The smoke annoyed him. At least, that was the reason he gave.

Marino stood among us, a storybook prince with his radiant features and thick turquoise sweater. "Shall we, fellas?" he said, eager to move this along.

Billy Drogna, our acting fire chief, stepped forward along with Phil Forrester, a volunteer. They each wore bright reversible school-bus yellow slickers with black arm stripes. These had been secured for the town's police and fire fighters courtesy of Made Right in a swap arrangement with the Blauer company out of Boston.

"Sure this won't electrocute me?" joked Marino.

"Fairly sure," deadpanned Billy.

The snow swirled down through the night sky, and the electric Christmas candles in the upper windows of town hall gave off a soft golden glow. Those townsfolk who'd taken the trouble now bunched together like shivering Pilgrims. Then, with Dan Marino at the switch, the holiday lights blinked on and the rough bark of the barren tree limbs shimmered from dotted lines of red and yellow and holiday blue.

Mrs. Sampson cued the Harding choir with a hearty "a one, and a two, and a three" and the children began singing "This Little Light of Mine." Chamber members and volunteer firefighters and police officers circled Marino like shy freshman at a college mixer, not quite sure what to say. Politely, we thanked him for coming and made a few tepid observations about how the NFL season was going. Privately, we were grateful that Marino did not appear angry to have come all this way, presumably from Pittsburgh, for such a paltry turnout. Of course, nobody wanted to mention this on the outside chance he hadn't yet noticed.

Jeremy Jr. cleared his throat and was about to say something when Marino clapped his gloved hands like the quarterback he was, ending this huddle.

"Nice town," he stated in that crisp wrap-up tone employed by news anchors concluding a segment. "By the way, which of you's the guy who got me to do this?"

Billy Drogna glanced at Mayor Luppert. Luppert looked to Todd Whelton. Todd, who considered PR his specialty, looked helplessly to Arch Robinson. Arch knew better, and nodded to Jeremy.

"He couldn't make it," said Jeremy.

"Gosh, I would have thought, you know, given how hard he worked to get this . . . "

"Personal problems," Jeremy hastened to explain.

"Well, tell him I got here and tell him thanks." Marino said this without any visible irony. "The guy is sure one persistent fellow."

Jeremy could not let this pass. "It was pretty much a team effort, Mr. Marino. If you know what I mean."

"Yep," said the quarterback, "Teamwork." With an easy stride he jogged back to his limo. The driver emerged to hold the door open for him. Before disappearing, Marino gave a friendly good-bye wave. Then he was gone.

For a full minute, no one spoke. Then, mostly to break the silence, Jeremy Jr. declared he was as surprised as anyone to see none other than Dan Marino, live and in person, at the Longview tree lighting. But the superstar's appearance did not, Junior hastened to add, soften his anger at Nick Whoever. In fact, he pointed out that this total lack of any advance notification concerning Marino's participation more or less negated any conceivable benefits the town might gain from it. "A job done right yields concrete, measurable results," he sniffed. "This most definitely did not."

Only later did we discover, again through the suddenly indefatigable efforts of the enterprising Earl Muntch, how Nick had been able to pull it off. The lucky break had been the NFL schedule. Marino was from Pittsburgh and his team, the Miami Dolphins, was scheduled to play the Steelers the Sunday after Thanksgiving. Nick had placed some phone calls, first to the Dolphins organization, then to the office of Marino's agent at IMG, then to the public relations company in New York that arranged Dan's commercial work and handled the flood of unwanted overtures the fabled quarterback received at the rate of ten per week.

"Put it in writing," the young lady had curtly told him.

"This event I'm talking about," Nick had emphasized, "comes up pretty soon."

"All appearance requests for talent must be put in writing."

It was like dealing with the telephone company back in their glory days as an unassailable monopoly. On the surface, it would all be very polite. Functionally, your request disappeared soon as you submitted it.

"I'll do that," Nick had persisted. "But I'm going to do a few more things you need to know about before you hang up. I'm going to make sure that Dan's father and brother know about this request. They're very good guys. And if they learn, and if Dan learns, that you did not even tell him about it – because I know that's what's running through your mind – if you do not even inform him, well, your office just might lose the Dan Marino account. Because he'll be mad. So, just for safety's sake, you'd be wise to pass the invitation. Directly to him. In its entirety. Okay?"

A bit more sympathetically, the young lady asked Nick to fax it to them (so all the details would be accurately conveyed) and she gave him their unpublished fax number.

Nick thanked her and said he would get it to her by the end of the day.

"Tell me again," the young woman said before hanging up, "who exactly are you?"

"Nobody. This tree lighting event is something Dan'll be doing for us nobodies. There's a lot of us out here."

....

T he night, as it turned out, was not quite over. Around mid-evening, simultaneous with the tree lighting ceremony, word began to circulate that the real Nick Nocero, the one who really did play tailback for Notre Dame and really did star in the Cotton Bowl and had never set foot in Longview and likely never would, was scheduled to be a guest on the Jay Leno Show, along with Cher and a former child actor on a defunct TV show who was considering a run for the US House of Representatives.

The trusty old phone tree kicked in. Maddy heard it from one of the football parents who'd heard it from Ray Friend, an elderly retiree who spent most evenings at the Riverview, who'd bumped into Gus Hoover shoveling snow outside the hotel and who kept his TV on seemingly all day and all night, thereby enabling him to catch the tail end of a network promo announcing Leno's guest lineup. We took pride in the efficiency of our phone trees. By 10 p.m., nearly everyone in Longview knew about the upcoming program.

In our darkened neighborhoods, peaceful as cemeteries with the new falling snow, nearly every house had its TV turned on. We were damn curious – curious yet wary and conflicted. Why would a top-rated TV program bother with anything so trivial? Perhaps if we knew more about the TV business we might have a better handle on the answer. For many, there was a troubling touch of masochism about the prospect of watching an interview with the real guy, like rubbing salt in our own self-inflicted wound. Still, on the Wednesday night before Turkey day, what else did we have to do?

Irma Hudson was at the stove preparing a cranberry sauce and sweet potato dish for tomorrow, her Panasonic perched atop the window box above the sink. Timmy was with her, helping with the peeling. He was a good kid that way, a good kid in most ways. Less TV and more homework was about Irma's only complaint when it came to Timmy. It was fortunate she couldn't afford one of those giant screen models, or else he might never pry himself away.

Harris Wilkins, Vince's dad, sat in his leather recliner facing the cherry wood bookcase that housed an entire 17-volume set of the Encyclopedia Britannica. Half a dozen polished trophies won by Vince and his two sisters occupied the shelf below the 24-inch Sony. Vince was in bed, resting up for the big game tomorrow. Coach Nick had wanted a 10:30 curfew on game nights and there was no reason to abandon the practice just because he turned out to be a fraud. Harris opened a Stroh's and settled back to watch alone.

Brett Rustich's new 34-inch Zenith console dominated his family's small living room. The set had been a Christmas present two years ago from Brett and his wife to the kids. Already, some of their happiest moments had been spent huddled around it, viewing the new Jurassic Park video the first week it was available, rooting for the Cleveland Indians in the World Series.

Flora McNulty watched with her widowed sister Ruth, who'd just moved back to town and was staying with Flora until she could find a job and afford her own place, which might be never. Ruth had been a Bobcats cheerleader and one of the prettiest in her day, although you would never know it to see her now, with those drooping eyes and graying hair erratically dyed.

Arch Robinson, just back from the tree lighting, poured himself a thimble of Dewar's, as was his habit before bedtime. Jacqueline, his wife of thirty-eight years, was already under the covers, leafing

through a copy of *Beautiful Home*. She was developing a late interest in interior design. The TV was tucked in a closed-door cabinet
she wanted to replace with something more Scandinavian. Arch
asked if Jacqueline would mind if he turned on the set, but he'd
already done so and was clicking the remote in search of NBC.

At the Legion Hall, the classic 1969 Superbowl was entering its
nail-biting fourth quarter and cocky Joe Namath was predicting victory. Nonetheless, the suggestion that they flip to Leno was unani-
mously approved. Guys quit the pool table to crowd around the bar.

Maddy told herself she simply wanted to see what the real guy
looked like. She had microwaved a bag of popcorn, seasoned it with
butter and a sprinkling of parmesan cheese, and plunked down on
the battered orange loveseat in what they called the wreck room, a
pun on the hyperactive play that over the years had dented the walls
and damaged the furniture.

Will and Brian were about the only ones not hovering around a
set. They'd taken their time coming home from the tree lighting on the
square, sloshing through town and up the long hill home, periodically
pausing to scrape together wet snowballs and test their aim against
tree trunks and mailboxes. Brian intended to sleep over at Will's. He
didn't want any part of whatever his mom was going through.

There were no cars and they could glide to and fro in the middle of
the road like skaters on the slippery surface, their footprints elongated
in the new snow. The beer and the pot and the turbulence of recent days
had made them uncharacteristically reflective, and a trifle spooky.

"Keeps snowing, by morning nobody'll know we even passed
this way." Brian said in reference to the trail of vivid footprints that
followed them through the pristine blanket of white.

"I will," said Will.

"Good man," said Brian.

They arrived home slightly before midnight. Whenever Will was
later than promised, he would invariably find his mom keeping a
vigil on the front steps, smoking a cigarette with her coat across her
shoulders like Washington at Valley Forge. Not seeing her perched

there was surprising, almost worrisome.

Will stomped the snow from his shoes as he barged through the door, Brian right behind. "Hi, Mom," he shouted once inside.

Maddy hollered from the den, "Get in here! Quick. The guy's on TV! The real Nick!"

Jay Leno, wrapping the segment, chuckled like a genial head-waiter. He was wishing Cher the best of luck with the release of her new album. Cher was her typical eyeful, dressed in a shimmering lavender blouse spotted with beige ovals that looked vaguely like breasts and that were situated in locations designed to encourage exactly this impression. Jay worked a daffy schtick of trying way too hard not to stare. He'd punctuate each exchange of dialogue by bulging his eyes in wild sweeping rotation, desperate to focus his vision anywhere but. Cher pretended to be blithely unaware of Jay's consternation.

As the house band launched into the familiar Fighting Irish fight song and Cher performed a gyration more akin to striptease than cheerleading, Jay announced, "When we come back, former Notre Dame football star Nick Nocero."

Following the commercial (cut-rate financing on a brand new General Motors car), the real Nick Nocero strode onto the set. He was broad shouldered, silver haired, deeply sun-tanned. If he had gained a few pounds since his playing days, it was not evident in his face, which remained clear-skinned and handsomely chiseled. He was dressed in a navy sports coat and a pink Ralph Lauren polo shirt that accentuated a youthful blush in his complexion. He would not have looked out of place in the winner's circle at Hialeah, beside a still-panting thoroughbred and a tiny jockey in colorful silks.

The real Nick Nocero plunked down on the sofa. You could tell by his manner he was comfortable with the limelight. Jay quickly established that Nick had been a renowned tailback in college, but that wasn't all. His fortunes had only improved since then. As a minority partner (along with two members of the Notre Dame Board of Trustees) in a Newport Beach real estate development and asset management company, his annual income now surpassed that of the average pro football player. Plus, as Leno noted, the real estate game was not one he'd have to retire from due to age or bad knees.

"So," Jay mused in his practiced deadpan, "you really think you guys got a chance tomorrow in that southeast Ohio all-county high school match-up?"

The real Nick Nocero played along, adopting the all-knowing manner of a broadcast booth analyst. "We stick to our game plan, play our game, stay with our strengths, don't get intimidated, we'll be all right."

Jay liked this. He leaned sideways to slap five. "Seriously, what's it like learning someone's out there living a life, and a pretty good one, masquerading as you? I mean, your wife ... "

"I promised her," cautioned the real Nick, "no wife jokes."

"Of course. We'll try to respect that."

Quickly, Jay summarized for those unfamiliar with the incident the basic situation (CNN and ESPN had been the primary national broadcast promulgators of the story, not NBC). He managed this in a few swift sentences. Jay wrung his hands and worried aloud about the phenomenon of identity theft. "So let's say I want to pretend I'm ... I'm ... President Clinton? What's to stop me?"

"In that town, nothing," cracked the real Nick.

Jay saw an opening and went for it. "So I could go there, to Longview, print up a resume on something resembling White House stationary, fine quality paper stock, nothing cheap, and probably land a pretty good job. Banking maybe. Or dentistry."

"Use plenty of Novocain," cackled the real Nick, "and nobody'd be the wiser."

"I could run for office? Be the mayor? Get the girl?"

"You could pull all that off," drolly interjected band leader Kevin Eubanks from the wing, "just by showing up as yourself, Jay Leno, star of the Tonight Show."

This was starting to veer, and Jay adroitly reeled it in. "Seriously," he intoned, tucking in his chin, "how does all this make you feel?"

The real Nick grew suddenly sober. The affable smile vanished.

"Listen, there's always been con men. Like they say, suckers born every hour. But you've got to wonder about an entire town that falls for it. We're not just talking about gullible high school kids. Or a few dropouts on the day shift, or geezers who'll salute anything in shoulder pads. From what I hear, this was an entire town, stem to stern."

Jay scrunched his mouth like he'd bitten into a lemon. "Some place, huh?"

"I did some research about Longview. You want to see what I found?"

Jay played it straight. "What?"

"Nothing. Zip. Nobody famous. Historically-speaking, nothing ever happened."

"Until now, of course," Jay smirked. With a flick of the hand in which he held a pencil, Jay cued his musicians that it was time. The band launched a mellow, jazz-inflected riff on the Notre Dame fight song, plunking bass and tinkling piano.

"Makes you wonder," the real Nick breezily concluded, "what the heck they teach 'em in their schools."

There should have been someone there to defend us, to stand up and set the record straight. History, it's said, is written by the victors. We could only hang our heads in doleful agreement.

Greater calamities, more acute and more profound, would soon enough eclipse our minor ignominy. Late-night viewers and newspaper readers and talk show devotees would in due time be diverted by newer sideshows. Longview would soon be forgotten. As we had been all along, and as we probably preferred to be. Those were the only consoling thoughts available as we climbed into bed and fitfully tried to fall asleep.

It was after midnight. Fat snowflakes continued fluttering down. Our houses were dark and our streets were ghostly silent and we were nearly drifting off to a long awaited slumber when the phones again began to ring.

CHAPTER ㉜

....

P ete Ledger's headlights carved through the grayness, turning up Iroquois Road from the tracks. Pete ran the only taxi service in town. It operated out of his apartment or during what he liked to call "office hours" at the Riverview, and consisted of an '87 Impala with him as the sole cabbie. Nick had phoned Pete the night before to set it up.

An inch of snow had fallen overnight, forming a thin blanket across the front lawn of the apartment complex. Gray and white were the predominant hues of the landscape. It was very quiet. No traffic, no pedestrians. Not a creature stirring. The Grand Prix was parked out front. Nick had mailed the key to Lou, along with one last monthly payment. The envelope, which Lou would not receive until the weekend, included a brief note on purloined Made Right stationary that was true as far as it went: "Thanks. Sorry."

It was 6:30 on the nose when Pete pulled up. We're a town of punctual people. That was another respect in which Nick fit right in. He was already waiting on his doorstep and Pete had the sense that he'd been out there for some time. His canvas duffel squatted at curbside, along with a lightweight Dacron suitcase he'd purchased at Emmy's Thrift Shop in the basement beneath Ramsay's. Pete popped open the Impala's trunk, and made space for the luggage by shoving aside a pizza box, the tire jack and a rusting can of brake fluid. Nick lowered the duffel, then the suitcase.

"Train depot," Nick said quietly, slipping into the back seat. As if Pete or any of us needed to be told Nick's destination.

It must have rankled Nick to have to slink away like an illicit midnight lover, as if nothing had ever happened, or worse, as if whatever had happened didn't really matter. In the rearview, Pete saw a forlorn face, eyes wide yet noticing nothing. He'd seen that type of blank stare before, wives fleeing husbands, boyfriends who'd discovered what they did not want to. The drive to the depot was ten minutes. Pete tried mentioning the weather ("winter coming on early, they say") but he received no reply.

Marie set her alarm for 6 a.m. The drive to the depot was less than two miles. She wanted enough time for one last conversation. There was a scene she'd been piecing together in her mind over the years and this would be the occasion. It didn't need to last long. The dialogue was terse, direct, almost minimalist, but a few lines each. He was free to go, she would tell Nick, free to board the train and say good-bye to the only woman of character who would ever believe in him so fiercely.

There would a while to talk, assuming the train was on time. That would be ample. She knew how this scene would unfold, where she wanted it to go, what she would say and how he would respond. It would be one final play with the clock ticking down, the type of crunch time predicament Nick had once professed to put so much stock in. She'd been rehearsing.

The roads were slick from the dusting. On the hill at the crest of East Hunter, Marie was forced to drastically reduce speed. Driving along Arrowhead, she recited her lines, practicing aloud as she'd done countless times to perfect her minor speaking part in "The Music Man." The right words would be crucial. The right words succinctly stated might yield a result different from the one they were helplessly spiraling toward like dishwater down the drain. With the heater in her Taurus on the fritz, her words came in frigid white puffs. "I wish that your dreams come true," she practiced saying calmly. Then, engulfed by the onrushing rumble of the approaching train, she would turn and proudly walk away.

It rankled her that Nick had not visited last night, but it did not surprise her. She understood that he wanted to avoid a last "scene." Tough, she needed one. There was a special potency, he'd once told her, in having it all come down to one last play. He'd been speaking specifically about Timmy Hudson's field goal but she felt, even then, that he was speaking more broadly, as if he'd been slyly coaching her for this very occasion, unwittingly prepping her for what she now had to do. This would be her final play. And his.

She knew how his facial muscles would tense at each exchange. He had a way of crinkling his eyes when he was thinking intently, as if he suffered an astigmatism that he struggled to correct through force of will. He would insist that leaving town was his one and only option. He would be stoic, a man of few words, a man of granite. That part came easily to him. He could do it in his sleep. He would become a chunk of polished granite. She'd have to find a way to crack through.

There was magic, she believed, in the words they would speak to each other. Poignant words could alter events. Ms. Averson, the youth theater director, had tried to convince Marie she had the stuff to play a leading part if only she could master the art of putting more feeling into her lines. Today the problem would be keeping her emotions in check. "Nick," she would inform him, "I don't need to stay in the same place forever."

A faint-sounding honk like a plastic New Year's party horn was audible above the groan of the Taurus engine. The bleat lasted several seconds. The dashboard clock was hopeless, frozen at 11:19 for at least the past week. Did trains ever arrive early?

Accelerating down Arrowhead, she rocketed into an uncontrolled skid for what seemed like the length of a football field before the brakes found some grip. The distant rumble of the train grew unmistakably louder. At the bottom of the hill, nerves jangled from the skid, panicked by the onset of crunch time, she swung left and . . . the parking lot was packed. Automobiles bunched like bees around the hive, and the swarm of new arrivals was creating congestion back to the footbridge.

Whoa! What the heck?

Cars trolled the gravel slope of the railroad bed for vacant slots. Vehicles were wedged at unorthodox angles everywhere space permitted and several were double-parked where it did not. Up on the platform, a crowd had amassed, and more were streaming from the other side of the tracks. Through the chaos of oncoming headlights and the vapor of too much traffic, our angled silhouettes resembled nothing so much as a guerilla army on night patrol moving with stealthy determination.

Marie slammed behind a dusty pickup and sprinted frantically for the depot.

A gyrating human chain, a twisting strand of Longview DNA, stretched the length of the platform. There were parents, neighbors, colleagues, merchants, Made Right workers, legionnaires, perhaps a hundred altogether, with more arriving by the minute. Nick was not exactly trapped, but if he wanted to get free of us he would have to make a very determined dash against the flow.

Immediately following the Leno show, our trusty phone trees had been reactivated. To this day we're not certain who initiated it. Several have taken credit – another example of the adage that success has many fathers. The message conveyed was succinct and needed no further elucidation: Nick was leaving by train first thing in the morning. Each person who showed up was as surprised as the next one to discover he had company. Yep, we'd surprised ourselves. After all these years, who would've thought we knew so little about our own true natures? Who would have thought that so late in life we'd stumble on a latent part of ourselves, lurking beneath the surface, waiting for a chance to be revealed? We'd each expected to be the only one there. We each showed up braced to be the only one foolish enough to have dragged ourselves from bed so early on a chilly holiday morning for no good purpose that could be easily defined. Yet here we were.

When the first of us emerged from the parking lot, coming forward out of the darkness, we must have appeared to Nick like some grim lynching party in a cowboy flick, a gaggle of cowards banded together to collectively accomplish what we were unable to do individually. But we'd come in peace and we let him know it with welcoming arms. We hoped that would assuage his fears, at least with regard to our intentions. Which were . . . which were what? We weren't really sure.

Nick's duffel and suitcase lay at his feet. There was exhaustion in his eyes but another quality also, sparked by the chill November air. He looked to be truly, deeply, sincerely, amazed. None of us will ever forget that look, that wild leap of involuntary delight on Nick's face, like a child who'd actually seen Santa. We didn't know yet what we would say or do, but good-bye did not seem sufficient.

More townsfolk poured onto the platform, people we'd known since childhood and people we knew only by sight, faces recognized from the check-out line at the grocery or the back row of PTA meetings or a Memorial Day softball game at Riverview Park. Brenda was there and in the dim light she might have been mistaken for one of the high school cheerleaders with her lithe exuberance, up on her tiptoes trying for a better view. The Captain, seeing her frustration, agreed to give her a boost and soon she was climbing onto his mountain man's back, a full head higher than the crowd.

Nick was the centerpiece of our attention but we couldn't help glancing at our neighbors, bathed in murky gray light, and as we did so a thought emerged, like a soap bubble slowly finding its shape. It was something we'd not had the imagination nor the courage to previously consider: if we were willing to agree there was more to Nick than his evident shortcomings, more that was indisputably decent and good, then damn, the same could be true of us.

246

Marie tried to push through to the inner circle surrounding Nick, but Rita Wilkens blocked her path like a member of the defensive line, and she wasn't budging. Rita kicked aside Nick's duffel to get even closer. She wanted to be heard.

"That TV commercial? Image is everything? Not here, Mr. Remke. Not us."

Brian stood tall in his blue and gold Longview letter jacket and gray sweat pants. His hair was tousled from sleep. Will at his side looked no better.

"Big game today, coach," Will said. "We need you."

"Here's my problem," Brian stated matter-of-factly, like someone thinking out loud. "You leave and I'll probably feel guilty and wind up having to write you a long letter telling how the game went. Who did what, who played well, which plays worked, blah, blah, blah. Thing is, coach, I ain't got time for that. Got those college applications to fill out."

With a muffled hum of its German-made brakes, the Amtrak pulled to a dead halt.

"Union'll find you something," Ashong stated confidently. "Least till they shut us down."

"Land of unlimited opportunity, used autos is," shouted out Lou, who had not succeeded in getting closer than the third or fourth ring of townsfolk encircling Nick. He wore an old beaver coat that made him look like a tipsy booster from the roaring 20's. "You got a standing offer with me."

The silver doors on the Amtrak zipped open. The conductor, dressed in blue-gray vest and pillbox-type cap, stepped down. James Sawyer surveyed our mob, not quite believing what he was seeing. It took him a moment to ascertain it was not a protest demonstration, though he had no idea what it actually was. "All aboard!" he hollered. When we didn't respond, he hollered once more, abiding by the protocol.

Marie now had an unobstructed view to Nick and what she saw was a brand new ball game.

"Everybody here," Sawyer asked with incredulity, "heading west?"

Marie drew a deep gulp of the crisp air, taking in the rolling sea of faces she was so deeply proud to live among. "No, sir. There's been a mistake. Everyone's staying right where we are."

Brian hoisted Nick's old canvas duffel. Will lifted the suitcase. Marie slipped her arm through Nick's and as they moved down the depot platform, more or less tracing the exact footsteps Nick had taken upon arriving here little more than two months ago, they were joined by a procession consisting of a healthy percentage of the entire town of Longview. We were like a flotilla escorting the mother ship to safe harbor. At last we had the grand communal gathering our civic leaders had been hoping for. No holiday lights, no grade school choir, no marching band, no inspirational oratory. Just us.

The conductor stepped back onto the train. Before signaling to the engineer to move out, he looked us over one last time, just to make sure there was nothing glaring he'd missed. His gaze settled on Nick, as though trying to place him. The sturdy build, the square jaw and deep-set eyes, the unsteady hitch in his gait may have stuck in his memory. But Sawyer encountered a great many faces that piqued his curiosity. His one occupational regret was that he rarely learned whatever happened next in their lives, these long distance passengers in the night.

Sawyer cried out one last time, just to be safe, "All aboard."

With exaggerated flaps of our uplifted hands, and in perfect unison, we waved the train good-bye.

....

A football game was played that Thanksgiving morning in Longview, Ohio. Kickoff occurred promptly at noon, as was the tradition for this annual Superbowl clash. The temperature was a cool 41 degrees with a light wind out of the northwest. The sky was tinged with a gray that hinted of silver. The air held a thick smoky quality, a fragrance of crisp leaves singed in distant upwind fields. Sunshine would have been welcome, but it wasn't in the forecast.

Nick Remke roamed the sideline. He'd been nominally demoted to his former role as behind-the-scene assistant to Bertram Sherman, but there was no doubt who was in charge or who ought to be.

A tin whistle hung on a leather shoelace around Nick's neck. The dark blue hooded sweatshirt with gold trim that he wore might once have been construed as Fighting Irish but today we knew it to be purely hometown colors. He had no hat. His close-cropped silver-gray hair matched as perfectly as a painter's sample the hue of the sky. He stood tall yet moved gingerly. You could say there was determination in his eyes, but this stillness and concentration could just as easily have suggested something like serenity. And in his heart? It's possible that no man has ever been happier.

On the barren hills beyond the field, the thin layer of snow was so bright it seemed as though the sun was beginning to break through.

In the abandoned limestone quarry known as Bruno's Pit, just beyond the far end zone, a congress of migrating geese was resting up, as they did every year around this time, before winging further south.

Made Right loomed high on its bluff, beleaguered fortress bracing for another siege.

Below, the broad river flowing past with dull invisible force was the gravel gray of deepest time.

On Made Right field where the grass was tinged a pale wintry brown, our fightin' Bobcats, all thirty-four of them, huddled up, running in place, thumping shoulder pads, clapping hands to keep warm.

In the far end of the stands, the Longview High band, under the determined direction of Larry Delp, was doing its best in frosty conditions that crimped the tone on the brass instruments. Fortunately, "When the Saints" was a number that did not require a pitch-perfect performance to be recognizable. Even in this choppy rendition, the tune had the capacity to lift us up, up, up . . .

We rose to our feet and began to sing. Lou and his cronies took turns – it was a game they sometimes played at the hall – trying to outdo each other with flamboyant imitations of crooners they admired, Sinatra, Elvis, Hank. It was great fun, for them, and their voices boomed to megaphone levels as they traded licks like jazz musicians in a cutting session.

"When those Bobcats go ma-a-a-arching i-i-n!"

In our grandstand seats, we were as antsy for the game to begin as the Bobcats were. You'd glance around and see people slapping fives as though a touchdown had already been scored. In the back row by the twenty-five, a group of guys, and not just Legion fellows, were busily placing petty-ante bets on a range of arcane categories (combined score at half-time, number of third downs converted), not just the final outcome. Gus Hoover, sporting a thick fold of dollar bills wrapped around each finger of his gloveless hands, appeared to be the ringleader of this enterprise; we had no idea who was minding the Ohio. At the north end of the field, beyond the end zone, Tuna prowled a private patch of turf. He'd switched to his cozier athletic wear, sporting an insulated Cleveland Browns overcoat, the type that the players on the sidelines throw over their shoulders to keep warm during those frigid December afternoons. You had to look hard to notice, but from the stream of vapor puffing rhythmically from his mouth it appeared as though he too was singing.

The Ziglars had not yet arrived and there was speculation they might not show at all. For another intriguing rumor had begun to formulate, one that was every bit as flimsy and insubstantial as a newly blown soap bubble, and still it took flight and floated enticingly among us. The Koreans, it was said, had finally become fed up with us. We were simply too poorly managed (the debacle over Nick's hiring), too unruly (the shooting incident), and too controversial (the Tonight Show infamy) to be worth it. Could it be true? We had no way of knowing. Again, all we could be certain of was that, for reasons that probably had little to do with our meager comprehension of free trade agreements and the global economy, it pleased us to think so. Whatever this looming deal had been about, it had never seemed like a good one for most of us. That the shrewd, disciplined, risk-adverse Koreans might have grown wary of our seemingly mercurial ways was a joke that you had to live in Longview to fully appreciate. Jay Leno's audience would not have seen the humor in it.

Regardless, the rumor that the Korean deal might be heading south provided another reason for us, all of us, to unleash our full-throated voices in a great choral roar and stomp those loose aluminum planks with the thunder of an invading army and thump our gloved hands together with a fierceness that had nothing to do with a desire for warmth.

Lou turned to Marie. She was seated in the row behind him. Her cheeks were rosy and the natural tint of her hair was highlighted by a purple band. She had white mittens on her hands, and a thick white woolen scarf at her neck. She was the only one in our section who was not singing. She wasn't even standing up like everyone else in traditional anticipation of the opening kick-off.

"Biggest game of his career," Lou complained loudly as he twisted around to gain her attention. "What's up? You sure as heck don't seem very excited."

Marie shot him a benign yet dismissive stare, eyes comically wide and unblinking, mouth slacked to an oval shape that perfectly conveyed her "duh, isn't it obvious?" response. Even as a schoolgirl this look had been part of her repertoire, long before she had any right to deploy it.

Marie called out in response to Lou, but her words were engulfed by the roar of the crowd as the two teams trotted onto the field. Lou cupped his hand to his ear, miming the fact that he had not heard a thing she'd said. Neither had we.

These past two months had been one wild excursion with the top down and more hairpin turns than anyone needed. This vaunted Big Game that had everyone so jacked up with anticipation was, from Marie's perspective, a long-awaited opportunity to kick back and finally relax.

Once again, she shouted her reply to Lou, straining to be heard above the clamor of our trampling feet. "Daddy," she shouted, her white mittens cupped around her mouth for amplification. "I already know."

"Know what?" Lou shrugged his shoulders and spread his arms to underscore his incomprehension. By now, we all were listening.

"I already know," Marie hollered with a ferocity that was as jolting as a cry for help but came from an opposite impulse, from exultation and sweet relief, from a giddy taunting of the fates and joy in its purest human form. "I already know," she shouted, "who wins!"

This time we all heard her. And this time we all agreed.

†††

Made in the USA
Monee, IL
23 August 2022

12348202R00152